Illusion
Is More Precise
Than Precision

Illusion Is More Precise Than Precision

The Poetry of Marianne Moore

Darlene Williams Erickson

The University of Alabama Press

Tuscaloosa • London

∞

The paper on which this book is printed meets the minimum requirements of
American Standard for Information Science-Permanence of Paper for Printed
Library Materials, ANSI Z39.48-1984.

Library of Congress Cataloging-in-Publication Data

Erickson, Darlene Williams, 1941-
    Illusion is more precise than precision : the poetry of Marianne
Moore / Darlene Williams Erickson.
        p.   cm.
    Includes bibliographical references and index.
    ISBN 0-8173-0570-X (alk. paper)
    1. Moore, Marianne, 1887-1972—Criticism and interpretation.
I. Title.
PS3525.05616Z66   1992
811'.52—dc20   91-29795
                                                         CIP

British Library Cataloguing-in-Publication Data available

to Larry Erickson

Again the sun!
    anew each day; and new and new and new,
    that comes into and steadies my soul.

Marianne Moore, "The Pangolin"

and to Dawn Holt Anderson (1938–88)

    . . . He
sees deep and is glad, who
    accedes to mortality
and in his imprisonment rises
upon himself as
the sea in a chasm, struggling to be
free and unable to be,
    in its surrendering
    finds its continuing.

Marianne Moore, "What Are Years?"

Contents

Acknowledgments

Previously unpublished material by Marianne Moore is used by permission of Marianne Craig Moore, Literary Executor for the Estate of Marianne Moore. All rights reserved. (A note of gratitude to Miss Moore for her graciousness, patience, and assistance in reading this manuscript and encouraging its publication.)

Special thanks to Eileen Cahill and Leslie Morris of the Rosenbach Museum and Library in Philadelphia for assistance in using unpublished letters, notebooks, and other materials in the preparation of this book. The Rosenbach grants permission for the quotation of material from the Moore collection in this book.

The cover photograph of Marianne Moore by Richard Avedon was made in New York City on 4 January 1958 and is used by permission of Richard Avedon.

Material by W. H. Auden in the Moore Collection of the Rosenbach Museum & Library is used by permission of the estate of W. H. Auden and authorized by Curtis Brown, Ltd.

Excerpts from the unpublished letters of Elizabeth Bishop are used with the permission of her Estate, copyright © 1991 by Alice Helen Methfessel.

Materials from "The Machinery of Grace," a senior honors thesis prepared by Elizabeth Bradburn at Amherst College, used by permission of the author. The thesis is located in the Amherst College Archives.

Unpublished papers by Amy Clampitt are used by permission of the author. (A collection of essays by Amy Clampitt, including one about Marianne Moore, was published by the University of Michigan Press in 1991.) A special thanks to Amy Clampitt for her generosity in sharing ideas about Marianne Moore's poetic techniques.

Unpublished materials by T. S. Eliot in the Moore archive at the Rosenbach Museum and Library are used by courtesy of Mrs. Valerie Eliot and Faber and Faber Limited.

Previously unpublished material by Ezra Pound, copyright © 1992 by the Trustees of the Ezra Pound Literary Property Trust, is used by permission of New Directions Publishing Corp. and Faber and Faber Limited, agents.

Previously unpublished materials by Wallace Stevens in the Rosenbach Museum and Library are used by permission of Holly Stevens.

Previously unpublished material by William Carlos Williams, copyright © 1992 by William Eric Williams and Paul H. Williams, is used by permission of New Directions Publishing Corp., agents.

Poems by Marianne Moore as they appeared in *Observations*, published by the Dial Press, 1924, including "The Past Is the Present," "Roses Only," and "Black Earth," are in the Public Domain. "Diligence is to Magic as Magic is to Flight," "The Fish," and "The Student" are quoted by permission of Marianne Craig Moore, Literary Executor for the Estate of Marianne Moore.

"No Swan So Fine," "Those Various Scalpels," "When I Buy Pictures," "Novices," "Marriage," and "An Octopus," as well as brief portions of "In the Days of Prismatic Colour," "England," and "The Frigate Pelican" are reprinted with permission of Macmillan Publishing Company from *The Collected Poems of Marianne Moore*, Copyright © 1935 by Marianne Moore, renewed 1963 by Marianne Moore and T. S. Eliot. "The Mind Is an Enchanting Thing," "Four Quartz Crystal Clocks," "What Are Years?" and "The Pangolin" are reprinted with permission of Macmillan Publishing Company from *The Collected Poems of Marianne Moore*. Copyright © 1941 and renewed 1969, by Marianne Moore. "His Shield," "Armour's Undermining Modesty" and "The Steeple-Jack" are reprinted with permission of Macmillan Publishing Company from *The Collected Poems of Marianne Moore* by Marianne Moore. Copyright © 1951 by Marianne Moore, renewed 1979 by Lawrence E. Brinn and Louise Crane. Lines from "The Student" are reprinted with permission of Macmillan Publishing Company from *What Are Years* by Marianne Moore. Copyright © 1941, and renewed 1969, by Marianne Moore. European rights to reprint passages of certain poems from *The Complete Poems of Marianne Moore* and *Selected Poems of Marianne Moore* by Marianne Moore are granted by Faber and Faber Ltd., London.

"Logic and 'The Magic Flute'" Copyright © 1956 by Marianne Moore, from *The Complete Poems of Marianne Moore* by Marianne Moore is used by permission of Viking Penguin, a division of Penguin Books USA Inc. "The Steeple-Jack," Copyright 1951 © 1970 by Marianne Moore, © renewed 1979 by Lawrence E. Brinn and Louise Crane, Executors of the Estate of Marianne Moore. "O to Be a Dragon," Copyright © 1957 by Marianne Moore, renewed 1985 by Lawrence E. Brinn and Louise Crane, Executors of the Estate of Marianne Moore. "Charity Overcoming Envy," Copyright © 1963 by Marianne Moore. "The Mind, Intractable Thing," Copyright © 1965 by Marianne Moore from *The Complete Poems of Marianne Moore* by Marianne Moore. Used by permission of Viking Penguin, a division of Penguin Books USA Inc.

Excerpts of a previously unpublished letter from John Ashbery to Marianne Moore housed in the Moore archive at the Rosenbach Museum and Library are used by permission of John Ashbery.

Quotations from the books of Job and Sirach (Ecclesiasticus) are taken from the 1609 Douai-Rheims translation of the Old Testament (DR) and from the New American Bible of 1970 (NAB).

I wish to express my appreciation to previous Moore scholars who have paved the way to new insights into Moore's poems and who have enriched my own work with the texts; I particularly acknowledge the work of Donald Hall, John Slatin, Margaret Holley, and Bonnie Costello. Special thanks also to Patricia C. Willis who kindly "put me on the scent," to Nicole Mitchell of the University of Alabama Press for continued support, to William C. Pratt and John G. Parks of Miami University at Oxford for suggestions and encouragement, to my copyeditor, Craig Noll, for extraordinary diligence and patience, to librarian Rhoda Boyer for her friendship and persistence, and to my husband, Larry, for his confidence and perseverance, to Larry and Mary for believing in me, and for D. G. for inspiration when all else failed.

Marianne Moore Chronology

1887 Born 15 November in Kirkwood, Missouri

1894 Family moves to Carlisle, Pennsylvania (age 7)

1896 Begins preparatory education at Metzger Institute, Carlisle (age 8)

1905 Finishes high school; enters Bryn Mawr College (age 17)

1909 Receives A.B.; enrolls at Carlisle Commercial College (age 21)

1910 Completes commercial courses (age 22)

1911 First visits with her mother to England and Paris during the summer; begins teaching commercial subjects at U.S. Industrial Indian School, Carlisle (age 23)

1915 First poems appear in the *Egoist* (London), *Poetry* (Chicago), and *Others* (New York) (age 27–28)

1916 Moves to Chatham, New Jersey, where she and her mother keep house for her brother, John Warner Moore, pastor of Ogden Memorial Church (age 28)

1918 Moves with mother to New York City; works as secretary and private tutor in a girls' school (age 30–31)

1921 Publication of *Poems* by Egoist Press (England); takes part-time job in Hudson Park Branch of New York Public Library (age 33–34)

1924 Dial Press publishes *Observations* and awards her $2,000 in recognition of "unusual literary value" (age 36–37)

1925 Becomes acting editor of the *Dial* magazine (age 37)

1926 Assumes job as editor of the *Dial* (age 38)

1928 First poem to be translated, "A Grave," appears in *Anthologie de la nouvelle poésie* (age 40)

1929 The *Dial* ceases publication; she and her mother move to Brooklyn; devotes full time to writing (age 41)

1935 Brings out *Selected Poems*, introduced by T. S. Eliot (age 47)

1936 *The Pangolin and Other Verse* (age 48)

1941 *What Are Years* (age 53)

1944 *Nevertheless* (age 56)

1945 *Rock Crystal: A Christmas Tale*, by Adalbert Stifter, translated by Elizabeth Mayer and Marianne Moore; receives Guggenheim Fellowship (age 57)

1947 Elected to National Institute of Arts and Letters; mother dies. During this period she begins wearing the tricorne hat and cape as her personal trademark (her mother had fashioned the first cape in 1905, and she had worn a cape in college). (age 59)

1949 Wilson College confers Litt.D., first of sixteen honorary degrees from American colleges and universities (age 61)

1951 *Collected Poems* published; receives a Pulitzer Prize and National Book Award (age 63)

1953 Visiting lecturer at Bryn Mawr College, which gives her M. Carey Thomas award; *Collected Poems* wins Bollingen Prize. Brooklyn's Youth United for a Better Tomorrow selects her for Youth Oscar; *Women's Home Companion* chooses her as one of the six most successful women of the year (age 65)

1954 *Gedichte*, bilingual edition of her poetry, published in Germany; the translation of *Fables of La Fontaine* is published (age 66)

1955 *Predelictions*, selected essays and reviews, is published; elected member of the American Academy of Arts and Letters (age 67)

1956 *Like a Bulwark* (age 68)

1959 *O to Be a Dragon* (age 71)

1961 *A Marianne Moore Reader* (age 73)

1962 National Institute of Arts and Letters observes her seventy-fifth birthday; Brandeis University awards her a prize and medal for outstanding achievement in poetry; *The Absentee* (age 75)

1963 *Puss in Boots*, *Cinderella*, and *Sleeping Beauty* retold (age 75)

1964 *The Arctic Ox. Festschrift for Marianne Moore's Seventy-Seventh Birthday*, by Various Hands, and *Omaggio a Marianne Moore* are published (age 77)

1965 Moves to Manhattan; *Tell Me, Tell Me* appears (age 78)

1967 *Complete Poems* published; receives Edward MacDowell Medal and Poetry Society of America's Gold Medal; receives the Croix de Chevalier des Arts et Lettres (age 79)

1968 Wins National Medal for Literature; throws out first baseball of the season at Yankee Stadium (age 80)

1969 Named "Senior Citizen of the Year" in New York Conference on Aging; receives honorary degree, her last, from Harvard (age 81)

1970 Publishes final poems, "The Magician's Retreat" and "Prevalent at One Time"; becomes semi-invalid (age 82–83)

1972 Dies 5 February in New York City (age 84)

1981 *The Complete Poems of Marianne Moore*, definitive edition, with the author's final revisions.

1986 *The Complete Prose of Marianne Moore*

Illusion
Is More Precise
Than Precision

The Wizard
in Words

> O imagnifico,
> wizard in words—poet, was it, as
> Alfred Panzini defined you?
> Weren't you refracting just now
> on my eye's half-closed triptych
>   the image, enhanced, of a glen—
>   Marianne Moore, "The Mind, Intractable Thing"

D. H. Lawrence once observed that "it is hard to hear a new voice, as hard as it is to listen to an unknown language. . . . The world fears a new experience more than it fears anything. Because a new experience displaces many old experiences. And it is like trying to use muscles that have perhaps never been used, or that have been going stiff for ages. It hurts horribly."[1] Although Marianne Moore's voice has been widely heard since her poetry was first published in 1915, it is a new voice in the sense in which D. H. Lawrence is speaking here. It is new not only because Moore was one of the few truly great technical originals that this century has produced but also because Moore used her verse to demonstrate a fresh, if age-old, epistemology. That way of knowing moved in a direction that still surprises her readers and continues to challenge her critics.

Just as D. H. Lawrence surmised it would be, hearing this new voice of Marianne Moore is difficult, almost like listening to an unknown language. And it is difficult for many reasons that most critics have never entirely understood. Even her staunchest supporters admit that Moore's works "can be exasperating in their allusions to the things we cannot quite grasp, filled with jarring combinations of images."[2] I suggest that a central difficulty with understanding Moore's verse is that readers and critics have been measuring her work against the wrong experiential models, using yardsticks that simply will not work, instead of learning to appreciate the discourse from its own original perspectives. I am not sure that Moore herself always understood the revolution she was so quietly effecting, for although she maintained great confidence in her work and took a healthy if humble pride in it, she remained a product of her own milieu. She does not appear to have seen herself as any kind of early spokeswoman for feminism. And John M. Slatin is probably correct when he suggests in *The Savage's Romance: The Poetry of Marianne Moore* that Moore was continuously measuring her style and content against the models of her male contemporaries and accommodating her work to what she may have perceived as a master's voice. And she often heard that master voice in the criticism of T. S. Eliot.[3] But her greatest successes always came when Moore followed her own instincts to produce poetry which told the *truths* (not merely the truth) about reality. "What is more precise than precision?" she asked in "Armor's Undermining Modesty." Her answer: illusion.[4] Moore was, it would seem, content to live with contradiction, paradox, ambiguity, intuition, ecstasy, and magic because those were far closer to the truth than anyone else's abstract precision.

I argue here that Marianne Moore came to poetry with the ways of knowing consonant with a woman's worldview, a woman's epistemology. At the same time, hers was a mind scientifically trained, one groomed for precision and innately attentive to detail. Moore took that training and that precision and turned it into something she herself perceived as nothing short of magical, for she discovered and to a real degree invented the means of speaking the truth about reality in a woman's voice that tended toward refracting (her own word choice in the epigraph above), bending, breaking apart, not toward the usual attempts at synthesizing and ordering the details of human perception.

In their landmark book *Women's Ways of Knowing*, researchers Belenky, Clinchy, Goldberger, and Tarule argue that most studies of human epistemology have tended to omit women from their consideration and have typically been content to look for ways in which women conform to or diverge from patterns found in the model studies of men. Attributes typically associated with the masculine are abstract critical thought and the search for objective, or "scientific," truth. The mental processes involved in considering the abstract and the impersonal have traditionally been labeled thinking and are attributed to men, while those that deal with personal and interpersonal experience as a route to thought fall under the rubric of intuition or even emotion and have tended to be associated with women.[5] That is not to suggest that both men and women are not both thinking and intuitive human beings. But over time, the art of thinking and abstraction tended to be valued more highly than the less easily explained process called intuition. One must be careful not to perceive the ways of knowing under consideration here as merely the differences between deductive and inductive reasoning. Moore's sense of intuition, of what she humorously came to call her sense of illusion, was far more complex than simple induction. It is inextricably bound up in her own uniquely feminine method of comprehending her world.

In *The Feminization of American Culture*, Ann Douglas has suggested that part of the legacy of the Victorian past has been a move toward a literature of inclusiveness rather than a literature of limitation.[6] That sense of inclusiveness, according to Douglas, marks an increasing awareness of the positive epistemological strategies one can learn from the feminine mind. Joseph Campbell has also suggested that the female represents what "in Kantian terminology we call the forms of sensibility. She is time and space itself, and the mystery beyond her is beyond all pairs of opposites. So it isn't male and it isn't female. It neither is nor is not. But everything is within her, so that the gods are her children. Everything you can think of, everything you can see, is a production of the Goddess."[7] Campbell's vision is another way of describing the feminine sense of inclusiveness. We are only beginning to understand the true symbiotic relationship of what the Chinese ancients called the yin and the yang as active parts of all human beings, male and female. Feminine thinking, including the tendency toward inclusiveness, can only add to human knowledge and to the broadening of human understanding.

As a great intellect and as a woman, Moore tended to operate in the world of intuition and inclusion quite naturally, and she happened very early onto the idea that human access to truth has many avenues, many voices. Carol Gilligan supports this very point in her study *In a Different Voice*, observing that "sensitivity to the needs of others and the assumption of responsibility for taking care lead women to voices other than their own and to include in their judgment other points of view. . . . The reluctance to judge may itself be indicative of the care and concern for others that infuse the psychology of women's development."[8]

To look at it another way, Moore moved instinctively into what critic Mikhail Bakhtin has called polyphony, the freedom for the points of view of others to reveal themselves.[9] But that very openness to various points of view and to ambiguities of meaning tends to confuse many of Moore's readers, especially those who are used to looking for a synthesis of meaning, for an abstraction, for what has been called a moral in a poem.

The perception that human access to objective truth might be relative is an important dimension of contemporary reasoning. There is evidence of a real effort in the last half of the twentieth century to move away from traditional learning as "banking," wherein the active expert deposits "true knowledge" into the minds of the passive learner. The epistemology of our time comprehends that truth, at least to its human perceivers, is probably relative, that the meaning of an event depends on the context in which that event occurs; relativism pervades all aspects of life. Knowledge, even so-called scientific knowledge, is constructed, not given; contextual, not absolute; mutable, not fixed.[10] Certainly such seemingly disparate avenues as the study of science or the development of the visual arts in the twentieth century explore that kind of relativity. It is also an important dimension of modernism.

Moore knew, as she herself put it in the titles of two essays, that she had a "burning desire to be explicit," a "mania for straight writing." But once she committed herself to telling the truth, her poetry seldom seemed explicit or straight. Rather it takes the careful reader into the interstices, into the highest level of human understanding, into the realm of what philosopher Henri Bergson called intuition. "All I can say," Moore wrote, "is that one must be as clear as one's natural reticence allows one to be."[11] If one would tell the truth, one must tell it as accurately and precisely as one can, even if that means admitting that those insights are fragmentary, incongruous, and kaleidoscopic, what Moore would come to see as image-laden, as imagination-induced—in short, as magical—all words from the same root and clearly connected, from Marianne Moore's point of view. Language is by its very nature a kind of magic because it puts names on what can be both seen (imaged) and then re-imaged in the mind (imagined).

In great music and dance, for example, one catches an occasional glimpse of the beautiful representation of truth, as in Mozart's *Magic Flute*. But the glimpse is so momentary, so fragmentary, as to leave only a flash of insight into the reality it signals. It cannot be held, only re-called, and then imperfectly. Any pursuit of the truth, of the genuine, will always take the selective mind beyond what mere words or sounds or movements and the realities they represent and can capture, into a world just beyond the reckoning of the usual human consciousness, a world of something very much like magic. For Marianne Moore, illusion is more precise than precision. And that illusion, that magic of intuition, is an important part of a woman's way of knowing; it is a new epistemology only because so few women have ever had the opportunity to give it voice. But as D. H. Lawrence suggested about any new voice, the liter-ary world is suspicious of and uncomfortable with the work of Marianne Moore because it represents a new experience and because by its very nature it displaces many old experiences.

The main purpose of this study, then, is to examine the poetic tech-niques of Marianne Moore to show how she executes a precision so exact that it can tap the real source of human creativity: the image, the imag-ination, magic—what Moore calls "divine fire, a perquisite of the gods."[12] I will show that Moore's was a woman's way of knowing, an epistemology that valued both order and inclusiveness. I will argue fur-ther that Moore came to cast herself wryly as a wonder, a conjurer, an "imagnifico," a "wizard in words." Of profound impact on my vision of Moore's technique and her worldview is an awareness of her pervasive sense of humor, which permeates the work to a degree not yet explored by any critic, but long suspected by her admirers. As Donald Hall first pointed out in *Marianne Moore: The Cage and the Animal*, such discon-nection of mind may be an affront to logic, but it is imagination's way of life. "Imagination sees a crazy, underlying connection, be it linguistic or visual, that permits seemingly disparate things to be conjoined in the mind."[13] Part of the facade of the magician, the spell Moore taught her-self to cast, is an enchantment rich with an appreciation for the in-congruous. She finds the joy of laughter, but a laughter of such a special kind that one must learn to recognize and enjoy it. Moore once spoke of a respected colleague's "susceptibility to happiness." That susceptibility was shared by Moore herself. For Moore was a remarkably comic spirit, in the truest, most classical sense of the word. Hers were indeed "con-juries that endure," another apparent contradiction in terms. Moore's magic was solid stuff; the power of the visible was the invisible; her imaginary gardens have real toads. What I am addressing here is the fact that like the work of any great magician, Moore's work was the result of a remarkable care, precision, and timing—and her magic show involved both an array of subjects and a volley of techniques unlike any attempted before her.

There is no doubt that Moore's discourse is worthy of effort, and yet it is still in real need of the critical tools to make it accessible. As early as 1918, Ezra Pound wrote to Moore, "You will never sell more than five hundred copies, as your work demands mental attention . . . [but] Your stuff holds my eye."[14] Hilda Doolittle (known as H.D.), who, along with Annie Winifred Ellerman (who took the byname Bryher), arranged for the first publication of a book of poems by Moore, wrote in 1916 that Moore "turns her perfect craft as the perfect craftsman must inevitably do, to some direct presentation of beauty, cut in flowing lines, but so delicately that the very screen she carves seems to stand only in that serene palace of her own world of inspiration—frail, yet as all beautiful things are, absolutely hard—and destined to endure."[15] T. S. Eliot, in his introduction to Moore's *Selected Poems* of 1935, makes the most famous pronouncement: "Miss Moore's poems form part of the small body of durable poetry written in our time."[16] He had responded even before to the publication of *Observations* by suggesting that Marianne Moore already had imitators and that her poetry was "too good to be appreciated anywhere."[17] William Carlos Williams said of her work, "It is the white of a clarity beyond the facts." He was enchanted by her techniques from the beginning, writing that "Miss Moore gets great pleasure from wiping soiled words or cutting them clean out, removing the aureoles that have been pasted about them or taking them bodily from greasy contexts. For the compositions which Miss Moore intends, each word should first stand crystal clear with no attachments; not even an aroma."[18]

Few would deny both Moore's excellence and her complexity, but as the poet Amy Clampitt declared in a paper presented at the Moore centenary in 1987, it is time that the world expends some energy "getting to know Marianne Moore." Her poetry is worth our effort and badly in need of the visual, verbal, and syntactic tools to approach it. Three recent book-length studies—Bonnie Costello's *Marianne Moore: Imaginary Possessions* (1981), John M. Slatin's *Savage's Romance: The Poetry of Marianne Moore* (1986), and Margaret Holley's *Poetry of Marianne Moore: A Study in Voice and Value* (1987)—have made useful contributions to Moore study, with all three critics providing useful approaches to Moore's themes and techniques. In this book I examine representative texts themselves and offer the serious student of Marianne Moore some consistently successful strategies for dealing with the discourse from both technical and epistemological perspectives.

Each poem offers its own set of challenges; Moore never used the same set of techniques in exactly the same way twice. And one philosophical decision tended to build upon and to presuppose another; they are all-inclusive. But a systematic approach to her style, syntax, and strategies makes access possible. As T. S. Eliot warned in a letter to Moore in 1934, "At your simplest you baffle those who love 'simple' poetry; and so one might as well put on difficult stuff at once, and only bid for readers who are willing and accustomed to take a little trouble over poetry."[19]

Bonnie Costello has suggested that Moore was very sensitive to the image, to the visual. Somewhat akin to Thoreau imagining himself the owner of various farm properties in "Where I Lived and What I Lived For" in *Walden*, in "When I Buy Pictures" Moore found herself considering those times when "I may regard myself as the imaginary possessor" of various objets d'art. Such possession gives Moore the chance to experiment with the ownership of something perfectly beautiful or something which may allow the pursuit of the genuine, the pursuit of truth, with what Moore calls her recklessness, her ardor. "How did I come to be an artist?" she responds to Donald Hall's question with one of her famous borrowed quotations (the many voices she always heard), her objets trouvés, this one from George Grosz, "Endless curiosity, observation, research—and a great amount of joy in the thing."[20] For Moore it was, after all, a matter of taking an informed liking to things and choosing to like and to examine the many dimensions of most any object or idea.

This was certainly the worldview suggested by Henri Bergson, French philosopher and winner of the Nobel Prize for literature in 1927. Bergson's studies of time led him to value what he saw as the highest level of human understanding: intuition—the world of the poet, the saint, and the philosopher. From one point of view, this is the world of magic, although not in the usual sense of the word. For this kind of enchantment is accomplished by excellence in conception and execution. Getting to such magic, regardless of the art form one uses, is done only with infinite care, timing, and precision. "Magic" is not made of mystery, but by hard and meticulous work, a labor of which the audience is not usually aware. This hard work is the true realm of the conjurer. Thus Bergson could praise the kind of "open society" which valued the intuitive mind of the poet, the prophet, the hero, and the saint, characters from Moore's own playbill. Never one to operate in the world of the expected, Moore's rabbit in the hat would become an elephant, a jerboa, a jellyfish, a frigate pelican, a pangolin, a whale, a snail, an ostrich, and a giraffe, although her preferences would frequently turn to dragons or plumet basilisks, which did, after all, portray "mythology's wish / to be interchangeably man and fish" ("The Plumet Basilisk"). ("Humor saves a few steps," Moore wrote in "The Pangolin"—"it saves years.")

Beneath, then, the veneer of this small and diffident woman lay one of the most remarkable poetic voices of the twentieth century, an artist for whom life proved an exhilarating experience. Many male critics have applauded Moore's poetry, although they frequently seem at some loss to explain its effectiveness. Andrew J. Kappel has called Moore's poetry a "triumphant demonstration of repeated mastery of the chaos that surrounds us." Through her quiet and repeated acts of will, Moore devised the means, not of escaping the world as Eliot had, nor of savoring it as Stevens would, but of transforming it, and of doing so on her own epistemological terms—with gusto.[21] Kappel is aware that Moore's ways of knowing connect with the world, with the earth, that they do more than merely intellectualize about it, but he does not stop to analyze the nature of what he calls her mastery. And although William Carlos Williams was consistent in his praise of Moore's work, he seems to marvel that a woman could have produced it. Marianne Moore's is a "talent which diminishes the tom-toming of the hollow men of a wasteland to irrelevant pitter-patter. Nothing is hollow or waste in the imagination of Marianne Moore. How so slight a woman can so roar, like a secret Niagara and with so gracious an inference, is one with all the mysteries, where strength masquerading as weakness—a woman, a frail woman—bewilders us. The magic name of Marianne Moore has been among my most cherished possessions."[22]

Reading her with a poet's perception, Donald Hall first asked that readers consider the common root in the words "image," "imagination," and "magic," for it seems clear that Marianne Moore has made precisely that connection in her own work.[23] Actually most critics who think and write about Marianne Moore slip quite readily and almost unconsciously into a metaphor of magic. Moore scholar Bonnie Costello, for example, writes that her "poetry turns out to be the magic trick . . . which absorbs us in its dazzling sleight-of-hand, in which we glimpse the genuine before it turns into the poet once again."[24] And Randall Jarrell writes in "The Humble Animal" that Moore's "forms have the lacy, mathematical extravagance of snowflakes, seem as arbitrary as the prohibitions of fairy tales; but they work as those work—disregard them and everything goes to pieces. Her forms, tricks and all, are like the aria of the Queen of Night: the intricate and artificial elaboration that not only does not conflict with emotion, it is its vehicle." Jarrell likens Moore's methods and mannerisms to the Cheshire cat's smile, which bewitched one for some time after the smile was gone.[25]

And Miss Moore herself offers great support for the critics' tendency to speak in such terms. Her own predilection for words of enchantment is evident in her poetry and prose. In fact, it is difficult to find a work by Moore without some kind of "magic" in it. Some of them are obvious: "The Wizard in Words," "Diligence Is to Magic As Progress Is to Flight," "The Mind Is an Enchanting Thing," "Logic and 'The Magic Flute,'" "Conjuries That Endure," "Sea Unicorns and Land Unicorns," "Sojourn in the Whale," "Snakes, Mongooses, Snake-Charmers, and the Like," "O to Be a Dragon," "My Crow Pluto," "Apparition of Splendor," and "Puss in Boots." Other words of enchantment appear in lines of the poetry itself, like the famous "imaginary gardens with real toads in them" (in "Poetry," *Selected Poems*) or "the power of the visible is the invisible" (in "He 'Digesteth Harde Yron'"). In "The Plumet Basilisk,"

> the basilisk portrays
> mythology's wish
> to be interchangeably man and fish.

"Spenser's Ireland" offers that

> . . . their pride,
> like the enchanter's,
> is in care, not madness.

"Sojourn in the Whale" declares, "You have been compelled by hags to spin / gold thread from straw." Moore spoke of "the conjuring wand of Henry James"[26] and suggested that Wallace Stevens's "method of hints and disguises should have Mercury as consultant-magician."[27]

Writing about the mystery of Anna Pavlova's dancing, Marianne Moore says, "One suggests that she so intently thought the illusion she wished to create that it made her illusive—hands and feet obeying imagination in a way that compensated for any flaw."[28] In another essay, entitled

"Subject, Predicate, Object," first published in 1957, Moore says, "Dazzled, speechless—an alchemist without implements—one thinks of poetry as divine fire, a perquisite of the gods. When under the spell of admiration or gratitude, I have hazarded a line, it never occurred to me that anyone might think I imagined myself a poet."[29] One must never take lightly Marianne Moore's use of any word. She always invites— demands—myriad considerations of a word and its origins, leaving us, as she does here, with disquieting ambiguity. Look at the phrase long enough, and the word "imagine" deconstructs itself into image and magic—and the famous Moore modesty takes on a new dimension. With startling legerdemain she presses the reader toward the truth, as Costello has suggested, and just for a moment we glimpse the genuine, in this case the fact that Marianne Moore is playing with the word "imagine" and we see an entirely opposite meaning in the passage. Moore's natural modesty may not be modesty at all. She imagined, imaged, made her work—as if by magic.

I will argue further that Miss Moore also taps the power of her own faith to establish a woman's sense of order and meaning over chaos, although her expression of that faith is almost always carefully camou- flaged in the works. When discussing writing in her essay "A Burning Desire to Be Explicit," Moore recalled Faulkner's ultimate defense of the whole business of writing: "It should help a man endure by lifting up his heart." With characteristic aplomb, Moore added only, "It should."[30] But to lift the human spirit, one must engage the power of the imagina- tion to glimpse the reality beyond the obvious. Moore's method, like that of the great magician always involves precision. All execution must be perfectly and precisely timed, and the materials she chooses, although frequently common objects and words from daily life, must be meticu- lously arranged and turned so that the audience can be taken to the outer edges of perception and made to find the genuine, the "rock / crystal thing to see" ("The Hero"). This is indeed an enchanted thing. And as Moore herself so deftly says in "The Monkeys," if such enchantment seems unusual or abnormal, she is "supreme in [her] abnormality." She is the imagnifico, the wizard in words.

In support of this perception, consider that one of Marianne Moore's two final poems, written in 1970, just two years before her death at age eighty-four, is entitled "The Magician's Retreat." Ostensibly the poem was occasioned by a small color reproduction of René Magritte's painting *Domain of Lights* from the *New York Times Magazine*. According to

Moore scholar Patricia C. Willis, Moore also owned a copy of *Arts Magazine*, which carried an article about the work of an eighteenth-century visionary architect, Jean-Jacques Lequeu.[31] On the cover appeared "Repaire des magiciens" (The magician's retreat), an eerie architectural drawing of a Gothic house complete with niches for magicians in pointed hats and elephant gargoyles on the facade. Evidently the two pictures took Miss Moore's fancy because she took the title from the drawing and wrote it at the top of the clipping showing Magritte's painting.

At first glance, the poem inspired by the painting and the illustration appears to describe an eerie house:

The Magician's Retreat

of moderate height
(I have seen it)
cloudy but bright inside
like a moonstone,
while a yellow glow
from a shutter-crack shone,
and a blue glow from the lamppost
close to the front door.
It left nothing of which to complain,
nothing more to obtain,
consummately plain.

A black tree mass rose at the back
almost touching the eaves
with the definiteness of Magritte,
was above all discreet.

Had it not been for a repeated metaphor about Moore used by William Carlos Williams and preserved in his *Autobiography* and *Selected Essays* (and verified as existing in Miss Moore's consciousness by the Donald Hall interview of 1961),[32] the reader might not perceive the subtle connection between the "consummately plain" little house, which was "above all discreet," and Marianne Moore's poignant perception of herself. William Carlos Williams wrote that Marianne Moore was "like a rafter holding up the superstructure of our uncompleted building, a caryatid, her red hair plaited and wound twice about the fine skull . . . she was surely one of the main supports of the new order."[33] ("I didn't hold anybody up," Moore responded in the Donald Hall interview.) In his

Selected Essays, Williams also described Moore as "straight up and down like the two-by-fours of a building under construction."[34] It scarcely takes the leap of a jerboa or the quicksilver ferocity of a plumet basilisk to alert the Moore reader that the comic imagination had been called into play. Thus the house of "moderate height" which the poet has seen becomes the poet herself, cloudy on the outside, but "bright inside / like a moonstone." With bright mind still glowing in the gathering darkness and blue eyes still shining, the poet, though "consummately plain," leaves "nothing of which to complain." With characteristic good humor, as she feels herself sinking into the "black tree mass" of infinity, Marianne Moore teases us into laughing with her that she is "above all discreet." For if we have seen the final, real-life caricature Moore created for herself—her flowing cape and tricorne hat, her "yellow glow" of wit and humor—we know that her discretion, her armor, has always been part of the facade which has covered the performance of the imagnifico.

Moore's choice of the word "retreat" is also interesting. If indeed the poem is about her as well as it is about the two houses, she is characterizing herself as a magician—and not only speaking of the privacy of her own person but also sounding a retreat in another sense, that of her withdrawal, at the end of her life, from the active battle in which she had struggled for so long. And a battle it must have been, particularly for a woman whose intellectual credibility was sometimes in question merely because she was a woman. Representative of the kind of thinking common to some members of the Stieglitz circle, for example, Mexican caricaturist Marius de Zayas wrote a poem called "Femme!" for *291* in 1915. In the poem woman possesses "pas d'intellectuelisme," "pas de forme,' and is "pas le miroir de son mâle." She is instead "matérialité pure."[35] By implication man is her opposite: "cérébral" and "intellectuel"; he possesses "forme" and is "spiritualité pure." It took a woman of rare self-assurance to succeed in such a milieu and to create and maintain her own voice.

Researcher Carol Gilligan has written, "At a time when efforts are being made to eradicate discrimination between the sexes in the search for social equality and justice, the differences between the sexes are being rediscovered in the social sciences . . . the presumed neutrality of science, like that of language itself, gives way to the recognition that the categories of knowledge are human constructions."[36] It is not so much the discovery of real differences between the sexes that one fears but instead the continued value judgment that one way of knowing is by its very nature superior to another, that to be successful in the arts or in the academy, one must "think like a man." By walking a very delicate course, Marianne Moore succeeded in maintaining the credibility of her own epistemology while continuing to dazzle her critics with her conjuries. It is my contention that Marianne Moore's is a new discourse worth the struggle to understand because it speaks brilliantly in a woman's voice. Given the attention it deserves, that voice will continue to displace, as it already has displaced, many old experiences. Moore demonstrates what has seldom been demonstrated so effectively before: a woman's way of knowing. Illusion can be more precise than precision—if one is a wizard in words.

CHAPTER 1

What Are Years?

One of Marianne Moore's most subtle and pervasive themes was that of time. Many if not most of her poems discuss time and duration either directly or indirectly, dealing in one way or another with the scientific and philosophical principles about time that fascinated her and her modernist colleagues. For at the root of Moore's perception of time is, paradoxically, the explanation of her own value as a woman and as an artist and her position as an optimistic believer in a force beyond the limitations of her own place and time.

In their book entitled *Einstein as Myth and Muse*, Friedman and Donley make the assertion that from the turn of the twentieth century until 1922, revolutions were occurring in the world of ideas that went far beyond the usual cyclic and temporary revolts of a younger generation against its elders. One cannot separate revolutionary ideas into tidy compartments of "science," "philosophy," or "art." New ways of thinking and seeing in one always affect the logic of the others. So it was not mere coincidence that in 1921 Albert Einstein won the Nobel Prize in physics, and one year later T. S. Eliot published *The Waste Land* while James Joyce published *Ulysses*. (In 1921 Marianne Moore's friends had published her first major book of poetry, *Poems*, and in 1924 another book of poems appeared, entitled *Observations*. The latter title suggests a kind of scientific perspective directed by her own interest and training in biology and perhaps inspired by Eliot's *Prufrock and Other Observations*, published in 1917.) And in 1927 a French philosopher won the Nobel Prize in literature—Henri Bergson, whose major work, first published in 1889, was entitled *Time and Free Will.* Bergson's ideas had long been widely discussed, both in philosophical and literary circles, for they dealt with the new revolutions in scientific thought from Darwin through Einstein that seemed to undermine the metaphysical and epistemological assumptions that had formed the basis of human thought for centuries. (One must remember that time and space are both philosophical and scientific [i.e., physical] principles. Even Aristotle discusses time in "The Physics." The line between mathematics and philosophy is surprisingly thin; both time and space are attempts to measure the unmeasurable through human—that is to say, scientific—means.)

This was certainly not the first revolution inaugurated by the redefinition of scientific principles. One has only to recall the impact of the ideas of Galileo to realize that such major reexaminations have altered the perspectives of generations. But twentieth-century physics offered two new worldviews, relativity and quantum theory, which differed so drastically from the conventional views of scientists that philosophers and artists were forced to reassess their own concepts of truth, order, beauty, and time. Modern painters, for example, began to explore whole new methods of spatial ordering. Musicians were busy redefining the rules of harmony. And modern writers came to reexamine every facet of the ways they ordered words and the ideas those words represented. Guillaume Appolinaire's *l'esprit nouveau* and Ezra Pound's dictum "Make it new!" eventually became the rallying cry of the literary modernists. In his book *Time and Western Man*, Wyndham Lewis observed that "point for point what I had observed on the literary, social and artistic plane was reproduced upon the philosophic and theoretic: and with startling identity, the main notion or colour at the bottom of the theoretical system was precisely the same thing as what was to be observed throughout the social and literary life of the day."[1] Many artists were invigorated by the new ideas. William Carlos Williams, for example, described the intellectual atmosphere as "a springtime of the mind."[2] But for others and for their audiences the new ideas of the avant-garde seemed inane; they contradicted common sense, observable reality, and traditional styles. And the negative reaction sometimes turned violent. There were riots at exhibitions and performances. There was furor at the "deviltry" of a Darwin or an Einstein. Such reactions were, from a later perspective, understandable. For the alterations required of the average person's perceptions of reality were staggering. At base was the notion of relativity, a new kind of mutability or ambiguity about basic concepts, in a world that seemed confusing enough already.

But confusing or not, the concept of relativity could not be dismissed; it had to be assimilated into the epistemology of the twentieth century. In May 1921, *Dial* art editor Thomas Jewell Craven wrote: "Professor Einstein's revolutionary theory is the latest example of the external kinship between art and science. . . . The fixed coordinates upon which the Newtonian measurements were erected have their parallel in more than one artistic manifestation . . . and it is this abstract quality which establishes the analogy between the old art and the classical mechanics. Professor Einstein's general theory of relativity has shaken the whole physical structure."[3]

Literary theory and practice needed reinterpretation and validation in the face of the new science and the new philosophy, and Marianne Moore was in a unique position to address that need. She could examine science from a new and personal perspective. She had always been interested in scientific observation and the recording of precise detail. She had even considered a career in medicine as a continuation of a major in biology at Bryn Mawr. In a discussion of what they call "separate knowing," Belenky, Clinchy, Goldberger, and Tarule suggest that most women who attend traditional elite liberal arts colleges (like Bryn Mawr) have been taught methods of critical thinking that ultimately lead the students to "the way *They* want you to think, in short, to learn to think like a man."[4] But almost from the beginning Moore valued her own epistemology; she had a tendency to explore her own ways of knowing. She was not particularly successful in English, for example; one professor remarked, "Please, a little lucidity. Your obscurity becomes greater and greater."[5]

Her first job, one she never talked about in print, was with Melvil Dewey, whose principles of organization and "scientific" methodization and accuracy, the Dewey decimal system, seem to have proved too much for the shy Bryn Mawr graduate. Moore left Dewey's employment at Lake Placid in upstate New York after only two months. (She did not work again for nearly a year.) Moore admitted to her mother that the detailed, repetitive, high-pressured work had not suited her. Dewey's reformed spelling system, based on his own scientific principles of spelling (note the missing "le" at the end of his own first name), may have seemed the final indignity to Moore.[6] Nonetheless Moore retained systems of organization throughout her lifetime and wrote frequently about her appreciation of precision, accuracy, and scientific discoveries, although often with a complex ambivalence. (She remained very attentive to the intricacies of orthography.)

As a matter of fact, Moore seems to have settled early on an essential connection beween science and its precision and the intentions and practice of the artist. In a letter written years later to William Carlos Williams, she remarked: "I lean on Pasteur. . . . I regard art—writing, I mean—to be more science than art, if it is to go beyond the writer; and marvel that we put up with haymows of selfexpression that is fluffy and unscientific."[7] It may have been a need to bridge the gap between science and poetry that directed Moore toward Bergson and his consideration of time.

Before Bergson, time was viewed in three distinct phases: the present must always be happening somewhere between what we call the past and the future. However, most have agreed that time has an oddly experiential quality; sometimes, at least as far as our immediate experience is concerned, time seems to speed up, while at other times it seems to move unendurably slowly, leading one to believe that objective and measurable time must be somehow independent of subjective time as it is experienced. Thus these two experiences of time, the chronological and the psychological, often seem at odds. It was this diffeerence that led Bergson to his new theory of time in the early part of the twentieth century. As he wrote to the American pragmatist William James, "I saw to my great astonishment, that scientific time does not endure . . . that positive science consists essentially in the attempt to eliminate duration."[8] Bergson's *Time and Free Will: An Essay on the Immediate Data of Consciousness* (1899) attempted to establish the notion of duration (*durée*), or lived time, as opposed to the spatialized concept of a clock measured by science. One must never confuse duration with extension, succession with simultaneity, or quality with quantity. And *durée reale*, which Bergson described as image after image in a spectrum of a thousand shades, does really exist in a kind of eternal now. However it can be known only by intuition, the highest stage in the human mind. Thus Bergson could praise the "open society" which valued the intuitive mind of the poet, the prophet, the hero, and the saint. In *Creative Evolution* (1909) Bergson went on to defend evolution by demonstrating that it supported *durée*, or permanence, at the same time that it produced the élan vital, the vital impulse that is continually generating new forms. Evolution is, in short, creative, not mechanistic.

Bergson's philosophy found in William James an enthusiastic reader who brought the ideas to America. Since we know that by the fall of 1907, Marianne Moore had become friends with Peggy James, Henry's niece and William's daughter, some early acquaintance with Bergsonian theory seems possible.[9] But whether or not the ideas were taken from Bergsonian texts directly or from discussions about ideas that were merely "in the air," Moore seems to have been processing Bergsonian ways of thinking. Part of what may have made Bergson's ideas so attractive to Moore, and to other artists and poets, was that he made a significant connection between time, intuition, and the arts. His philosophical position justified the arts and validated their worth at the very time that scientific theories seemed to be negating their value. For Bergson believed that through intuition, the artist develops a power most human beings rarely use. When one moves beyond being a doer to being a knower, one rises to real intuition, the highest stage in the evolution of human understanding. Thus an intelligent young woman like Marianne Moore could place the highest value on her "burning desire to be explicit." She could put her powers of scientific observation, what she would call her preoccupation with the minutiae, to the service of the highest stage in the evolution of human understanding: intuition. Such a life focus was clearly an idea derived from Bergsonian thought.

But Moore's interest in Bergson went beyond the generality of this theory of intuition and the arts. She was also interested in his view that scientific attempts to measure time actually misrepresent its reality. Human beings experience time as continuous; only "spatialized" time measured by clocks is taken to have separate units (i.e., seconds, minutes, hours). These units are merely conventionally accepted measures imposed by human beings upon an ultimately vital, and continuously immediate, experience. In *Time and Free Will*, Bergson argued that scientific time does not really endure, because one psychologically perceived fact and one perceived moment is always different from any other. Such views placed Bergson in direct opposition to the French positivist movement, then in its ascendancy. For the positivist, the scientific world seemed to offer—at least eventually—the keys to all knowledge because it could measure and explain the logical reasons behind all things. Bergson never accepted that position; science could provide details, but it could never substitute for the magic of intuition. It is evident that Bergson conceived of the functions of the artist and the intuitive metaphysician as very similar.[10] So, there are two profoundly different ways of knowing: the one, which reaches its perfection in science, is analytic, spatializing, and conceptualizing, tending to see things as solid and discontinuous. The other is an intuition that is universal, immediate, reaching by sympathy to the heart. The first is useful for getting ordinary things done, but it fails to reach essential realities precisely because it leaves out duration (*durée*) and its perpetual flux, which is inexpressible as scientific fact and can be grasped only by intuition. Nonetheless, the two aspects of knowing and of time exist in a complementary relationship. Precisely in that relationship Moore would find her own raison d'être.

By 1915, the twenty-eight-year-old Moore had already been considering the meaning of time for several years, weighing its ramifications in some of her earliest, but in many ways, most difficult works. In fact, the contemporary reader frequently has to move carefully into the disarming simplicity of some of the earlier poems with a keen awareness of their actual complexity. "The Past Is the Present" is an interesting example.

The Past Is the Present

> If external action is effete
> and rhyme is outmoded,
>   I shall revert to you,
> Habakkuk, as on a recent occasion I was goaded
>   into doing by XY, who was speaking of unrhymed verse.
> This man said—I think that I repeat
>   his identical words:
>   "Hebrew poetry is
>   prose with a sort of heightened consciousness. 'Ecstasy affords
>   the occasion and expediency determines the form.'"
>
> *Observations*

It is difficult to approach this poem, first published in the December 1915 issue of *Poetry* magazine, without placing it in the context of Moore's interaction with other modernist poets, a subject of which she always remained wary. It is clear that some of the poem's perceptions are similar to those of other modernist poets, particularly those of Pound and Eliot, although it is not always possible to trace the interaction of the ideas. However, it seems probable that most early modernists were familiar with Bergsonian ideas; they were virtually in the air. As Kreymborg described the encounters of the young modernists in *Troubador*, there was "a joyous bewilderment in the discovery that other men and women were working in a field they themselves felt they had chosen in solitude. . . . Each of them had been cultivating a garden in the secrecy of his own isolation."[11] We know that Moore knew enough about Pound and his work before her first European trip in 1911 to purchase Pound's *Personae* and *Exultations* in London a year before the official beginning of the renaissance of poetry in the little magazines.[12]

We also know that she read the 1914 issue of the Vorticist magazine *Blast*, at the Library of Congress 2 March 1915.[13] Pound published *Cathay* in April 1915, eight months before the publication of Moore's "The Past Is the Present." In another essay published in 1915, this one in *Poetry* magazine, Pound declared, "It is possible that this century may find a new Greece in China."[14] Hugh Kenner has pointed out that *Cathay* is more than a collection of poetic translations created by a master translator; it demonstrates the way the calcified poetic language of one culture may become a viable model for the modern poetic language of an entirely different culture.[15] As John M. Slatin has commented, Moore's "new Greece" was not Chinese poetry, however, but Hebrew verse.

Moore's exposure to the Hebrew language through a series of lectures given in 1914–15 by a Presbyterian minister, E. H. Kellogg, in Carlisle, Pennsylvania, predates Pound's publication of the Fenollosa *Essay* by four years, but she quite probably had seen *Cathay* much earlier. And that exposure does suggest that Moore may have found some of the same lessons Pound had discovered about making an ancient poetic language an active model for a modern one. (From another perspective, T. S. Eliot also explored the role of the past in refining new works of art in a Bergsonian mode in *Tradition and the Individual Talent* in 1919.) It is obvious that Moore was already exploring the intricate relationship of the past and the present in a way analogous to the explorations of Pound and Eliot.

The title takes an unmitigated stand: "The Past Is the Present." In later poems about time such as "No Swan So Fine" and "Four Quartz Crystal Clocks," Moore proceeds to her thesis a bit more circuitously. This time the conclusion is announced at the outset, except it appears to contradict itself: one entity is declared to be another—the past is the present, a paradox. The theme deals particularly with time as it affects art. It examines the new poetic techniques and theories and how one might respond to the need to "make it new" in each succeeding generation.

The poem is only ten lines long; it is set in a syllabic pattern of 9, 6, 6, 15, 15, with a rhyme scheme of *a b x b x* and *a c x c x*. It is more abstract than visual, the only vivid and musical word being the memorable "Habakkuk." The syntax is couched in the conditional "if," complicating the entire message by hinging everything on the possibility/probability that "external action is effete / and rhyme is outmoded." If, therefore, literary styles and techniques of the recent past are obsolete, the poet must look for a style other than the unwholesome, unproductive, sterile modes of Victorian decadence. The choice of the word "effete" is a very interesting one. The word suggests sterility, an inability to reproduce. It is as though Bergson's élan vital, the vital impulse that evolves into new forms of life, has been rendered impotent. For positive, creative evolution to continue, the poet must seek a new direction. "External action," suggestive of a narrative or a sequential plot, is declared outdated, as is rhyme, which has become banal by overuse. (Note, though, that Moore does use rhyme, although of a more subtle, less conventional character.) Searching for a new idea, the poet sets out to find linguistic patterns not already explored and rendered "effete" in English poetry. She finds a literary precursor so little known (as was the case with Pound's Chinese and Provençal models) as to retain its freshness, at least in the English language.

Habakkuk was a minor Hebrew prophet of about the seventh century B.C. and the author of a book of the Bible bearing his name. The series of lectures given by the Reverend E. H. Kellogg, evidently the "XY" who "goaded" her into recognizing the quality of Hebrew verse, occasioned a new look at language and the way it works. Moore had also read A. R. Gordon's *Poets of the Old Testament* and four volumes by George Adam Smith which he had contributed to a series called *The Expositor's Bible*. As John Slatin has noted, the linguistic principles Moore extracted from her sources are remarkably similar to the principles Pound takes from his studies of the Fenollosa Notebooks. Slatin argues, in fact, that Pound *is* the carefully disguised Habakkuk, Moore's real connection between new inspiration and another linguistic model.[16] That thesis remains somewhat academic; the important point is that whatever the catalyst, Moore turned to Hebrew, not to Chinese, to derive her guiding principles.

"Hebrew is a phonetic tongue," Kellogg apparently told his audience, and "it is a language of pictures [with] very little inflection. Every word has in it a picture and often a picture of an action—'movies.'"[17] This entry was made in Moore's notebooks in 1914. In 1915 Moore quotes Kellogg as saying that "there is an image in the heart of every Hebrew word."[18] In addition to this emphasis on the pictorial quality of Hebrew, Moore's sources share with Pound's Fenollosa a conviction about the importance of verbs of action. Another essential characteristic of Hebrew verse is the frequent use of semantic parallelism, resulting in a stately balance of ideas. Hebrew scholar Mowinckel has called the effect *Gedankenreim*, "thought rhyme," indeed a useful way of approaching Moore's own syntactic structures. Also, Hebrew verse avoids end rhyme, although assonance, consonance, and internal rhyme are highly valued, connections Moore seems clearly to have made. It also seems valid to assume that the distinctions between prose and verse are blurred in Hebrew poetry, at least by Western standards, another of Moore's guiding principles. And although it is not possible to re-create accurately the original pronunciation of ancient Hebrew, it seems reasonable to argue that some kind of syllabic count may have been used. (The sources Moore would have known felt confident that Hebrew verse was quantitative. Contemporary scholars differ on that judgment.)[19]

It is clear from Slatin's research that Moore later openly recognized the connections she had made with Hebrew poetry to those Pound had made with Chinese in the Fenollosa manuscripts. After Pound's Fenollosa *Essay* was published in 1919 (four years after the Kellogg lectures and the publication of "The Past Is the Present"), Moore took the subject up again in her notebooks. By 1921, she had combined the two ideas in the poem "England," with "the sublimated wisdom of China" and "the cataclysmic torrent of emotion / compressed in the verbs of the Hebrew language." It is impossible to know whether the connection seemed new to her at that time or had already been at work earlier in her poem of 1915. "England" ends with a kind of Emersonian reasoning:

> The flower and fruit of all that noted superiority—
> if not stumbled upon in America,
> must one imagine that it is not there?
> It has never been confined to one locality.

Moore had indeed long been looking for a new American superiority in poetry. She is "goaded" into "reverting" to the past to find both a new source of the *élan vital* and a better way of capturing the *durée*, the time represented by the permanence of art. She finds her inspiration in an almost magical-sounding name, Habakkuk, and the structures of Hebrew poetry. Although Moore liked to think of herself as an original, she was too well-read to be naive about the meaning of that word. Years later, Moore wrote, "Humility indeed is armor, for it realizes that it is impossible to be original, in the sense of doing something that has never been thought of before."[20]

Thus by 1915, Moore had already been experimenting with new connections from the past, those connections themselves one kind of originality. She was achieving verse by syllabic count rather than by the inflected metrics of most English stanzas, using prose rhythms, trying new standards of rhyme, and employing unusual parallels of thought. She always called the effects she achieved "natural," saying, "When I am as complete as I like to be, I seem unable to get an effect plain enough."[21] It is probably impossible to re-create Moore's contemporary literary inspirations; as Amy Clampitt says, "She did everything she could to cover her tracks."[22] But Moore was interested in images, whether that interest is traced to Hebrew poetry, Imagism, Bergson, or all three. When Donald Hall asked, "Was imagism a help to you?" in his interview with Moore, she quickly replied, "No. I wondered why anyone would adopt the term . . . I was rather sorry to be a pariah, or at least that I had no connection with anything."[23] But there are clues that Moore was somehow affected by the spirit of Imagism, although she seems to have rejected some of its tenets such as the concentration of images in short poems. (Moore's poetry is sometimes almost totally devoid of imagery, as in "The Past Is the Present," and she certainly generated some long poems.) Nor did she reject rhyme. (Moore created new systems of light rhyme and became, as T. S. Eliot would write, its "greatest living master.")[24] One must recall too that Kellogg had described Hebrew verse as "a language of pictures"; every word is "a picture of an action—'movies.'" Also note that the final chapter of Bergson's classic, *L'Evolution créatrice*, was entitled "The Cinematographical Mechanism of Thought and the Mechanistic Illusion," in which he argued that nature is a continuing series of images, a becoming. So if Moore was an Imagist (and I think one must admit that she was), her sense of the "image" had many sources.

When Pound wrote of Ford Madox Ford in 1914, "I find him significant and revolutionary because of his insistence upon clarity and precision, upon the prose tradition," he was paralleling Moore's own theories and even her statement in "The Past Is the Present" that "Hebrew poetry is / prose with a sort of heightened consciousness." It is probably impossible to know who borrowed what from whom. Ford's famous pronouncement in *New Freewoman* (15 December 1915), the magazine which would become the *Egoist*, that he believed "poetry should be written at least as well as prose" also parallels his comments in *Outlook* (11 April 1914) that "literature is pared to its essentials, in conformity with the principle that art is greatest which most economises its means." In the 16 May issue of the same magazine he wrote, "Life was a sequence of impressions; there was to be no superfluity, no bombast, only a 'quiet voice,' just quietly saying things in her own way. As for poetic diction, the poet should use such language as he ordinarily uses."[25] Moore became that "quiet voice" just quietly saying things. In an unpublished poem entitled "Why That Question?" written about 1919, Moore wonders, "What is the difference between prose and poetry— / If it is one?" She answers, "There may / Be a difference, only no one says who is sure."[26]

Thus, by 1915, the twenty-eight-year-old poet had already declared that for her "The Past Is the Present" and had connected it with her own poetic formula of syllabic verse, precise pictorial images, carefully selected verbs, masterful parallels, light rhyme, and natural voice, from which she would depart only twice in her lifetime. (Moore experimented briefly with free verse in 1921 to 1925 with "When I Buy Pictures," "A Graveyard," and "The Monkey Puzzle," among others, the first of her poems to appear in the *Dial*. She again returned to free verse in 1967, when she converted three poems, by then over forty years old, into free verse. She offered no explanation for the conversion.) But for most of her poetic career, Moore maintained her original style derived from Hebrew poetry: "prose with a sort of heightened consciousness."

The word she chooses in "The Past Is the Present" to describe her inspiration is magical again ("ecstasy"), but the forms come from expediency, from the dictates of practical hard work and necessity. As she wrote to Pound in a letter dated 9 January 1919, "Any verse that I have written has been an arrangement of stanzas, each stanza being an exact duplicate of every other stanza. I have occasionally been at pains to make an arrangement of lines and rhymes that I liked, repeat itself, but the form of the original stanza of anything I have written has been a matter of expediency, hit upon by being approximately suitable to the subject."[27]

Once again, it is precision and accuracy that serve the ecstasy—the illusion. And she reasons, as Bergson had argued, that events in real time are not merely the products of past events; they contain an element of novelty as well as being rich with the past. (This idea is close to Eliot's consciousness of the past in the present in *Tradition and the Individual Talent.*) When, as Bergson had described it, the élan vital seems to stall, it is the work of the poet to demonstrate that "The Past Is the Present," by helping the reader grasp the real nature of the duration, the permanence of art, and at the same time the value of nurturing the vital impulse that unites all creation by generating "new" forms that both celebrate and complete the old ones. For the truly creative poet, the intuition that the past is the present is both humbling and invigorating, for it places her own work against a backdrop of excellence, within the rhythms and echoes of which she must perform, and at the same time it makes her aware of the choices she must exercise to "make it new." She had already decided that true originality lay in finding forms from the past and making them operate in the present. As far as the future is concerned, that was the only choice the true poet could make.

Moore's examination of the dimensions of time became increasingly complex and visual after her years with *Dial.* ("The Monkey Puzzle," written in 1925, was Moore's last poem for seven and a half years; soon after its publication, she was named editor of the *Dial,* and until it closed its doors in 1929, she did not publish any of her own poetic work; she did not begin publishing again until June 1932.) By the time of "No Swan So Fine," appearing first in *Poetry* 41 (October 1932), Miss Moore's sense of time, in a Bergsonian sense, had become very sophisticated and far more visual than the rather abstract philosophical treatment in "The Past Is the Present."

No Swan So Fine

"No water so still as the
    dead fountains of Versailles." No swan,
with swart blind look askance
and gondoliering legs, so fine
    as the chintz china one with fawn-
brown eyes and toothed gold
collar on to show whose bird it was.

Lodged in the Louis Fifteenth
    candelabrum-tree of cockscomb-
tinted buttons, dahlias,
sea-urchins, and everlastings,

it perches on the branching foam
of polished sculptured
flowers—at ease and tall. The king is dead.

In this poem one finds the syllabic stanza pattern 6–7, 8, 6–7, 8, 8, 5, 9. The pattern is altered only in the last line, where the addition of one syllable disrupts the pattern and forces the reader to break the pace. That phrase commands special attention: "The king is dead." Each seven-line stanza has end rhymes only in lines 2 and 5. But what lingers in the ear is the repetition of more than thirty "s," or "z," or "ch" sounds, which gives the poem an unusual sibilance. Perhaps it is meant to capture the hushed stillness of the Versailles fountains. Or more probably, the large number of sibilants may suggest the sound made by the whistling swan, the "swan song" romantically believed to be sung by the dying swan. The term "swan" has a literary meaning too; it has come to mean the poet, one who sings sweetly a song of unusual beauty, excellence, or purity. Thus, with the most delicate of signals, Moore sets up a "swan song" for both the ear and the mind.

In *A Homemade World*, Hugh Kenner discusses Moore's work in a chapter called "Disliking It." Here he argues, among other things, that Moore's "poems are not for the voice; she sensed this in reading them badly."[28] One cannot deny that Moore was a poor reader of her own works, but that is not proof that the poems were not intended for the ear as well as for the eye. The great care taken with the sibilance of the swan's song in this poem belies such an easy judgment. The entire subject of Moore's subtle auditory expertise is only beginning to unfold among her critics, especially among critics who are themselves poets. As Kenner himself has noted in an earlier essay, "Miss Moore's formalisms are so tactful they will not make themselves heard."[29] Kenner provides further insight into Moore's experiments with sound when he offers a consideration of Moore's poem "Bird-Witted," demonstrating her phenomenal control of bird sounds, suggesting that "no poem is more careful of its sounds, husbanding its effects, and expanding them at an exact moment." Kenner further explains that Pound had praised Arnaut Daniel in the *ABC of Reading* (1934) for making the birds sing "IN HIS WORDS," and then repeating the strophic pattern over and over, "WITH the words making sense." Kenner suggests that Miss Moore's 1935 "Bird-Witted" "brings to Daniel's tradition of the musical irregular stanza his own particularities of observation." Arnaut's birds are emblems of spring;

Moore's "squeak, shuffle, miss their footing, on the tree and in the mind." The mother bird's song is deeper, more resonant than that of her nestlings.[30] In fact, as John Slatin has pointed out, the stanza about the mother bird offers no visual details at all; it is entirely devoted to sound.[31] (The reading of several of Moore's poems by Laurie Heineman in a recent *Voices and Visions* telecast points the way toward capturing their auditory quality.) Reading Moore's poems takes special care and talent, but the tonal result can be as exquisite as the visual or the intellectual effect. One need not miss the controlled and hypnotic sibilance in "No Swan So Fine," in spite of Moore's "tactful formalism."

To return to the theme of the poem, as Patricia C. Willis has recorded in *Marianne Moore: Visions into Verse*, Moore collected and classified several bits of information which resulted, over a period of years, in the generation of these stanzas.[32] In 1930 she offered condolences to the English critic George Saintsbury on the passing of his friend, Lord Balfour. Later that year, she noticed a Christie's sale announcement in the *Illustrated London News* for a pair of Louis XV candelabra, "the property of the late Lord Balfour." She carefully sketched one of the pair on a page of her notebook.[33] About a year later, Moore read an article by Percy Philip in the *New York Times Magazine* entitled "Versailles Reborn: A Moonlight Drama." The article had been prompted by the restoration of Versailles, sponsored by the Rockefeller Foundation. Philip wrote a drama, imagining that the statues protested the dullness of Versailles without the court of King Louis. Moore clipped one of the pictures accompanying the article and wrote above it a caption from another article: "There is no water so still as the dead fountains of Versailles." Willis suggests that a third element in the poem centering on a theme of "passing" was probably the fact that Moore was writing the poem for the twentieth anniversary number of *Poetry* magazine. Rumors were circulating that the magazine would cease publication that year; thus the poem may have been intended as a kind of "swan song," in a most delicate sense of that idea.

The poem opens with a quotation about the past, about "the dead fountains at Versailles." Once a place of sparkling light, life, and activity, the stilled fountains, although resurrected, as it were, seem almost frozen in their beauty and their stillness. Only echoes of another era, ghosts from another moment in history, inhabit the environs now. Similarly, there is no living swan like the chintz china one lodged in the Louis XV candelabrum captured in time among the carved dahlias, sea urchins, and (appropriately) everlastings. Unlike the real swan, with its peculiar dark, blind look, its superior attitude, and its webbed feet propelling its body, like a Venetian gondolier guiding his gondola, the carved swan seems "at ease and tall," its "toothed gold / collar on to show whose bird it was." The work of art is, in its way, owned by its creator, the artist, and therefore does not have a will, a destiny of its own. It does, however, have a kind of permanence in time as well as a posed elegance, carefully colored and polished to perfection. The real swan, by contrast, may appear a bit foolish as it takes its gondoliering sea legs ashore and waddles up the river bank. One senses, though, that the artwork swan, although it has its own kind of duration, is somehow deficient. It lacks Bergson's élan vital—that vital impulse that is continually developing and generating new life. It cannot offer even the most rudimentary movement, the most elementary change of expression.

Moore's attitude toward artifice sometimes seems clear, as in these lines from "To Statecraft Embalmed" (1915): "As if a death-mask could ever replace / life's faulty excellence!" Reality, even with its flaws, seems preferable to the perfection achieved in art. The real swan, "with swart blind look askance / and gondoliering legs," is always better than the chintz china one. But is that what Moore says syntactically in this poem? As Donald Hall has pointed out, one must not be too quick to assume simple irony in Marianne Moore. She may well be saying precisely what she means, not intending that the reader infer the opposite. There is something in itself ironic about a criticism of artifice embedded in the superrefined stanzas of "No Swan So Fine."[34] If Moore is so opposed to artifice, why does she work to produce art (i.e., poetry) at all? Or why did she labor so patiently to sketch the swan candelabrum if she found it less beautiful than a real swan?

What Moore is saying is beyond the expected, beyond the either-or. Executing a woman's way of knowing, Moore is including paradoxical ways of looking at the same thing; she is refracting rather than synthesizing. She is operating in the realm of magic, performing an extraordinary balancing act—about time and a relativity of values. She is, I would suggest, offering a kind of Hegelian dialectic in her thesis, antithesis, and synthesis, although the argument is never really brought to a permanent solution. There is no swan so fine as the chintz china one; but the real swan has vital qualities no artifice can duplicate; yet both kinds of swans have real importance to the human beings who observe them. In one sense, time and real swans are always passing; hence one must make some effort to capture permanence in an always-changing and less-than-perfect world. One kind of time, whether measured in milliseconds or in dynasties, becomes history; it passes on, leaving only the human attempts at catching *durée* in works of art. The gondoliering swan represents that kind of time, one in movement, in process, one that is and will be replicated by swanness throughout time, although each swan will be a unique unrepeatable individual, having its own peculiar quality of the élan vital. The other swan, the "chintz china one," represents another kind of time, the *durée*, the swan above time that has an existence beyond the limitation of days and years. It is interesting that Moore has the china swan perched among everlastings, flowers that keep their color and shape beyond their actual life span, retaining a kind of beauty even when dried and preserved. So too is the quality of the swan created by artifice. Here is a permanence, not unlike that of Keats's "Grecian Urn."

But Moore's use of the words "chintz" and "china" to describe the china swan makes another interesting qualification. Chintz has a fascinating etymology. It is a Hindu, Sanskrit word meaning multicolored or bright. But over time, the beautiful glazed cotton cloth called chintz has been tinged by the pejorative. Since the late 1850s, some chintz cloth has come to be thought of as sleazy or tawdry.[35] Thus Moore causes careful readers to qualify their judgments again. If the poem is not ironic, (and Hall argues that it may not be), Moore seems to be saying that no real swan is "so fine / as the chintz china one." And yet the very word "chintz," which may only mean "brightly colored" in its candelabrum-tree of carved flowers, tugs at the mind. For it may also suggest a showiness, a contrived artifice, like the era of the Versailles fountains, now rendered "so still," even when preserved in the new life of art. And china, although beautiful, is also fragile, as was the era of Versailles. Moore makes reference to an era like that of the court of Versailles in another poem, "Nothing Will Cure the Sick Lion But to Eat an Ape." She writes,

> Perceiving that in the masked ball
> attitude, there is a hollowness
> that beauty's light momentum can't redeem.

That "hollowness," no matter how artfully captured in the renovation of Versailles (or in the china swan), remains shallow. It may be beautiful and brightly colored, but it is showy, fragile, and hollow nonetheless, a perfect enactment of its time.

The living swan, with "gondoliering legs," though it has locomotion and can look with apparent disapproval at the world around it, still suffers from a blind limitation in time and history. The sculptured bird enjoys the ability to be complete, to stand tall and at ease, to operate from an established and permanent perspective. The china swan, the work of art, must replace the real one for an era that is gone; it provides duration and gives us a glimpse of an era's values, as well as its version of perfect beauty.

But there remains one all-important phrase in the poem. When one hears "The king is dead," the unspoken response should also be heard: "Long live the king!" One must be ready to welcome new realities and new art forms when the old ones have passed, although one may have some access to the past and to an existence beyond time through art. Thus Willis's intuition that the poem may have to do with passing, and perhaps even the passing of a particular magazine of the arts, seems valid. The poem can be seen as an accolade to *Poetry*'s support of the arts, and at the same time a kind of swan song, a consolation for the possibility of its demise by reminding those associated with the magazine of their part in capturing permanence and beauty in a changing world. Nonetheless, any institution, even one associated with what at one point must have seemed the avant-garde, must be ready to greet the new king. That is the only realistic thing to do. Perhaps one should even smile at the "hollowness" of what once had seemed so glittering and so fine as well as at the realities that art represented. And once again Moore has surprised the careful reader, has done her magic with painstaking precision and accuracy, giving us an awareness that is not the expected view about time, history, and art. She has achieved Bergson's charge to the poet to move beyond being merely a doer to becoming a knower. The poet has brought the attentive reader to a new dimension of a multifaceted truth, to a real intuition, which is for Bergson the highest stage in the evolution of understanding.

One of the most striking instances of Marianne Moore's creative interpretation of Bergsonian ideas was initiated some years later when she opened her phone bill in 1939 and read an enclosure from New York Bell which described "The world's Most Accurate 'CLOCKS'" housed in a "time vault" at the Bell Telephone Laboratories in New York at precisely

41°C. Moore's synthesizing mind and tongue-in-cheek wit produced the following mock-scientific poem:

Four Quartz Crystal Clocks

There are four vibrators, the world's exactest clocks;
    and these quartz time-pieces that tell
time intervals to other clocks,
    these workless clocks work well;
independently the same, kept in
    the 41° Bell
       Laboratory time

vault. Checked by a comparator with Arlington,
    they punctualize the "radio,
cinéma," and "presse,"—a group the
    Giraudoux truth-bureau
of hoped-for accuracy has termed
    "instruments of truth." We know—
       as Jean Giraudoux says,

certain Arabs have not heard—that Napoleon
    is dead; that a quartz prism when
the temperature changes, feels
    the change and that the then
electrified alternate edges
    oppositely charged, threaten
       careful timing; so that

this water-clear crystal as the Greeks used to say,
    this "clear ice" must be kept at the
same coolness. Repetition, with
    the scientist, should be
synonymous with accuracy.
    The lemur-student can see
       that an aye-aye is not

an angwan-tíbo, potto, or loris. The sea-
    side burden should not embarrass
the bell-boy with the buoy-ball
    endeavoring to pass
hotel patronesses; nor could a

                practiced ear confuse the glass
                    eyes for taxidermists

            with eye-glasses from the optometrist. And as
                MEridian-7 one-two
            one-two gives, each fifteenth second
                in the same voice, the new
            data—"The time will be" so and so—
                you realize that "when you
                    hear the signal," you'll be

            hearing Jupiter or jour pater, the day god—
                the salvaged son of Father Time—
            telling the cannibal Chronos
                (eater of his proxime
            newborn progeny) that punctuality
                is not a crime.

In order to understand a poem like "Four Quartz Crystal Clocks," one must be ready to deal both with the text itself and with the techniques and issues being toyed with by the mind that produced it. It is easy enough to observe typical Moore externals like the rhythms, based on a syllabic pattern of 11–12, 8, 8, 6, 9, 7, 6 syllables per line respectively, or to note a rhyme scheme of $x\ a\ x\ a\ x\ a\ x$. Moore offers three rhymes per stanza with an intricate pattern of approximate rhymes and the beautiful echoes of sound throughout. Note, for example, the predominate sounds in stanzas 2, 4, and 5.

            stanza 2, "oo" sounds: punctualize, group, Giraudoux, truth,
                    bureau, accuracy, instruments, truth, Giraudoux;
            stanza 4, hard "c" sounds: clear, crystal, clear ice, kept,
                    coolness, accuracy;
            stanza 5, "s" sounds: loris, seaside, should, embarrass, pass,
                    patronesses, glass, eyes, taxidermists.

Moore spoke openly of her dislike for rhyme in the usual sense but wrote of her "own fondness for the unaccented rhyme devices . . . from an instinctive effort to ensure naturalness."[36] Thus the carefully controlled patterns of sound are part of Moore's music, which she worked unceasingly to produce. Early drafts of several poems exhibit musical notation and tonal goals like "Solfeggietto."[37] She echoes Bergson almost exactly when she speaks of the poet's sense of sound "in the use of which the poet becomes a kind of hypnotist."[38] Bergson wrote:

> The object of art is to put to sleep the active or rather resistant powers of our personality, and thus to bring us into a state of perfect responsiveness, in which we realize the idea that is suggested to us and sympathize with the feeling that is expressed. In the process of art we shall find, in a weakened form, a refined and in some measure spiritualized version of the process used to induce the state of hypnosis. . . . the poet is he with whom feelings develop into images, and the images themselves into words which translate them while obeying the laws of rhythm.[39]

Far from rejecting rhyme or rhythm as poetic devices, Moore simply reinterpreted them, disguising them with great subtlety in her efforts to "make it new."

In "Four Quartz Crystal Clocks," Moore also heightens rhythm with the precision of a clocklike pattern established through the predictably regular but decidedly background rhythms of the regular syllabic count (as opposed to a pattern of stressed and unstressed syllables). The rhythm is repeated through six stanzas. Note the repetition of "t" and hard "c" sounds, forming an oddly syncopated "ticktock" sound pattern:

> and these quartz time-pieces that tell
> time intervals to other clocks,
> these workless clocks work well.

In the final stanza, Moore alters the pattern by changing the syllabic count and rhyme scheme, as well as the number of lines, but the "t" and "c" patterns continue, sometimes muted to a "ch" and punctuated by "p"'s. Such patterns were never accidents with Moore, although she liked to speak of them as natural rhythms. She worked out such designs with colored pencils so she could carefully control the effects she was working to achieve. It seems reasonable to surmise that the careful alteration in the final stanza causes the reader to stop the rhythmic "ticktock" pattern and respond in a different way to the final thoughts of the poem.

Every reader has to meet the etymological challenge of analyzing Moore's choice of words and references, particularly things like an "aye-

aye is not / an angwan-tíbo, potto, or loris," and the puzzling references to the "Giraudoux truth-bureau." Moore must have loved words and their history, for it is impossible to work well with almost any of her poems without a good dictionary. In "Armor's Undermining Modesty" she warns that "even gifted scholars lose their way / through faulty etymology." Moore's intricate puns require deft mental gymnastics from her readers, as in lines like "the bell-boy with the buoy-ball" or

> . . . nor could a
>   practiced ear confuse the glass
>   eyes for taxidermists
> with eye-glasses from the optometrist.

Contemporary poet Amy Clampitt argues that Moore's sense of humor has been unduly ignored by her critics.[40] Moore's fastidiousness sometimes effectively covers her wit—and one must learn to appreciate the delight she takes in words like "exactest," or in puns like "bell-boy and buoy-ball." Only the reader who is on Moore's intellectual wavelength can enjoy her invitation to celebrate the endless panoply of words and sounds that language offers. On the actual manuscript of this poem Moore writes, "I won't stake my life on it that the inferences are all crystal clear."[41] To the audience who would appreciate Marianne Moore, the understatement itself offers both an implied joke and an echo of the "crystal" of the title.

In 1972, Gary Lane put Moore's poetic oeuvre through an IBM 360 computer "to help the reader study the uniquely precise imagination of Marianne Moore."[42] It is astounding to discover that Moore used thousands of words only once and that she exercised extraordinary willpower in choosing to use even commonplace words, what one might identify as favorite words, with great self-control. Only nine words were used as frequently as twenty-two times, for example, and they included "am," "why," "whom," "work," and "don't." Even great favorites such as "humility" and "shield" were used only four times each, "affection" and "elephant" only three. As she herself has suggested, omissions are not accidents. But even these important particularities fall into perspective only when one begins to sense that Moore, in her uniquely witty way, is playing with contemporary intellectual arguments about time.

The theme triggered by the leaflet in Marianne Moore's phone bill slowly starts to come into focus. There are four quartz timepieces, the world's most exact clocks. They are the quintessential example of what science can produce. As the leaflet says, "When properly cut and inserted in a suitable circuit, they will control the rate of electric vibration to an accuracy of one part in a million."[43] These remarkably accurate clocks even regulate the frequencies of radio stations, thus keeping the "radio, / cinéma" and "presse" on time. They are themselves further verified by comparing their accuracy with readings at the U.S. Naval Observatory at Arlington.

The words "cinéma" and "presse" signal a change to a French vocabulary, as Moore seems to switch abruptly to the "Giraudoux truth-bureau" and to Giraudoux's own communication that "certain Arabs have not heard—that Napoleon / is dead." Jean Giraudoux was a French playwright and novelist best known for his witty and satiric fantasies— for, one might say, his creative intuitions. His creative works, however, often on "classical" subjects (*Siegfried, Judith, Amphytrion 38, Electra, The Enchanted, Ondine, The Apollo of Bellac,* and *Duel of Angels* [titles in English translations]) were overshadowed at the end of his life, when in 1939 he was put in charge of disseminating war information for the French government. His performance in this position was not appreciated and proved to be the first step in his decline as an artist. Thus this brilliant, intuitive writer, capable of reinterpreting the great myths of humankind, was reduced to the transmission of "hoped-for accuracy" when he tells us that "certain Arabs have not heard—that Napoleon / is dead." At the same time, the lines function to make a point about time and its relativity. The truth is accessible to any group of human beings only at such time as they hear it. Truth may be in some kind of permanent existence outside time, but that has little effect on the uninformed Arabs whose perspective, whose relativity, is something far different from the readers of this poem, or from Giraudoux's truth-bureau.

Moore returns to the quartz crystal, what the Greeks used to call "clear ice" (again, a classical echo), to tell us that

> . . . repetition, with
>   the scientist, should be
> synonymous with accuracy.

Moore had more than a passing fascination with the term "crystal," using it to great effect in three other poems and in an English translation of a French work by Adalbert Stifter, *Rock Crystal: A Christmas Tale.* In "The Hero," she says of the hero,

> . . . He's not out
> seeing a sight but the rock
> crystal thing to see—the startling El Greco
> brimming with inner light—that
> covets nothing that it has let go.

In "England" she says of the East,

> . . . Its emotional
> shorthand and jade cockroaches, its rock crystal and its
>   imperturbability,
> all of museum quality.

In "Novices" she writes,

> king, steward, and harper, seated amidships while the jade and
>   the rock crystal course about in solution,
> their suavity surmounts the surf—
> the willowy wit, the transparent equation of Isaiah, Jeremiah,
>   Ezekiel, Daniel.

In Moore's mind, rock crystal has something to do with the permanent quality of art, Bergson's "real time" or *durée*, even with truth, but paradoxically, this permanence is only through the intuition of the artist and the "magic" of the imagination. (There is also a reference to a "crystal peak" in "An Octopus," the point when the poet and the reader reach the highest pinnacle in both the real and the symbolic ascent of the mountain, perhaps meant as the ascent toward truth.)

Moore turns again to an appreciation of the quartz crystal clocks and their scientific accuracy. It is, however, an accuracy based on repetition, a repetition achieved, as Bergson had described, through "spatialized" time measured by clocks that have been assigned separate units of measure, units arbitrarily assigned by a human mind, no matter how accurately they are measured. The ideas of seconds, minutes, and hours are the constructs of the human mind. Thus repetition has become synonymous with accuracy—which it is not. Try as we will to make any two milliseconds alike, they never really are, as the details of history make clear. No amount of repetition can change that reality.

Consider the lemur-student, one studying monkeys, for example. Even the ordinary student can see that an aye-aye, a species of lemur (a small, nocturnal, quadrumanous mammal, closely allied to the monkey), and an angwan-tíbo (a small, West African monkeylike creature with a rudimentary tail), a potto (a red-gray lemurlike monkey), and a loris (a slow-moving lemur from Ceylon and Java) are not quite the same thing. They are similar but present themselves with essential differences. Careful scientific description recognizes those differences, so the names are not mere repetitions. So too one would not confuse a bell-boy with a buoy-ball or confuse the glass eyes made for a taxidermist with eyeglasses from the optometrist. The sounds may stray perilously close, may tease the mind into toying with the interrelationships of idea and sound, but any confusion of the meanings of such words would be ludicrous.

So when one calls "MEridian-7 one-two / one-two" and the recorded voice announces that "'The time will be' so and so" "when you hear the signal," one must realize the limitations of such scientific "accuracy." What one is really hearing is the human mind superimposing its own measures upon reality, just as surely as if one were hearing the voice of "the salvaged son of Father Time," Jupiter, the "day god," telling Chronos that punctuality is not a crime. In fact in the myth (with echoes of the classical allusions of Giraudoux), there may be a better intuition of the truth about time than there is in the precision of scientific accuracy as represented by the four quartz crystal clocks. Indeed, "punctuality / is not a crime," but it has its limitations. It may tell part of the truth, but only a part of it.

Moore commits a deliberately ambiguous spelling error in this final irregular stanza. If, as she once wrote, "omissions are not accidents," one might safely assume that neither are additions accidents. The Roman god Saturn was called Cronos by the Greeks, not Chronos. *Chronos* means simply "time" in Greek and appears in English as a combining form (e.g., "chronometer"). It was Cronos, son of Uranus and father of Zeus or Jupiter, who ate his newborn progeny—and Saturn/Cronos whom the Romans remembered in their annual Saturnalia, a time of peace, forgiveness of debt, and equality, a time when differences were put aside and friends made presents to one another. At this winter feast, slaves sat at table while their masters served them, to show the natural equality of human beings and to dramatize that things belonged equally to all in the reign of Saturn/Cronos.

Moore startles the careful reader by putting the two together again: Chronos, the time created by science, one kind of Father Time, and Cronos, the mythical Father Time intuited by the imagination. Which is superior? Can there be equality as there was at the ancient Roman Saturnalia? The poem ends enigmatically: "punctuality / is not a crime." There is nothing wrong (i.e., criminal) with science, with punctuality, with scientific "accuracy," as long as one understands that it is not totally accurate. It offers one kind of time, one aspect of accuracy; but the poet can offer another. Whatever time is, each millisecond of it is a different, somehow never-to-be repeated instant. The "magic" insight of the poet may offer a truth at least as durable in Bergson's parlance as that of the scientist or the historian, for it can re-create the flash of a truth beyond a moment. Thus illusion, in Marianne Moore's view, is more precise than precision. But the two are, in some profound way, interrelated. For without accuracy, without precision, an important dimension of reality is lost. To return to her letter to William Carlos Williams, writing is "more science than art, if it is to go beyond the writer" into the consciousness of the reader.[44] The imagnifico, as she called him, the magician must be at work again, creating her illusions with the precision and accuracy that make her magic work in the minds of her audience, but doing so by being disarmingly precise—so precise, in fact, that one may not notice the artifice.

In 1941, Moore published a book of poetry entitled *What Are Years?* which included "Four Quartz Crystal Clocks." The title poem, first published in the *Kenyon Review* for summer 1940, also examines the concept of time, as the title implies, but in a way far different from the examination in "The Past Is the Present," "No Swan So Fine," or "Four Quartz Crystal Clocks." In this poem the impetus rises not from a glimpse of the past epitomized by a magical name like Habakkuk, a work of visual art like the candelabrum, or something Moore had read like the brochure in her telephone bill. There is no extraordinary image, to use the word in Moore's sense, around which to hinge the complex set of ideas she wanted to share. Laurence Stapleton has pointed out that "this grave and beautiful poem has no predecessors in Marianne Moore's poems . . . it is a plainsong rather than a sonata or fugue."[45] By Moore's standards the poem is fairly traditional and straightforward, indeed a kind of plainsong. It is not surprising that both Louis Untermeyer and F. O. Matthiessen would choose it for inclusion in *Modern American Poetry* and *The Oxford Book of American Verse* respectively in 1950. On the surface, at least, it seems accessible even to the average reader, one unfamiliar with the intricacies of Moore's work. The entire poem is nine sentences long (the text includes the title) and makes a philosophical and moral statement about time.

What Are Years?

What is our innocence,
what is our guilt? All are
   naked, none is safe. And whence
is courage: the unanswered question,
the resolute doubt,—
dumbly calling, deafly listening—that
in misfortune, even death,
     encourages others
     and in its defeat, stirs

   the soul to be strong? He
sees deep and is glad, who
   accedes to mortality
and in his imprisonment rises
upon himself as
the sea in a chasm, struggling to be
free and unable to be,
     in its surrendering
     finds it continuing.

   So he who strongly feels,
behaves. The very bird,
   grown taller as he sings, steels
his form straight up. Though he is captive,
his mighty singing
says, satisfaction is a lowly
thing, how pure a thing is joy.
     This is mortality,
     this is eternity.

[handwritten marginalia: "let come accept ambiguity + humanness"]

[handwritten marginalia: "to himSELF, to mortality"]

The poem is interesting for many reasons, but one of them is surely the fact that Moore always named it as one of her own favorites. She "thinks it is solid, perhaps best written of all her works."[46] It is also a synthesis of many of Moore's favorite metaphors: the sea in a chasm, a singing bird, courage in the face of fear of defeat, humility, and self-protectiveness. And the finish, as Donald Hall has pointed out, is meticulous. The syllabic count in this poem of three stanzas is very exact: 6, 6, 7, 9, 5, 9, 7, 6, 6. Each stanza has nine lines with lines 8 and 9 forming a kind of aphoristic rhymed couplet, a technique Moore rarely used. The rhyme is approximate in a pattern of *a x a x x b b c c* (surrendering/continuing, lowly/joy, others/stirs), and the text is heavily alliterative. The poem asks four questions: What are years? What is our innocence? What is our guilt? and Whence is courage? Following the Hebrew models described in "The Past Is the Present," Moore sets up a system of parallels, the "thought rhyme" so descriptive of Hebrew poetry. The parallels are almost all oxymorons, one idea paired with its opposite: innocence/guilt, naked/safe, unanswered/resolute, dumbly calling/deafly listening, struggling to be free/unable to be, surrendering/continuing, mortality/eternity. Each oxymoron is its own small dialectic, creating a system of particular tensions. Those tensions are most apt, for they are descriptive of the poet as hero, using the balancing of many forces so that he "steels / his form straight up" and attains a rationale for courage.

As the title suggests, the poem is couched in the ultimate question about time: What are years? Whether one speaks of time in the sense of a measurable extension or an intuited mode, the question with Moore is always complex. As in "Four Quartz Crystal Clocks" Moore is pitting scientific or historical time, something measurable and sequential (and something which runs out for all mortal beings) against time which is the *eternal now*, as it were God's (or the gods') time: eternity. But it is on both systems that she predicates her questions and her solutions.

The poem is spoken very much from an adult perspective. (Moore was about fifty-three at the time of its composition.) The reader familiar with Moore's work will quickly discern that the theme is not as mundane and as easily understood as it may at first appear. The poem begins with a distinctly adult question, one not unlike Blake's great study of innocence and experience. "What is our innocence, / what is our guilt?" The answer comes immediately, but not from an easily ascertained connection. (Moore once wrote: "Wallace Stevens, referring to poetry under the metaphor of a lion, says, 'It can kill a man.' Yet the lion's leap would be mitigated almost to harmlessness if the lion were clawless, so precision is both impact and exactitude, as with surgery.")[47] It is that surgical

precision one finds in the answer to Moore's own question about innocence and guilt. "All are / naked, none is safe." Cutting away all disguises, all the veneers of civilization, Moore declares what every adult
knows: in time, no one is armored against sin and guilt; no one is safe
from hurt; no one is totally self-confident and self-sustaining. All of us
are vulnerable beyond our ability to express that vulnerability: that is the
agonizing truth, the lion's claw.

To point up this terrible vulnerability, this ambiguity, Moore employs
the Hebrew patterns of thought rhyme, the oxymorons (naked/safe, un-
answered/resolute, etc.), which describe the conflicting tensions of the
human condition. We want assurance, clarity, and truth but find only
relativity and contradiction in our own "scientific" search for truth.
Sometimes we see clues in the phenomenal courage of others that there
is a moral certitude, a reason for human dignity, hope, and confidence;
perhaps there is even a Supreme Being. Donald Hall saw Moore as a
religious woman who "thinks she reads the Bible everyday," yet doc-
trinally her Christianity is not evident in her poetry. Although religious
faith may underlie her philosophy, "man on his own, self-sustaining is
the figure emerging from the poetry."[48] People seem to be advised to
practice Christian virtues but to rely on themselves for help and protection. Nonetheless, as Margaret Holley has pointed out, Moore's work
contains "an ideal of serenity and wisdom" which one does not find in
most modernist writers.[49] Moore's spiritual principles, and most as-
suredly her regular Bible reading, provided a bedrock of stability and
style which writers like Pound, Stevens, Lawrence, Hart Crane, and the
early Eliot seldom matched. There is even a biblical cadence in "What
Are Years?" Moore often remarked that her favorite book of the Bible was
the Book of Job, and the poem echoes biblical passages of Job quite
directly: "Naked came I out of my mother's womb, and naked shall I
return thither" (1:21, DR); "The life of man upon earth is a warfare"
(7:1, DR); and "Who cometh forth like a flower, and is destroyed, and
fleeth as a shadow, and never continueth in the same state" (14:2, DR).
And yet at the end, out of the whirlwind (40:1), the Lord says to Job:
"Clothe thyself with beauty, and set thyself up on high: and be glorious"
(40:5, DR).

Like Job, the poet searches for courage and for answers to doubts and
questions. But we seem to call out "dumbly" and listen "deafly." Moore
includes all of us in this perception: "All are / naked, none is safe."
This is not only a poem about an individual's vulnerability and armoring,

it also reaches toward a universal. We all sometimes see human bravery—even in the face of death—and are inspired by the example of others, who seem to find the courage we seek even in defeat, misfortune, and death. And we take some consolation in their bravery—but we still need answers to understand how that heroism is attained. The date of this poem, 1940, places it during a time of great stress for all Americans, and for the entire Western world. The horrors of the war in Europe were most distressing to Moore's own sense of security, occasioned in particular by her brother Warner's naval commission and a fear that he might be pressed into action. Having lost their two male protectors, both the grandfather and the father, the remaining Moore family—mother, daughter, and brother—were extremely close. They needed each other with an intimacy greater than most families might feel. Moore's sense of security always remained tightly involved in this family circle, and her sense of security, like that of many other Americans, was disturbed by the news of the growing conflict in Europe and the inevitability of American involvement.

Reading the working notes of "What Are Years?" one finds other surprises. Early drafts suggest that Moore was dealing with the death of an individual, perhaps a child. The first worksheets for the poem make note of Chaucer's "Prioress's Tale," wherein the little clergeon continues to sing after his death. Reading Moore's personal notebooks and letters, one also finds that these years brought frequent illnesses to Moore, and more especially to her mother, so mortality, on all fronts, seems to have been uppermost in the poet's consciousness. (Mrs. Moore died in 1947 after a lengthy illness. Letters from all of Marianne Moore's friends during these years ask about her mother's health; every friend understood their deep bond, one far beyond the usual relationship of mother and daughter.)

Moore had always been suspicious of emotion. Early in her career, she copied into her reading notebook: "Women are highly responsive to the attractions of the arts, of letters, of music. They do not understand them better . . . but they like them better."[50] Tess Gallagher has discussed the dilemma of women writers after the turn of the twentieth century. In an article about Marianne Moore, "Throwing the Scarecrows from the Garden," Gallagher quotes George Eliot: "Women have not to prove that they can be emotional and rhapsodic and spiritualistic, everyone believes that already. They have to prove that they are capable of accurate thought, serious study, and continuous self-command."[51] These goals of accurate thought and continuous self-command were precisely Moore's personal quest. She remained wary of dealing with any issue from a merely emotional (i.e., "womanly") perspective. So it is with great infrequency that she enters directly upon so undisguisedly emotional a set of issues as those expressed in "What Are Years?" without the protection of a central image or figure, and without the armor of irony or humor. But by age fifty-three, as Margaret Holley posits in *The Poetry of Marianne Moore: A Study in Voice and Value*, Moore had developed a "sense of voice," a confidence in her own poetic control.[52] The overriding fact of the Second World War, whose tragedies she addressed, were now demonstrated by a marked moral mode of speech, indicative not of an individual poet searching for a means to "make it new" but of a poet speaking of and for an entire people ("What is our innocence, / what is our guilt?"). She offers a resoundingly optimistic and moralistic view of time and how one can deal with it, a view with biblical overtones in style, message, and tone.

Like Job's world, Moore's and America's own world seemed beset by mortal disaster. One needed a positive resolution in a world beset by so much doubt. Thus the unresolved dialectics of "No Swan So Fine" or the ironic humor of a piece like "Four Quartz Crystal Clocks" seemed out of place in a world already full of ambiguity, fear, and lack of resolution. Like all other Americans, Moore had to learn ways of facing and dealing with the terrors of war. To do so, she had to learn to face her own fears, to explore them, and to overcome them. Her fears were all too human: mortality, death, the achievement of *durée*, permanence in time and history—and a chance to contribute something vital and alive to the élan vital, the continuance of the human race.

Her metaphor for facing innermost terror was always the same: the sea. Donald Hall has argued that the metaphysical dangers that haunted Moore's earlier poems are by the early forties objectified in the reality of a world on the edge of war. The reality of that danger seems to have made the means of protection more explicit. Where danger was amorphous, aloofness and reticence served as protection. The armoring recommended in the poems of the forties is no longer withdrawal into an inexplicit and rather aristocratic reticence. It is instead an inward armoring of self, which includes the courage to participate actively in human affairs.[53] To achieve that inward armoring, Moore turns to some of the metaphors of earlier poems, bringing them this time to a meaningful resolution. The "sea in a chasm, struggling to be / free and unable to be," echoes the principle that "water seeks its own level" ("Sojourn in the Whale," 1917). In "The Fish" (1918) there is also a negative finality in the sea, for

> . . . the chasm-side is
> dead.
> Repeated
>   evidence has proved that it can live
>   on what can not revive
>   its youth. The sea grows old in it.

In "What Are years?" there is a resolution to the destruction of youth, the press of time: one "sees deep and is glad, who / accedes to mortality," and "in its surrendering / finds it continuing." The only *durée*, the only way to ensure preservation of the vital impulse of life itself, is to stop struggling and to surrender oneself to a system larger than anything humans can devise. Whether one measures time in psychological experiences or by scientific measures, one must learn to master time by surrendering oneself to its mastery—yet another paradox, another oxymoron. "So he who strongly feels, / behaves" provides a most interesting choice of verbs. To behave means not only to act properly but also to be a haven, to afford oneself protection. In "The Student," written in 1932, Moore wrote of her heroic student that he

> . . . is too reclusive for
>   some things to seem to touch
> him; not because he
>   has no feeling but because he has too much.
> > > *Collected Poems*

Analogously, the only real means of controlling strong feeling, particularly fear, is an act of will; one must behave, control, and direct emotion in a positive and heroic direction in order to make for oneself a safe haven. Like the singing bird, one must stand tall, sing, and "steel / his frame straight up." Like Job, one must understand that earthly satisfaction is a lowly thing. The perfect quest is for a pure thing: joy. If one finds that, one has found a secret that encompasses both mortality and eternity. "Clothe thyself with beauty, and set thyself on high: and be glorious" (Job 40:10). To do that is to achieve power over both kinds of time: psychological and scientific, eternity and mortality. As Moore recalled in *Tell Me, Tell Me,* Faulkner's ultimate defense of the whole business of writing was absolutely right: "It should make man endure by lifting up his heart." Her singing bird grows taller as it sings. Its mighty singing, its joy in being part of life, surmounts both mortality and eternity.

And so we find in these four poems a poet's exploration of time from four very different perspectives and in four different styles. (Moore never pursued the same theme twice in the same way.) But the common thread that unites them is their exploration of the many dimensions of time and history and the poet's place in that exploration. And behind that exploration are the philosophical principles of Henri Bergson, whose concepts of the relationship of art and science had a great impact on the development of twentieth-century modernism. For he helped thinkers deal with new concepts of science and epistemology, particularly with evolution and relativity, and he defended and retained the value of intuition—the mode of the poet, the hero, the prophet, and the saint—a value that might have been submerged in the early years of the twentieth century. Bergson encouraged creativity as part of the élan vital, which valued the new and made change and individuals seem both natural and necessary. At the same time, he valued the past and the passing, the *durée*, the permanence of the eternal now which is an innate part of all time and history as well. For Moore, that meant locating herself in time and learning the real meaning of originality, as well as how one might effect the permanence of what has passed and is passing as she does in "The Past Is the Present." It meant exploring the relationship between art and reality, between the *durée* and the élan vital, in "No Swan So Fine." It also meant focusing her humor and her insight on the limitations of both scientific time and mythological time as measured in "Four Quartz Crystal Clocks." Finally, it meant granting her a rare chance to deal with ultimate questions about grace, serenity, wisdom, and joy in "What Are Years?"

All the while, Moore could take pride in her work, in Bergson's world of the poet and the hero—the world of intuition—wherein she could take careful readers to that remarkable place wherein one catches glimpses of the truth, glimpses so momentary as to leave only a flash of insight into the deepest reality. This indeed is the world of magic. But this kind of enchantment can be achieved only with infinite care, choice timing, and precision—with scientific accuracy. This is the world of the conjurer, the imagnifico, the wizard of words. As Moore had suggested (with Bergson's blessing), illusion is more precise than precision, for it takes one to the highest stage of human understanding: intuition.

CHAPTER 2

When I Buy Pictures

If Moore was interested philosophically in the meaning of time and the value of intuition, she found it necessary to work out her discourse by using the most precise sensual tools at her disposal; for her, both sight and sound were "scientifically" her best methods of conjury. But as Bonnie Costello has demonstrated in her book *Marianne Moore: Imaginary Possessions*, Moore's dominant sense was that of sight.[1] Her metaphors are predicated on a visual resemblance, and as Hugh Kenner has suggested, even her stanzas are usually arranged by their appearance on the printed page.[2] Certainly her poems are filled with visual imagery executed with astounding care and precision. Patricia C. Willis's 1987 catalogue *Marianne Moore: Vision into Verse*, published on the occasion of an exhibition of Moore's work at the Rosenbach Museum and Library in Philadelphia, clearly establishes visual connections to the production of many of Moore's most complex and interesting poems. It could certainly be argued that almost every poem Moore produced can be traced to an art object, a picture she had seen, a postcard she had collected, or even to sketches she herself had made. Unlike many of her colleagues, Moore rarely produced a poem from "life" but rather from an actual painting she had seen, or a photo, print, or reproduction she owned.

Moore's interest in the plastic arts was long-standing. After she and her mother and brother had moved from St. Louis to Pennsylvania after her grandfather's death in 1894 (Mrs. Moore eventually taught at the

Presbyterian Metzger Institute for girls at Carlisle), the family was be-
friended by the Norcross family. (Dr. Norcross was pastor of the Second
Presbyterian Church.) By 1900, three Norcross daughters had graduated
from Bryn Mawr, which would become Marianne Moore's alma mater.
The youngest, Mary, worked at the college for two years before she returned to Carlisle to pursue a career in arts and crafts, enrolling in
workshops at the Boston Society for Arts and Crafts founded by Charles
Eliot Norton, professor of fine arts at Harvard. In 1904 and 1905, Mary
Norcross took on the task of preparing Moore for her matriculation exams
at Bryn Mawr. The influence of Mary Norcross probably had a great deal
to do with Moore's continued interest in the expertly crafted objets d'art
which she worked into many of her poems. When Donald Hall asked
about Moore's Bryn Mawr days in his interview; "At what point did poetry become world-shaking for you?" Moore responded, "Never! I believe I was interested in painting then. . . . I remember Mrs. Otis
Skinner asked at Commencement time, the year I was graduated, 'What
would you like to be?' 'A painter,' I said."[3] And from the beginning,
Moore's interests often lay beyond the works of art that had been declared
excellent by someone else. She always trusted her own instincts and
judgments and valued her own assessment of excellence where others
might have missed it.

Moore loved museums, and she worked for the New York Public Library, giving her continued access to the visual arts themselves and to
critical evaluations of them. Her exposure to the world of art also received inspiration when, in the summer of 1911, she visited England
and France. The tour took Moore and her mother to the Lake District,
Glasgow, Edinburgh, Stratford, Oxford, and London. Art galleries and
museums, as well as literary shrines, filled their itinerary. Moore's reactions to the trip are accessible to us through her vivid and whimsical
letters about her experiences to her brother, Warner. Moore delighted in
almost everything she saw, from armor to the work of Morris, Burne-
Jones, and the other Pre-Raphaelites. She visited the British Museum
and the National Portrait Gallery but also found time to purchase something from the literary avant-garde, Ezra Pound's *Personae* and *Exultations* in Elkin Mathew's London bookshop. In one of her amusing letters
to Warner, this one dated 13 July 1911, Moore wrote: "London has my
goat. We never see anything that I don't want to see 90 thousand other
things of the same stripe, nymphs excepted. There is a great outbreak of

them in the galleries."[4] She remarked that she enjoyed Hogarth's *Rake's Progress* and was particularly fascinated by anything Egyptian, noting especially that "the mummies are a very fine assortment, and there are grave servants enough to people the kingdom. They have mummied cats, reptiles, dogs, bulls, jackals and humans, lots of faience (bead-ornaments) and fine examples of wrappings. Also many of the cases had portraits in them."[5] Moore's interest in Egypt would be regenerated in 1922, when she and the rest of the world experienced the Egyptomania that followed Howard Carter's discovery of Tutankhamen's tomb. References to Egyptian art figure prominently in Moore's work. (See "Novices," "To Statecraft Embalmed," "The Jerboa," "The Icosasphere," and "An Egyptian Pulled Glass Bottle in the Shape of a Fish.")

Moore was not always pleased with what she found. When the mother and daughter went to Paris, Moore discovered that the Louvre was full of "rotten Rubens," probably related to the outbreak of nymphs in London. But the Dürer exhibition delighted her, a reference she returned to frequently in her poetry. And she purchased a photographic reproduction of Rodin's *Penseur*. As Willis has pointed out, it would be hard to overestimate the importance of this trip to Moore's writing. The armory at Warwick castle and peacocks in the cedar trees appear in "People's Surroundings," an Oxford swan shows up in "Critics and Connoisseurs," an Elizabethan trencher she saw at the Bodleian inspired "Counseil to a Bachelor," and the ceiling stalls of St. George's Chapel, Windsor, are probably those described in "The Pangolin."[6]

At least as profound an impact on Moore's visual encounters occurred during her first trip to New York in 1915. Among her other experiences, Moore listed a visit to 291 Fifth Avenue, the Alfred Stieglitz Gallery, which did so much to promote modern art, as one of the most memorable events of her weeklong visit. Stieglitz showed her paintings by Picasso, Francis Picabia, and Marsden Hartley and even gave her personal copies of *Camera Work*. One of the issues featured a photograph of Gordon Craig, a revolutionary set designer, which she very much admired. (Craig always rated high praise from Moore; her poem "To a Man Working His Way through the Crowd" assigns him the positive characteristics of a lynx.) One of Moore's most pleasing memories of 291 Fifth Avenue was of a painting by John Marin of a seascape that she found particularly appealing, even when others were discounting it. She also visited the Daniel Gallery (early supporters of William and Marguerite Zorach and

Charles Demuth). She referred to a "magnificent photograph of Whitman" at the Kraft Gallery, indicating that she had been lucky enough to "make the rounds" of the avant-garde studios during her short stay in New York.

The point is that very early on, Moore was caught up in the enthusiasm of the best of the young modernist painters. Although she had probably not seen the famous Armory Show of 1913, which featured Constantin Brancuşi's *Kiss* and Marcel Duchamp's *Nude Descending a Staircase*, she read voraciously about it, making careful notes about the impact of such art and saving over a dozen articles about the show itself. She was also aware of theories at issue in even newer developments, having read Ezra Pound and Wyndham Lewis as they outlined their theories of Vorticism in their 1914–15 magazine *Blast*. In "Education of a Poet" (1963), she wrote, "After leaving Bryn Mawr, I came under the spell of the *English Review* edited by F. M. Ford (F. M. Hueffer) who wrote many of the book reviews—some of which I transcribed, having borrowed the copies. And *Blast*. The flavor of Wyndham Lewis meant a great deal to me."[7]

In the modernist period, the reciprocity of the arts was such that it "makes little sense to talk in hierarchial terms of painting as the model for poetry or vice versa."[8] Enthusiasm for the means to "make it new," what the French literary Cubists preferred to call *l'esprit nouveau*, ran through all artistic media, and they flourished by cross-fertilization. Painters and poets talked as feverishly as they wrote and painted. After the Armory Show—and led in America by the compelling conversations and leadership of artists like Duchamp and Picabia—new ideas were in the air, many of them European imports. New galleries were opened: the Daniels Gallery, the Bourgeois, *291*, and the Modern Gallery, financed by Walter Arensberg. Aided by Duchamp and Man Ray, Katherine Drier founded the Société Anonyme in 1920, the first modern art museum in America. Something as simple as the sale of fifty-seven separate halftone postcard reproductions of works shown at the Armory Show aided artists and writers in familiarizing themselves with the revolution in ideas these paintings signaled. In his book *The Visual Text of William Carlos Williams*, Henry Sayre has demonstrated that Williams learned one lesson especially from the painters with whom he associated throughout his life: "The advent of pattern or design in a work of art is a function of the imagination, and the justification for the artistic imagination is, in fact, its ability to order and compose its world."[9] There are certainly some sound analogies here to Moore's own methods of creating intricate visual and aural designs.

Hall notes that one group associated with the little magazine *Others* found as their entire raison d'être the belief that there should be more experimental alternatives to Harriet Monroe's *Poetry* and met frequently to discuss art and literature. Alfred Kreymborg and Walter Arensberg had brought *Others* into being and were publishing the work of many new writers, among them, Marianne Moore.

> The *Others* group gathered frequently for Sunday picnics at Kreymborg's "shack" in Grantwood, New Jersey. Williams, according to Kreymborg, was a sort of Don Quixote figure arriving wild and talkative in his rattletrap car. Stevens never came to the country but Arensberg did, once bringing along Marcel Duchamp. Mary Carolyn Davies . . . came frequently and occasionally brought Marianne Moore. Kreymborg remembers Moore as an astonishing person with Titian hair and a brilliant complexion and a mellifluous flow of polysyllables which kept every man in awe.[10]

William Carlos Williams and his wife, Floss, did their share of entertaining too. On 23 December 1919, Bill Williams penned this gentle invitation to his regal, if reserved, acquaintance, Marianne Moore: "Won't you come out with the rest on Sunday afternoon for tea and something else if we're lucky? I've been writing hasty and lewd letters to many of the rest of the crowd—in which you seem so out of place—so in place, like a red berry still hanging to the jaded rose bush. . . . it isn't so far from sacramental wine to drink." Marianne Moore responded, "I cannot feel sorry for the red berry when the bush is so full of sap."[11]

And she did attend the Williams party, as she had been attending such gatherings for several years. Moore said later, perhaps a bit bemused by her own youthful temerity: "It was the visit in 1916 that made me want to live there [New York City]. I don't know what put it into her [Miss Cawdrey of Carlisle] head to do it, or why she wasn't likely to have a better time without me. She was most skeptical of my venturing forth to bohemian parties. But I was fearless about that. In the first place, I didn't think anyone would try to harm me, but if they did I felt impervious. It never occurred to me that chaperones were important."[12]

One finds Moore turning up frequently and reading her work at gatherings of young modernist writers and artists. The Rosenbach collection owns a series of invitations from Marsden Hartley to Marianne Moore.[13] In *Troubadour: An Autobiography*, Alfred Kreymborg says that both he and Bill Williams "held the mind of Marianne Moore in absolute admiration. What [we] lacked in intellectual stability was freely and unconsciously supplied by her. Her familiarity with books on every conceivable theme astonished [us]."[14] Williams remembers Moore at one of Lola Ridge's parties with Marsden Hartley and Charles Demuth when she read "Those Various Scalpels."[15] The two painters were so taken with the literary excellence around them that they made literary attempts of their own. Marsden wrote "On the Hills of Caledonia," and Charles Demuth tried several genres, including a short story entitled "The Voyage Was Almost Over" and two plays, *Fantastic Lovers* and *The Azure Adder*. Other works—*You Must Come Over*, *A Painting: A Play*, and *Filling a Page: A Pantomime with Words*—were exploratory attempts to cross over the boundaries of artistic genres. For Demuth plot was certainly secondary to the creation of a pictorial tableau that was Symbolist in style and spirit.[16] Demuth's writing demonstrates elusive meaning and almost intentional obscurity, a trait many modern writers seemed to share. So apparently confident was Moore of the value of Demuth's opinion, that she complimented T. S. Eliot on 10 December 1923 by writing to him, "Charles Demuth spoke to me recently of the skill and the very perfect finish of your writing."[17]

The common goals of writers, sculptors, and painters caused them to exchange insights and to blur the lines between the arts. Dickran Rashjian deals with this exchange in *Skyscraper Primitives*, arguing convincingly that the very poetry many writers produced developed out of their response to Dada. He quotes William Carlos Williams: "No one knew consistently enough to formulate a 'movement.' We were restless, constrained, closedly allied with painters. Impressionism, dadaism, surrealism applied to both painting and the poem."[18]

In *Hieroglyphics of a New Speech: Cubism, Stieglitz, and the Early Poetry of William Carlos Williams*, Bram Dijkstra suggests that the basic concepts of Imagism were already contained in the theories of painting that took their cue from Cézanne. Stieglitz's *Camera Work* had stressed the very goals later described by T. S. Flint and Ezra Pound in *Poetry* as the tenets of Imagism. Painters were experimenting with the ways in which devices like poetic metaphor could cross the boundaries of nature by its conceptual license. Poets watched how painting engages the senses with its immediacy. The point is that whatever the scenario, working with the visual, with images, was in the air. And like the "red berry on the bush so full of sap," Moore was part of the extraordinarily creative world of the young modernists.

There is no doubt, then, that Moore was grounded in the visual, by temperament, talent, training, and experience. Her attention to visual detail is obvious in many poems, but perhaps in none more clearly than in "Those Various Scalpels," first published in the Bryn Mawr *Lantern* for the spring of 1917. No amount of paraphrasing can hope to do justice to Moore's succinct portrait reproduced below.

Those Various Scalpels,

those
various sounds consistently indistinct, like intermingled echoes
   struck from thin glasses successively at random—
      the inflection disguised: your hair, the tails of two
     fighting-cocks head to head in stone—
       like sculptured scimitars repeating the curve of your ears in
                  reverse order:
     your eyes, flowers of ice and snow

sown by tearing winds on the cordage of disabled ships; your
                     raised hand,
   an ambiguous signature: your cheeks, those rosettes
   of blood on the stone floors of French châteaux,
   with regard to which the guides are so affirmative—
     your other hand,

a bundle of lances all alike, partly hid by emeralds from Persia
   and the fractional magnificence of Florentine
     goldwork—a collection of little objects—
   sapphires set with emeralds, and pearls with a moonstone,
                    made fine
     with enamel in gray, yellow, and dragon-fly blue;
     a lemon, a pear

and three bunches of grapes, tied with silver: your dress, a
                  magnificent square
    cathedral tower of uniform
     and at the same time diverse appearance—a
   species of vertical vineyard rustling in the storm

of conventional opinion. Are they weapons or scalpels?
Whetted to brilliance

by the hard majesty of that sophistication which is superior to
opportunity,
these things are rich instruments with which to experiment.
But why dissect destiny with instruments
more highly specialized than components of destiny
itself?

It would be difficult to outdo Moore for sheer economy and biting accuracy of detail. If an essential dimension of Cubism was the reduction of figures to basic forms and the creation of austere, monochromatic figures, then there is in "Those Various Scalpels" a kind of Cubist flavor. This female figure, portrayed with both photographic detail and the insight of the great portrait painter, is a modern woman, but one represented with all of the characteristics of changing femininity that continue to alarm the contemporary world. She is communicated to the reader/viewer with brilliantly chosen visual details that reveal her innermost soul. Her hair is not soft and feminine but arranged like

. . . the tails of two
fighting-cocks head to head in stone—
like sculptured scimitars.

(The tails of the cocks are an interesting pun on the cocktail party, the backdrop of the entire portrait. Like the portrait painter, Moore is experimenting with motifs of language, not of shape.)

The metaphors are those of fighting, weapons, and violence, certainly not those of the traditional portraits of womanly grace and beauty. And the female's eyes, "flowers of ice and snow / sown by tearing winds on the cordage of disabled ships," continue the imagery of coldness, violence, and disaster. The roses on those cheeks are like the blood on the stone floors of French châteaux, images Moore may have remembered being pointed out by guides (who are "so affirmative") during her own European tour. What, after all, is affirmative about blood on stone, the evidence of one human being committing violence upon another, Byron's "Chillon" notwithstanding? But more significantly, what a dreadful association to draw while looking at a "beautiful," well-groomed woman.

The coup de grace of the poem reflects its title; the poet visualizes the hands as "a bundle of lances," all carefully groomed and disguised,

> . . . partly hid by emeralds from Persia
> and a fractional magnificence of Florentine
> goldwork.

Moore adds more color to the portrait with

> . . . a collection of little objects—
> sapphires set with emeralds, and pearls with a moonstone, made
> fine

> with enamel in gray, yellow, and dragon-fly blue.

The motif is that of "a lemon, a pear / and three bunches of grapes." The lady's dress is severe,

> . . . a magnificent square
> cathedral tower of uniform
> and at the same time diverse appearance.

It is an oddly knit "vertical vineyard rustling in the storm / of conventional opinion." Moore loved clothes, choosing her own with great care, almost like a costume designer creating a character through the careful selection of garments. She frequently made notes about fashion in her notebooks, taking careful information, for example, from Frank Parsons's *The Psychology of Dress* (1920).[19] She even wrote her own pieces on fashion, items like "Dress and Kindred Subjects," which appeared in *Women's Wear Daily* on 17 February 1965. So when she dresses this lady like a "square / cathedral tower," there are carefully chosen echoes of austerity and even a nunlike quality for the figure, but at the same time a very graphic picture of a buildinglike and formidable woman.

But it is to the hands, specifically the fingernails (those "lances"), to which the poet returns, asking, "Are they weapons or scalpels?" For in one aspect, this woman is like a warrior, armed to do battle in the arena of a sophisticated modern cocktail party (the "intermingled echoes / struck from thin glasses successively at random"). She is majestic in her armor of sophistication. But the poet remains ambivalent about her hard appearance. Her scalpels could be "rich instruments with which to experiment" rather than merely weapons to destroy. However, as the poem concludes, "why dissect destiny with instruments / more highly specialized than components of destiny itself?" Why use something as magnificent and highly specialized as human hands—and the human mind—for destruction or dissection, when they are the building tools of destiny?

It has always been assumed that Moore's precise portrait of this modern woman was based on someone she had observed or on a picture she had seen. It is worthy of conjecture that the woman may have been a portrait of Moore herself, at least a dimension of her personality that she sometimes saw emerging. She too was capable of dissection and of destruction. Several poems of this period verged on the destructive: "To a Steam Roller" (1915), "To Statecraft Embalmed" (1915), "Pedantic Literalist" (1916), "To Be Liked by You Would Be a Calamity" (1916). They are almost black and white in their harsh judgments, showing little patience with the offender. But by late 1916 and 1917, the harshness had begun to fade as Moore began to temper her judgments with a more mature and humane understanding. By "The Monkeys" (1917) and "To the Peacock of France" (1917), and certainly by "Melanchthon" (1918), there is a far more sympathetic treatment of human frailty. It is possible that Moore may have seen in the figure of the fighting cocks and the lady armed with weapons and scalpels of dissection a reflection of herself, an image she strove to correct. The reference to the dress like a cathedral tower might reinforce the argument, with Moore viewing herself as someone who watches the world from an ascetic and aesthetic distance (that red berry on the jaded rosebush).

Moore may also have decided at one point that scalpels and dissection were necessary tools of the artist; but after taking a long hard look at herself, she realized that her talents, her "instruments," were "more highly specialized" than that. They could become the "components of destiny itself." An additional support for the argument might come from Moore's choice of jewelry for her female figure. In "Voracities and Verities Sometimes Are Interacting," Moore wrote, "I don't like diamonds; / the emerald's 'grass-lamp glow' is better." If indeed the female figure is Moore herself, she assigns herself imaginary possessions that include "emeralds from Persia" and "sapphires set with emeralds." As a matter of fact, the myriad jewels, perhaps Moore's own many-faceted talents, weigh down the very hands they adorn.

Regardless of its model, this austere female figure is indelibly etched upon the reader's mind. It is obvious that the superb visual effect of this piece was Moore's final objective because a quick perusal of the text will demonstrate that Moore's usually exact syllabic count is forfeited to the more important goal of visual impact. The poem almost succeeds in being experienced as a picture might be. One cannot deny that there will always be differences in the two art forms. Literature, based on words, sounds, and syntax, must always be decoded linearly, while a painting is usually decoded as a single experience. Nonetheless, a fine painting can be appreciated for the excellence of its parts in the formation of the whole. And careful concentration and study help the viewer appreciate the integrity of the composition and perceive echoes of his or her own past experiences and responses. So too in literature it is possible for the artist, particularly the poet, to call up in the reader's mind an intuition so graphic as to approach pictorial quality. Granted, the writer cannot totally control the reader's imagination, but with precise word and image choices, the writer can come very close to re-creating a common visual experience, while at the same time challenging old ideologies and stereotypes of both the figure under consideration and the style of presentation.

In July 1921, Moore wrote to H. D.: "There has been an exhibition of modern work at Wanamaker's that has a great deal of flavor to it—a cross-eyed monk in browns by Max Weber and a wool map of New York in minute sketches by Marguerite Zorach. . . . Lachaise has a bronze statue originally called *Pudeur*, which he calls 'Standing Figure'—very elegant—and four dolphins with long, oval eyes diving side by side at different heights with a wave thrown in."[20]

In that same month Moore published a major poem about her own relationship to the arts, entitled "When I Buy Pictures." With a subtle dose of the famous Moore humor, she admits that for her, shopping for great pictures is an activity that exists largely in her mind. (Moore did own some lovely works of art, especially a series of Blake prints, several framed sketches by family members, and a lovely collection of animal figures after her animal poems. But these were almost entirely gifts from friends. The Moores were not wealthy people.) Instead, like Thoreau choosing pieces of property only in his imagination in *Walden*, Moore could save herself a great deal of bother and expense by becoming merely the "imaginary possessor" of great works of art. She could, in fact, possess whole galleries of beautiful things, if only in her mind.

When I Buy Pictures

or what is closer to the truth,
when I look at that of which I may regard myself as the
        imaginary possessor,
I fix upon what would give me pleasure in my average moments:
the satire upon curiosity in which no more is discernible
than the intensity of the mood;
or quite the opposite—the old thing, the medieval decorated hat-
         box,
in which there are hounds with waists diminishing like the waist
        of the hour-glass,
and deer and birds and seated people;
it may be no more than a square of parquetry; the literal
        biography perhaps,
in letters standing well apart upon a parchment-like expanse;
an artichoke in six varieties of blue; the snipe-legged
        hieroglyphic in three parts;
the silver fence protecting Adam's grave, or Michael taking Adam
        by the wrist.
Too stern an intellectual emphasis upon this quality or that
        detracts from one's enjoyment.
It must not wish to disarm anything; nor may the approved
        triumph easily be honored—
that which is great because something else is small.
It comes to this: of whatever sort it is,
it must be "lit with piercing glances into the life of things";
it must acknowledge the spiritual forces which have made it.

It is obvious that Moore had been doing a great deal of thinking about what she chooses to call pictures. Her standards of selection are unique because, as she says, she fixes upon "what would give me pleasure in my average moments." "Average moments" is a curious turn of phrase. For Moore, whatever her imaginary choices, art had become part of her everyday, her "average" life, and she could fancy herself surrounded by the best of everything. Some of the objects could produce "satire upon curiosity" (perhaps a Demuth), or in others "no more is discernible / than the intensity of the mood" (as perhaps in a Picasso or a Braque). At times she might prefer something quite the opposite, "the old thing" (such as an object she had seen in Europe or in her beloved museums), like "the medieval decorated hat-box / in which there are hounds with waists diminishing like the waist of the hour-glass," an object Mary Norcross might have treasured. And there are more museum pieces only a connoisseur might appreciate: "a square of parquetry," an actual "biography" formed by a beautifully framed series of letters mounted on "a parchment-like expanse." And there is an artichoke rendered in "six varieties of blue," a bizarre "snipe-legged hieroglyphic," and a picture of the Archangel Michael taking a dazed Adam by the hand.

Trusting in her own unerring sense of excellence at an instinctive level (a level not unlike Bergson's intuition, the highest level of human intelligence), Moore senses that "too stern an intellectual emphasis upon this quality or that detracts from one's enjoyment." And the work must give pleasure, albeit both an intellectual and an aesthetic one. The work need not be of such proportions as to disarm anything, nor must it be overpoweringly triumphant, great only "because something else is small." Size and magnitude of subject matter have nothing to do with greatness. Nor do genre, historicity, theme, color, realistic or abstract style, technique, or motif. These are really all trivial dimensions of what makes great art, at least for Marianne Moore. All that really matters is the work's ability to penetrate to the essence of things, to produce that illusion which is more precise than precision, what Moore would come to call the "rock crystal thing to see."

Moore concludes by articulating the only real measure she uses when she "buys" a picture. It must be "lit with piercing glances into the life of things," and "it must acknowledge the spiritual forces which have made it." Moore's references to "spiritual forces" have presented an enigmatic problem for Moore scholars and critics. The twentieth century has remained wary of such references, particularly if they suggest a religious solution to what is perceived as an intellectual and philosophical dilemma. But there is little doubt about Moore's own strong religious faith; she remained a devout Presbyterian throughout her lifetime. If one is to work with Moore's discourse, one must take her faith into account, utilizing the qualities of character that are based on Christian ethics, for a basic faith in something beyond herself informs both Moore's poems and her epistemology. Hall argues that "it seems unlikely that 'Supreme Belief' should be taken to mean belief in God. Rather . . . that Miss Moore is talking about a belief in life, an affirmation of life that includes acceptance, not avoidance of its perils."[21] It seems clear to me, however, that Moore's *is* an abiding faith in a Supreme Being.

Harold Bloom has commented that Moore was a "curious kind of devotional poet, with some authentic affinities to George Herbert," and that she "reminds us implicitly but constantly that any distinction between sacred and secular poetry is only a shibboleth of cultural politics." He adds that her poetry might be in danger of dwindling into moral essays ("an impossible form for our times"), were it not for her "wild allusiveness, her zest for quotations, and her essentially anarchic stance."[22] Moore's spiritual judgments offer a dimension far larger than the limitations of a particular woman's faith or even of a particular religion. It is a dimension that demands that the essential questions about the purposes of human existence be asked and ultimately be accommodated by some kind of willed affirmation. But the nature of that accommodation is left to each reader. All Moore asks is hope and belief in the power of the human spirit to endure.

As noted earlier, Moore loved the Book of Job; its metaphors and themes are often part of her poetry. She applauded the sustaining power of Job that allowed him to "contrive glory from ashes." And she was moved by the Job poet's vision of a Yahweh who celebrated his own creation with a majestic procession of beasts (including peacocks, unicorns, lions, behemoths, and even the great leviathan, denizens of Moore's own bestiary). Moore's creative instincts produced a similar celebration and an unflagging sense of faith in the essential variety and greatness of men and women and of all creation.

Moore's early insistence that great art must "acknowledge the spiritual forces which have made it" is a theme from which Moore never wavered. If Wallace Stevens was involved in the creation of the "Supreme Fiction," Moore had already found it. Her confidence in the innate goodness and potential of human beings is always reflected in her verses; there would always be glory in ashes. And that expression of confidence in the spiritual in art was already clear in Moore's criteria of choice in "When I Buy Pictures," first published in 1921.

By the time Moore wrote "Novices," first published in the *Dial* for February 1923, her tendency to combine both literary and artistic techniques and terminologies in her now very complex searches was evident. The poem marks a real difference from her previous work because of its very inclusiveness, its polyphony, its gathering of many voices, most all of them unexpected, at least given the poetic tradition of her day. Moore had begun to view her own work with greater confidence and assurance, although she understood that she too remained a kind of novice.

Novices

anatomize their work
in the sense in which Will Honeycomb was jilted by a duchess;
the little assumptions of the scared ego confusing the issue
so that they do not know "whether it is the buyer or the seller
          who gives the money"—
an abstruse idea plain to none but the artist,
the only seller who buys, and holds on to the money.
Because one expresses oneself and entitles it wisdom, one is not
         a fool. What an idea!
"Dracontine cockatrices, perfect and poisonous from the
         beginning,"
they present themselves as a contrast to sea-serpented regions
      "unlit by the half-lights of more conscious art."

Acquiring at thirty what at sixty they will be trying to forget,
blind to the right word, deaf to satire
which like "the smell of the cypress strengthens the nerves of the
         brain,"
averse from the antique
with "that tinge of sadness about it which a reflective mind
         always feels,
it is so little and so much"—
they write the sort of thing that would in their judgment interest
         a lady;
curious to know if we do not adore each letter of the alphabet
        that goes to make a word of it—
according to the Act of Congress, the sworn statement of the
        treasurer and all the rest of it—
the counterpart to what we are:
stupid man; men are strong and no one pays any attention:
stupid woman; women have charm, and how annoying they can be.
Yes, "the authors are wonderful people, particularly those that
         write the most,"
the masters of all languages, the supertadpoles of expression.
Accustomed to the recurring phosphorescence of antiquity,
the "much noble vagueness and indefinite jargon" of Plato,
the lucid movements of the royal yacht upon the learned scenery
         of Egypt—
king, steward, and harper, seated amidships while the jade and
        the rock crystal course about in solution,

their suavity surmounts the surf—
the willowy wit, the transparent equation of Isaiah, Jeremiah,
                                                    Ezekiel, Daniel.
Bored by "the detailless perspective of the sea," reiterative and
                                                    naïve,
and its chaos of rocks—the stuffy remarks of the Hebrews—
the good and alive young men demonstrate the assertion
that it is not necessary to be associated with that which has
                                                    annoyed one;
they have never made a statement which they found so easy to
                                                    prove—
"split like a glass against a wall"
in this "precipitate of dazzling impressions,
the spontaneous unforced passion of the Hebrew language—
an abyss of verbs full of reverberations and tempestuous energy"
in which action perpetuates action and angle is at variance with
                                                    angle
till submerged by the general action;
obscured by "fathomless suggestions of color,"
by incessantly panting lines of green, white with concussion,
in this drama of water against rocks—this "ocean of hurrying
                                                    consonants"
with its "great livid stains like long slabs of green marble,"
its "flashing lances of perpendicular lightning" and "molten fires
                                                    swallowed up,"
"with foam on its barriers,"
"crashing itself out in one long hiss of spray."

"Novices" is a difficult poem, demanding that the reader bring the same academic, artistic, literary, historical, and biblical references to bear that Moore did. She chose to deal now with abstractions, with ideas "split like a glass against a wall," a "precipitate of dazzling impressions," their metaphors set with angle "at variance with angle" and exhibiting language filled with "fathomless suggestions of color." Bonnie Costello was the first to observe that this poem's "collage of phrases, emphasis on infinitely crossing angles, contrasting colors, rapid succession of images and words beyond a syntactic hold are all elements of Cubist painting stressed by Gleizes and Metzinger."[23] In another poem of about the same time, "Bowls," Moore writes,

I learn that we are precisionists,
not citizens of Pompeii arrested in action
as a cross-section of one's correspondence would seem to imply.

The term "precisionist" cannot be passed over lightly. Moore liked the word "precision" and used it frequently, but "precisionist" had quite another meaning. It was the name assigned to American "Cubists" by Wolfgang Born in about 1920. Charles Demuth, whom Moore knew, was the leader of American Precisionism, a style whose artists were also called the New Classicists and the Immaculates. (Other friends, Georgia O'Keeffe and Charles Sheeler, were also dubbed Precisionists.) Actually the word came to "include virtually every artist who reduced an industrial theme to geometric shapes."[24] But it was the Cubist principle of multiplicity of viewpoint that enabled Demuth to distill into a single painting a variety of elapsed experiences and perspectives. The result approximated, or tried to, the experience of reading a novel or watching a theatrical performance, in which characters and places change. William Carlos Williams recommended that Demuth and other American painters and writers find American subjects and techniques more suited to the American idiom when they attempted to work with the European Cubist theories, thus the creation of what Born called Precisionism.

Moore seems impatient with some writers' and artists' vision of so-called Precisionism in "Bowls" if only because they delude themselves into believing that their work is truly modern, that they have broken with the past, an observation she had already proven was impossible in "The Past Is the Present." In "Bowls" she renounces "a policy of boorish indifference / to everything that has been said since the days of Matilda." Furthermore, she says she "shall purchase an etymological dictionary of modern English / that [she] may understand what is written," again reflecting Eliot's notion that a true historical sense "compels a man to write not only with his own generation in his bones, but with a feeling that the whole of the literature of Europe from Homer . . . has a simultaneous existence."[25] So one serious flaw of many novices is their tendency to discount the past, to be so foolish as to be blind to its existence.

By "Novices," Moore argues her case against what she observed were some of the errors of at least some practitioners of Dada, Cubism, or Precisionism, while at the same time utilizing Cubist, or perhaps more accurately Precisionist, techniques to accomplish the task. Moore is warning American novices, herself included, that although their techniques are useful, even fascinating, they must not dismiss the past, must not be "averse from the antique / with 'that tinge of sadness about it.'" To accomplish her goal, Moore creates two unforgettable paintings—or visions—of the sea.

There is so much included, so much action in the poem that the two visions of the sea are in some danger of being overshadowed by the artistry of their own execution, an effect which seems to me intentional. For how better to warn about the dangers of a technique than by demonstrating them. In the first picture, which does not culminate until halfway through the poem, Moore looks at the sea from the perspective of one kind of novice. This viewer is merely "bored by the detailless perspective of the sea." These "supertadpoles of expression," as she calls them, have become

> accustomed to the recurring phosphorescence of antiquity,
> the "much noble vagueness and indefinite jargon" of Plato
> the lucid movements of the royal yacht upon the learned scenery
> of Egypt.

Thus they miss the "rock crystal course[ing] about in solution." (Again Moore makes reference to "rock crystal," the existence of some kind of objective truth.) Their "suavity surmounts the surf." They miss "the willowy wit, the transparent equation of Isaiah, Jeremiah, Ezekiel, Daniel." They see only "the stuffy remarks of the Hebrews." These shallow young men have decided that it is just "not necessary to be associated with that which has annoyed one."

By contrast, other novices see "split like a glass against a wall" in this "precipitate of dazzling impressions, / the spontaneous unforced passion of the Hebrew language." They perceive a veritable

> ". . . abyss of verbs full of reverberations and tempestuous
> energy"
> in which action perpetuates action and angle is at variance with
> angle
> till submerged by the general action.

They see a "drama of water against rocks," "fathomless suggestions of color," "incessantly panting lines of green, white"—an entire "ocean of hurrying consonants." Note how Moore is interweaving literary and linguistic terms like "drama," "verbs," and "consonants" into her anatomized picture of a vitalized sea, a picture, incidentally, that is very much like the Cubists' multiplicity of viewpoints, which enabled the painter to focus on a variety of elapsed experiences and perspectives in time. Note also that this is anything but a boring "detailless perspective of the sea." It is alive "with its 'great livid stains like long slabs of green marble'" and "with foam on its barriers," "crashing itself out in one long hiss of spray." Most significantly for Moore, this second picture of the sea is lit with "flashing lances of perpendicular lightning" and "molten fires swallowed up," the "piercing glances into the life of things" which had become her criteria of greatness in "When I Buy Pictures." Admittedly, the novices of the second picture are not quite sure where to begin with what they see, but at least they do see it.

Moore's metaphor of the past as a cosmic, crashing, tumultuous, multicolored sea that is not boring or "detailless" at all but teeming with color and with life is an interesting variation on Eliot's attempts to explain the vitality of the past in relation to present art in "Tradition and the Individual Talent." Eliot's "monuments" from the past take on a wonderful simultaneity in *The Waste Land*, particularly at the end, when Eliot juxtaposes lines like:

> London Bridge is falling down falling down falling down
> *Poi s'ascose nel foco che gli affina*
> *Quando fiam uti chelidon*—O swallow swallow
> *Le Prince d'Aquitaine à la tour abolie.*

That same simultaneity, however, remains somewhat static and academic in *The Sacred Wood*.[26] But Moore's sense of the simultaneity of the past is very visual, a living painting of a sea alive with the creative possibilities of all time. Slatin has further pointed out that in Moore, "unaided, the eye sees that the wave is breaking; it takes an 'x-raylike inquisitive intensity' to perceive that the wave is composed of materials already extant, and that the rhythm of its movement was laid down at the Creation."[27] Thus Moore has traced the reader back even beyond Eliot's sense of the past, to the beginning of things, to "The Days of Prismatic Color" (1919), to the time when "there was no smoke and color was fine, not with the refinement of early civilization art, but because of its originality." And she has brought all of the elements together in a picture of the vital and elemental sea, a picture only enhanced by the richness of the great art and literature of the past.

But there is still another dimension of the poem, another layer of experience with the past, one circuitously woven, but undeniable nonetheless. For Moore means to lead us through that knowledge of the past which Eliot knew could be gained only by "great labour." (Yeats had also warned in "Adam's Curse" that one needs to understand that "women and poets must labour to be beautiful.") The first half of the poem is a challenging examination of many of the classic errors of artistic novices. It prepares the reader for a many-layered understanding, a collage, of the varying natures of novices. It readies the reader to view the two contrasting pictures of the sea and to realize which choice the serious artist, even though he or she remains a novice, must make. It does, however, require concentration and patience from the reader.

Costello is right to call the piece a collage, one of seemingly random comments about neophyte artists and writers, all organized thematically around the character of Will Honeycomb. "Novices" marks one of Moore's first poems created from a collage (from the French *coller*, "to glue"), a collection of disparate objects "glued" together. But her glued objects are not only visual, they are also collections of borrowed phrases, making the poem a verbal montage. (In a montage, the artist adds to the glued items materials from various sources, particularly items from printed matter.) Moore's poem is filled with quotations, a true polyphony, twelve separate sources acknowledged in her notes, everything from *The Decameron* to Leigh Hunt's *Autobiography*. Several were taken from A. R. Gordon's *The Poets of the Old Testament* and one from Anatole France. But Moore uses the collected references, pictures, and prose to create a sense of impatient anger in the poem as she discounts the naïveté of the "Dracontine cockatrices, perfect and poisonous from the beginning," who present themselves as having discovered amazing new ideas far superior to the old ones which were "unlit by the half-lights of more conscious art." This kind of artist, she tells us, is busy "acquiring at thirty what at sixty they will be trying to forget." Naively smug in their own immaturity, they are "deaf to satire / which like 'the smell of cypress strengthens the nerves of the brain.'"

It is around the artistic value of satire that Moore has set up her argument, and indeed her own intent in the poem: "Novices" is a satire. The selection opens with the figure of Will Honeycomb, a character taken from Addison and Steele's *Spectator Club*. Moore's reference to this classic Augustan satire may seem a bit incongruous at first, but in a kind of Cubist style, Moore is demanding the active intellectual involvement of her audience. As Calvin Tomkins writes in *The Bride and the Bachelors*, apropos of Marcel Duchamp, in both Cubism and Abstract Expressionism a "good deal of the new art both in this country and in Europe seems to make its appeal less to the eye than to the mind."[28] So Moore's reference to classical satire as represented by Will Honeycomb requires quick intellectual gymnastics from her readers. It is indeed an appeal less to the eye than to the mind.

Will Honeycomb is the eternal male chauvinist naïf, "an aging Gentleman," Steele tells us in No. 2 of *The Spectator*, "who is very ready at the sort of Discourse with which Men usually entertain women." With beautiful economy, Steele reports that "Time has made but very little Impression, either by Wrinkles on his Forehead, or Traces in his Brain." Honeycomb loves to entertain the assemblage with innuendos about women and flamboyant boasts about his prowess in their company. Steele says he is "that sort of Man who is usually called a well-bred Gentleman . . . where women are *not* concerned." But in spite of Honeycomb's continued boasting of conquests of ladies of the highest degree, and gratuitous information about their most private activities, by *Spectator* No. 530 Steele has him married off, not to a duchess at all, but to a farmer's daughter. So when Moore purports that "novices anatomize their work / in the sense in which Will Honeycomb was jilted by a duchess," she is suggesting that most novices, like Will Honeycomb, are characterized largely by talk, by bombast. They make so many little assumptions of the scared ego that they confuse the issue so that they don't even know who's selling and who's buying anymore. The work of a great satirist of that kind of bombast is lost upon them; they simply declare it boring, reiterative, and naive. After all, "it is not necessary to be associated with that which has annoyed" them. More important, they do not see themselves in Will Honeycomb; they probably do not even know who he was. Because they are deaf to satire, they will never know "the smell of the cypress [that] strengthens the nerves of the brain." They continue to "write the sort of thing that would in their judgment interest a lady; / curious to know if we do not adore each letter of the alphabet that goes to make a word of it."

Moore's choice of the womanizer, Will Honeycomb, beside this line about underestimating the intellectual capacity of women, added to the reference that she will renounce "a policy of boorish indifference / to everything that has been said since the days of Matilda" in the companion piece "Bowls," suggests that Moore is also working through her own reaction to the tendency of some male "novices" to discount the female mind as a worthy counterpart in the world of art and literature. By 1923, Moore's awareness of the limitations of being a woman in the art world had become keen. Not everyone was as kind and appreciative as William Carlos Williams. (Note that Moore traces the English language back not to Henry II, the first of the Plantagenets, the "father" of modern English, but instead to its [and Henry's] mother, the powerful Matilda, a reigning queen of England and empress of the Holy Roman Empire [1102–67]). Hers was a subtle but clear defense of her sex.

We may conjecture whether there was a particular novice that irritated the persona of the poem. Some of Marcel Duchamp's repartee could have provided that impetus. He claimed that Dada "was a way to get out of a state of mind—to avoid being influenced by one's immediate environment, or by the past; to get away from cliches—to get free." Later he said: "The dead should not be permitted to be so much stronger than the living. . . . We must learn to forget the past, to live our own lives in our own time."[29] It is easy to envision the pristine Miss Moore's reaction to Duchamp's attempt to submit the readymade urinal signed "R. Mutt" to an exhibition or perhaps his longtime commitment to *The Bride Stripped Bare by Her Bachelors, Even,* a work with possible antifemale reverberations.

Although Moore herself is certainly not always an easy poet to decipher, she was never intentionally obscure. Yet some of the novices of her acquaintance are proud that they are working in "an abstruse idea plain to none but the artist." Moore worried a great deal about the abstract becoming too obscure. In "In the Days of Prismatic Color," she had written,

> . . . complexity is not a crime, but carry
> it to the point of murkiness
> and nothing is plain.

To be abstract merely to confuse is the ploy of the eternal novice.

Like the work of many of its Cubist and Precisionist counterparts, I am not sure that "Novices" is entirely successful and accessible, except perhaps in the final precision of the two pictures of the sea, but it does represent a major breakthrough in Moore's attempts at applying the principles of Cubism and the artistic techniques of collage and montage to poetry. And it represents layers of meaning, of quickly changing perspectives, of metaphors set with angle "at variance with angle," of language filled with "fathomless suggestions of color." It is indeed a "precipitate of dazzling impressions" in which meaning may be subservient to overall effect. But at the same time, it is a daring flight, a bold attempt at a new kind of magic, one unparalleled as yet in her own work. Moore's words call up layers of ideas and images from literary history to linguistic X rays as they reinforce the inclusiveness of her meaning. Moore would be more successful with the same techniques in "Marriage" and "An Octopus," two masterful poems by any measure. But "Novices" is an important work by a "novice" who understands the significance of that word and who is ready for "the smell of the cypress [that] strengthens the nerves of the brain."

By the *Dial* years, 1925 to 1929, Moore had achieved a high degree of confidence in her knowledge of the world of the literary and the visual arts. Her association with the *Dial* occurred in the early twenties, when she met Scofield Thayer and James Sibley Watson, Jr., two wealthy, young Harvard graduates who had purchased the *Dial* from Randolph Bourne. Their goal was to turn it into a modernist journal of the highest standards. They meant the publication to be cosmopolitan, and to that end they hired foreign as well as American editors: Pound wrote from Paris, Eliot from London, Thomas Mann from Germany, and John Eglinton from Dublin. Thayer's interest in modern art (he had a fine personal collection) made him determined to publish prints by the finest modern artists. The *Dial*'s first issue featured works by Cézanne, Charles Demuth, John Marin, and Gaston Lachaise. Sibley and Hildegarde Watson, close personal friends of Marianne Moore's also held a major collection of the work of European and American modernists, so Moore would probably have seen many of the actual works of some of the greatest of the modernist painters and sculptors.

By 1920, the *Dial* was publishing the work of Marianne Moore, the woman who had in 1918 been "the only modernist poet in New York."[30] (Moore began doing book reviews for a section of the *Dial* called "Briefer Mentions" in 1920, and a number of her poems were published in various issues. There was even a rumor recorded by Williams in his *Autobiography* that by the midtwenties Scofield Thayer had proposed to

Marianne Moore, but there is little in their correspondence to support such a claim. The two seem to have worked their way through some minor editorial differences but appear to have remained only professional friends.) Moore's work had so impressed the owners of the magazine that by mid-1925, she had been persuaded to become acting editor of the *Dial*, ostensibly to give Thayer more time abroad, although he seems to have suffered some kind of nervous collapse. Thus by a rapidly unfolding set of circumstances, Moore found herself at the helm of one of the most prestigious publications of modernist literature and art in America. The *Dial* years found Moore writing with increasing confidence and insight, not only about literary figures and their works, but about artists and their productions.

Before the *Dial* editorship, in February 1916, a rather tentative-sounding Moore wrote the following, probably to William Rose Benét, "I mistrust my eligibility to appear in the Chimaera for prosaically, I am a novice, and poetically, I am a little sinister, I fear, to find favor in the eyes of you wits in chain mail."[31] There is something tantalizing about Moore's use of language here. When she says that she sees herself as a novice "prosaically," she could merely mean in prose, as opposed to "poetically," set later in the sentence. But prosaically also suggests that the work might be considered ordinary or commonplace. One is never surprised to find Moore implying two or more meanings at once. And the word "sinister," when used with armor or heraldry can mean merely on the left-hand side and, when juxtaposed beside "chain mail" later in the sentence, may associate with that. Yet "sinister" describing her own poetry might suggest that she understood that her work could be threatening or disastrous to her male colleagues, those "wits in chain mail." In that case the lines are cast more ironically than tentatively. But her "fear" could be that her work will not be appreciated by the men in protected positions of power; still, perhaps they are the ones who should beware of the sinister, who should walk in fear of disaster.

However one reads the 1916 passage, by February 1924 the self-proclaimed "prosaic novice" was speaking with assurance in praise of American versus European creativity when she wrote about an exhibit in Room 303 of the Anderson Gallery, singling out the work of John Marin, Marsden Hartley, Alfred Stieglitz, Charles Demuth, and Georgia O'Keeffe. Along with art critics Paul Rosenfeld and Henry McBride, Moore had become a major arbiter of modern art in the late twenties. And she continued to write important art criticism, including catalogue introductions, reviews of exhibitions, and articles which considered the whole question of the moral value of art and the role of the artist. It is useful to remember that until an artist has articulate critics, his or her work tends to remain obscure. Moore wrote critiques of new artists and reclaimed long-established ones, contributing opinions about Picasso, Cézanne, Brancuşi, Gauguin, Kandinsky, Klee, and Rodin as well as Brueghel, Blake, da Vinci, Dürer, and El Greco.

Sometimes phrases from her own poems crept into her prose—and sometimes her prose planted the seeds for poems yet to come. Certainly relevant to the present argument is this excerpt from Moore's article on artist E. McKnight Kauffer.

> Instinctiveness, imagination, and "the sense of artistic difficulty" with him, have interacted till we have an objectified logic of sensibility as inescapable as the colors *refracted* from a prism . . . Kauffer is a *parable of uncompromise*—a master of *illusion* . . . verifying Democritus' axiom, "Compression is the first *grace* of style." What is to be feared more than death? the man asked; the sage replied "Disillusion." Here, actually, we have a product in which unfalsified impulse safeguards *illusion*.[32] (emphasis mine)

Moore's major themes are represented: instinct, refraction, imagination, the value of artistic difficulty, illusion, compression, style, and grace. This echoed Moore's own brand of magic. Although the *Dial* kept Moore too busy to write any new poetry of her own, her experiences as critic, editor, and prose writer "contributed to the highly polished surfaces of her new work just as maturity of mind affected its content."[33] Much later, in 1958, for the April issue of *Arts*, Moore wrote about a painter for whom she had the utmost admiration. His name was Robert Andrew Parker, and her praises might well have been accolades for herself.

> Parker is one of the most accurate and at the same time most unliteral of painters. He combines the mystical and the actual, working both in an abstract and in a realistic way. . . .
>
> His subjects include animals, persons—individually and en masse; trees, isolated and thickset; architecture, ships, troop movements, the sea. . . . A cursive ease in the lines suggests a Rembrandt-like relish for the implement in hand; better yet,

there is a look of emotion synonymous with susceptibility to
happines. . . .
Robert Parker is a fantasist of great precision.[34]

One should not read casually Moore's unusual phrases about Parker—
and, I think, about herself. She speaks of his "look of emotion" and
"susceptibility to happiness" and says that he is a "fantasist of great
precision." The *Dial* years gave Moore a chance to experience an objective view of the works of others, and at the same time, it gave her a
chance to become objective about her own work. She too had a "susceptibility to happiness," hardly a common quality in *The Waste Land* years.
In 1984, Andrew Kappel wrote of Moore that she "created a triumphant
demonstration of repeated mastery of the chaos that surrounds us."[35]
Moore would pursue that ability to share her sense of order amid chaos
and her sense of joy. And Moore continued to be a "fantasist of great
precision."

"The Steeple-Jack" is an outstanding example of Moore's ability to
combine the mystical and the actual, perhaps the best illustration of
Moore's own ability to produce fantasy of great precision. It is probably
also the most pictorially successful of all Moore's poems.

The Steeple-Jack

Dürer would have seen a reason for living
    in a town like this, with eight stranded whales
to look at; with the sweet sea air coming into your house
on a fine day, from water etched
    with waves as formal as the scales
on a fish.

One by one in two's and three's, the seagulls keep
    flying back and forth over the town clock,
or sailing around the lighthouse without moving their wings—
rising steadily with a slight
    quiver of the body—or flock
mewing where

a sea the purple of the peacock's neck is
    paled to greenish azure as Dürer changed
the pine green of the Tyrol to peacock blue and guinea

gray. You can see a twenty-five-
    pound lobster; and fish nets arranged
to dry. The

whirlwind fife-and-drum of the storm bends the salt
    marsh grass, disturbs stars in the sky and the
star on the steeple; it is a privilege to see so
much confusion. Disguised by what
    might seem the opposite, the sea-
side flowers and

trees are favored by the fog so that you have
    the tropics at first hand: the trumpet-vine,
fox-glove, giant snap-dragon, a salpiglossis that has
spots and stripes; morning-glories, gourds,
    or moon-vines trained on fishing-twine
at the back door;

cat-tails, flags, blueberries and spiderwort,
    striped grass, lichens, sunflowers, asters, daisies—
yellow and crab-claw ragged sailors with green bracts—toad-
                                  plant,
petunias, ferns; pink lilies, blue
    ones, tigers; poppies; black sweet-peas.
The climate

is not right for the banyan, frangipani, or
    jack-fruit trees; or for exotic serpent
life. Ring lizard and snake-skin for the foot, if you see fit;
but here they've cats, not cobras, to
    keep down the rats. The diffident
little newt

with white pin-dots on black horizontal spaced-
    out bands lives here; yet there is nothing that
ambition can buy or take away. The college student
named Ambrose sits on the hillside
    with his not-native books and hat
and sees boats

at sea progress white and rigid as if in
    a groove. Liking an elegance of which

the source is not bravado, he knows by heart the antique
sugar-bowl shaped summer-house of
    interlacing slats, and the pitch
of the church

spire, not true, from which a man in scarlet lets
    down a rope as a spider spins a thread;
he might be part of a novel, but on the sidewalk a
sign says C. J. Poole, Steeple-Jack,
    in black and white; and one in red
and white says

Danger. The church portico has four fluted
    columns, each a single piece of stone, made
modester by white-wash. This would be a fit haven for
waifs, children, animals, prisoners,
    and presidents who have repaid
sin-driven

senators by not thinking about them. The
    place has a school-house, a post-office in a
store, fish-houses, hen-houses, a three-masted
    schooner on
the stocks. The hero, the student,
    the steeple-jack, each in his way,
is at home.

It could not be dangerous to be living
    in a town like this, of simple people,
who have a steeple-jack placing danger-signs by the church
while he is gilding the solid-
    pointed star, which on a steeple
stands for hope.

"The Steeple-Jack" appeared first in *Poetry* in June 1932. It was Moore's first poem after seven and one half years, a silence enforced by the *Dial* hiatus. T. S. Eliot chose it as the opening selection in his edition of *Selected Poems of Marianne Moore* in 1935. Thereafter it appeared first in *Collected Poems* in 1953. By the summer of 1934, Eliot was in correspondence with Moore about the new edition. On 20 June 1934, he wrote the following to Marianne Moore:

> If the chronological order were retained, I think dates ought to
> be given. But I am inclined to a reshuffle, which is more or less
> arbitrary in that it could be varied considerably without damage;
> and I enclose a tentative list for your approval.
>
> I want to start with the new poems hitherto uncollected, and
> shove some of the slighter pieces towards the end. At your
> simplest you baffle those who love "simple" poetry; and so one
> might as well put on difficult stuff at once, and only bid for the
> readers who are willing and accustomed to take a little trouble
> over poetry.[36]

"The Steeple-Jack" is "difficult stuff," certainly worthy of those who
are willing "to take a little trouble over poetry." Eliot's instincts about the
poem were correct; it is a masterpiece among Moore's pictorial works; it
is a masterpiece by any measure. Certainly paramount among its attributes is its remarkable brand of inclusiveness, of refraction.

Moore chooses to call up a particular artist in the reader's mind, Al-
brecht Dürer (1471–1528), a fifteenth-century German painter who was
founder of the German High Renaissance. Dürer's works rank among the
treasured "old things" from "When I Buy Pictures." Moore had been
fascinated by Dürer since her trip to Paris in 1919. References to the
German painter turn up in two other of Moore's poems, "Then the Ermine" ("like violets by Dürer") and "Apparition of Splendor," ("Dürer's
rhinoceros"). For the July 1928 issue of the *Dial*, Moore wrote an important review of an exhibition of Dürer prints at the New York Public Library. The seeds of "The Steeple-Jack" can be found in that review.
Moore begins by quoting Dürer: "In der Zeit verliche mir Gott Fleiss,
dass ich wol lernete" (Over time, God has granted me diligence, a lesson
I have learned well). As examples of Dürer's diligence, Moore refers to
her discovery that even his "mere journeyings are fervent—to the Dutch
coast to look at a stranded whale that washed to sea before he was able to
arrive; to Bologna to learn, as he says, 'the secrets of the art of perspective which a man is willing to teach me.'" Moore makes the point that the
"reliquary method of perpetuating magic" is ordinarily to be distrusted,
but not so with Dürer. Here was an artist who was the true imagnifico,
one for whom illusion was more precise than precision. Moore adds at
the end of her article that seeing such work "commits one to enlighten-
ment if not to emulation, and recognition of the capacity for newness
inclusive of oldness."[37] Here then, by any of Moore's measures, was a
master artist, not a novice, one who understood the newness of the past

and the value of diligence in granting access to truth through the magic of combining the mystical and the actual.

The poem opens by imagining that Dürer would have seen value in living in an American town with eight stranded whales to look at. After all, he had journeyed to the Dutch coast in the hope of seeing only one. Next Moore's mind—through her words—rapidly creates a Dürer-like black-and-white sketch of a town by the sea,

> . . . with the sweet sea air coming into your house
> . . . from water etched
>   with waves as formal as the scales
> on a fish.

The choice of the very word "etched" adverts to the Dürer technique, as does the formal arrangement of details: sea gulls flying "one by one in two's and three's" "back and forth over the town clock" or "sailing around the lighthouse without moving their wings." Interestingly, there is no security provided by the two symbols of human control over the universe, the lighthouse and the town clock; the sea gulls do not light there. Slowly, Moore begins to add color to her picture of the sea, color which towards the middle of the poem will overwhelm everything else. A flock is

> mewing where
> a sea the purple of the peacock's neck is
>   paled to greenish azure.

Slatin has noted that in 1508 Dürer wrote about his plan to produce a triptych called *The Assumption of the Virgin*, the central piece of which was destroyed in a fire in 1674. The loss of the painting may well have created in Moore the desire to honor Dürer with her own triptych: *Part of a Novel, Part of a Poem, Part of a Play*. ("The Steeple-Jack" is the central portrait in Moore's own poetic triptych.)[38] In her reading notebook Moore carefully recorded Dürer's own words about his plan for the use of color in *The Assumption* triptych.

> I have painted it with great care as you will see. It has also been done with the best colours I could get. It is painted with good ultramarine under & over, & over that again some 5 or 6 times & then after it was finished I painted it again twice over so that it

may last a long time. If it be kept clean I know it will remain
bright & fresh 500 years.[39]

But the painting did not remain bright and fresh for five hundred years,
in spite of Dürer's diligence. And Moore's own work may have been
meant to honor the Dürer loss by praising the painter's intent. Thus when
Moore writes that Dürer changed "the pine green of the Tyrol to peacock
blue and guinea / gray," there is a suggestion of the painter's magic, but
it is also Moore's own special kind of conjury, that which can be accomplished by diligence, precision—and color. The picture is enlarged by
the addition of more background etching: "fish nets arranged to dry."

In the second picture Moore created in "Novices," one can see a sea
alive and in movement, with its "great living stains like long slabs of
green marble," and the foam "crashing itself out in one long hiss of
spray." In "The Steeple-Jack" there is a "whirlwind fife-and-drum" storm
that brings life and movement when it

> . . . bends the salt
> marsh grass, disturbs the stars in the sky and the
> star on the steeple.

As Moore had suggested about those novices who were capable of seeing
the remarkable life of the sea in "Novices," here again "it is a privilege
to see so / much confusion." Out of this "precipitate of dazzling impressions," out of chaos, there is life; there is magic in the storm. The
limitations of a flat canvas, or even words on a page, could produce a
static picture, but Moore's precise details, like Dürer's, make the picture
come alive with movement through time.

In her book *Marianne Moore: The Poetry of Engagement*, Grace
Schulman has noted that "The Steeple-Jack" is a poem that puns relentlessly in the words "see" and "sea." Even the steeplejack himself is
C. (see) J. Poole (another kind of sea).[40] There seems little doubt that
Moore is asking the reader to "see" something significant in her land and
seascape about the "sea," always one of her favorite metaphors. One
must grant that Moore's intent is certainly visual.

Next, less like Dürer than like a verbal Henri Rousseau, Moore begins
to splash her canvas with color, imagining a scene "favored by the fog,"
but so vivid "that you have / the tropics at first hand." Moore's imaginary

gardens are lush almost beyond imagining, as she covers the canvas of
the mind with

> . . . the trumpet-vine,
> fox-glove, giant snap-dragon, a salpiglossis that has
> spots and stripes; morning-glories, gourds,
> or moon-vines . . .
> . . . sunflowers, asters, daisies—
> . . . .
> petunias, ferns; pink lilies, blue
> ones, tigers; poppies.

This Eden of Moore's imagining is so dizzying with color it approaches
the surreal. But Moore pulls the reader back from the recesses of the
unconscious and the suggestion of the exotic to the American east coast
by reminding us that

> the climate
> is not right for the banyan, frangipani, or
> jack-fruit trees.

John Slatin has made the useful point that none of the flowers Moore
places in her American garden are indigenous to North America. All
derive originally from tropical or subtropical areas and have become
domesticated on the American east coast, an important consideration
when one reaches toward the poem's total meaning.[41]

Finally, from the perspective of a new figure who is himself a novice, a
college student named Ambrose ("with his not-native books and hat"),
Moore retreats from the intense color of the flowers to complete the
sketch. Ambrose sees boats "at sea progress white and rigid as if in / a
groove." He knows by heart the "sugar-bowl shaped summer-house
of / interlacing slats," and he remembers the pitch of the church spire,
not true, "from which a man in scarlet lets / down a rope as a spider
spins a thread," and the church portico, which has four white fluted
columns.

The picture of the seaside town (perhaps one Moore had seen as a
young person in Maine; she told Barbara Kurz that the setting is "both
Brooklyn and various New England seacoast towns I had visited")[42] is
completed by a black-and-white sketch of

            . . . a school-house, a post-office in a
      store, fish-houses, hen-houses, a three-masted
            schooner on
      the stocks.

Moore's vivid word painting is finished, but as was the case with Dürer's reliquary method of perpetuating magic, the meaning of Moore's poem has only begun. For by the composition of "The Steeple-Jack," Moore seems to have decided that the ideas generated by both words and pictures could carry her to yet another dimension of human intuition: the instinctive recognition of danger in the world and how one can deal with it.

There are two pictures in "The Steeple-Jack," as there were in "Novices," but this time they occupy the same space. One is superimposed upon the other, and the reader experiences them at once, in a kind of gestalt. Seeing one, the reader cannot quite see the other. And when the first is in focus, the other fades.

One picture is Edenesque, an idyllic seaside town in which one senses security, safety, and happiness. The other picture, within the same visual field, verges on the sinister; the reader senses uneasiness, even danger. "The Steeple-Jack" tells the story of good and evil living side by side in the world, occupying, as it were, the same space. The difference between them is sometimes only one of perspective, perhaps seeing the same world and the same characters from Blake's *Age of Innocence* or his *Age of Experience*. But it is a vision which will not stand still; the careful viewer sees them both.

From the outset of the poem, there are contradictions. How does one square "sweet sea air coming into your house" with eight stranded, probably decaying whales on the sand? Or why do the sea gulls fly back and forth "with a slight / quiver of the body"? Like the whales, the twenty-five-pound lobster must be beached and is probably dead; it must be hung up to be weighed. The very irrationality and unpredictability of the "fife-and-drum . . . storm" "disturbs" the stars in the sky and the star of the steeple. Fife-and-drum music was a traditional call to battle; the storm comes on like the attack of a marauding army, disturbing the security of the peaceful village and its stability in the universe.

There is sometimes a fantastic, even a fairy-tale, quality about "The Steeple-Jack," if one remembers that fairy tales frequently project terror on what at first seems a commonplace world. (The children of Western culture have not been spared an awareness of danger in the world. Consider Jack and the Beanstalk, Snow White, Sleeping Beauty, Hansel and Gretel, and The Fisherman and His Wife.) In *The Uses of Enchantment: The Meaning and Importance of Fairy Tales* (1976), Bruno Bettleheim has shown that the fairy tale has served our culture by allowing people to deal with their deep-seated anxieties, fears, and conflicts in a way which grants a certain distance, as well as a comfortingly predictable structure. There is something of that comfort in Moore's poem. Instead of an "exotic serpent" in her Eden, there are merely "cats, not cobras, to / keep down the rats." (But nonetheless, there are rats.) And if that garden has as many frightening weeds as flowers (spiderwort, toad-plant, lichens, exotic tigers, poppies, and slapiglossis [related to the deadly nightshade]), they grow side by side among gentle asters, petunias, and daisies. It is a world of a thousand contradictions. It is a place of confusion, but as Moore reminds us, "it is a privilege to see so / much confusion."

The hero of this poem may be the steeplejack, who calls himself C. J. Poole (on one sign in black and white) and who warns his town of Danger on another sign (in red and white). Or he may not be the hero at all. The hero may be the narrator of the poem, that ubiquitous character, the Poet. Or it may even be the student, Ambrose, for he too is a character who is watched and described. But his is a life of detached scholarship. Instead of looking at the world, he sits with his back to it and remembers what he already "knows by heart" from his studies, which try to superimpose order on the world. But that order too is static, for it sees boats "at sea progress white and rigid as if in / a groove." The Poet, in contrast, is helping the audience "see" the truth in the "sea" of details she provides, paints in words, as it were. What one sees is indeed confusion, paradox, ambiguity. And that, says the Poet, is truly a privilege. It is also consonant with a woman's way of perceiving her world.

In *The Savage's Romance*, John Slatin has argued convincingly that the student, Ambrose, is a complex reference to St. Ambrose, a great bishop of the fourth-century church and thus a representation of good. Conversely, the steeplejack, the man in scarlet who lets down a rope as a spider spins a thread, is a reference to the devil, taken from Harold Donald Aberlies's *Little Known England*, which quotes an anecdote from John Leland that Moore copied into her reading diary in the fall of 1931.[43]

There is the spire and choir of St. Alkmund's where in the year 1533, upon Twelffe daye, in Shrowsburie, the Dyvyll appeared . . . when the Preest was at High Masse, with great tempteste and darknesse, so that as he pasyed through, he mounted upp the Steeple in the sayd churche, tering the wyers of the clock, and put the prynt of his clawes uppon the 4th bell, and tooke one of the pinnacles away with him, and for the Tyme stayed all the Bells in the churches within the said Towne, and they could neither toll nor ringe.[44]

I have no problem with those claims—except that they do not complete Moore's picture. At the same time, these figures may represent good and evil respectively, they quickly deconstruct into something else. It is an odd Satan/steeplejack who places danger signs by the church

> while he is gilding the solid
>   pointed star, which on a steeple
> stands for hope.

And it is an odd saint who merely sits on a hillside remembering only the truth he has committed to memory. The characters are not static symbols but ambiguous, ever-changing ones. They are characters drawn from a dangerously ambivalent reality.

In Moore's imagined Eden, the wheat grows right beside the tares. Frequently it is difficult to know which is which. And there is no balm of familiarity. Even native flowers, books, and hats may be "not-native" at all. But if one has "a susceptibility to happiness," a faith like Job's in the ability "to contrive glory from ashes," it is possible to celebrate even the confusion. The hero/poet finds joy in the very ambiguity and is not defeated by it. Like Dürer, the hero/poet records with great precision the details observed in the world, good and bad alike, and celebrates the privilege of having the ability to see them. Two verses from the Book of Job seem particularly applicable here: "Nothing on earth is done without cause; sorrow does not spring out of the ground" (5:6), and "In destruction and famine thou shalt laugh; thou shalt not be afraid of the beasts of the earth" (5:22).

But as the Poet says, the pitch of the church spire is "not true," and wise people need to understand that all is not as simple as they may want it to be. Only unthinking people believe that

    it could not be dangerous to be living
        in a town like this, of simple people,
    who have a steeple-jack placing danger-signs by the church
    while he is gilding the solid-
        pointed star, which on a steeple
    stands for hope.

One has the obligation of remaining sensitive to the sinister side of Eden, even while one is enjoying the blessed aspects of it. An awareness of that fact makes it "a privilege to see so / much confusion."

There is a maddening quality to "The Steeple-Jack," a poem in which the mystical rests happily beside the actual and the abstract is expressed in realistic details. It is a fantasy rendered in verbal brush strokes of infinite precision, with one set of positive attributes superimposed upon the same field of vision composed of negative ones. It is not an easy or comfortable world to live in—but there really is no other one. It is a fairy tale in Bettleheim's sense of allowing the reader to deal with deep-seated anxieties, fears, and conflicts by granting them a certain distance. But at the same time it invites the reader to celebrate confusion and ambiguity, because they are part of the nature of the real world and always part of a woman's way of knowing. It is also an artistic work that is "lit with piercing glances into the life of things." And it is the work of one, like Job, who can laugh, who senses something larger than herself that orders things, someone who can acknowledge "the spiritual forces that have made" her world.

Moore's experiments with the effects of the visual in poetry did not stop with "The Steeple-Jack." In fact, Moore rarely worked without an art object, painting, or picture to draw upon. But in some of her very best work she became the artist herself, using words to come very close to creating verbal experiences so vivid they are retained like pictures in the reader's mind. An awareness of Moore's interest in the world of the visual arts enhances an understanding of her work. Whether she is creating a verbal portrait as in "Those Various Scalpels," creating a collage/montage as she does in "Novices," or painting a symbolic landscape as in "The Steeple-Jack," Moore's ability to make magic by becoming a fantasist of great precision is an important dimension of her poetry.

CHAPTER 3

Objets Trouvés and Readymades

As noted in the Introduction, D. H. Lawrence has warned that it is always hard to listen to a new voice, as hard as it is to listen to a new language. And new voices, new ways of experiencing reality, always engender fear because they displace the comfort of old experiences, although they ultimately cause new growth and new insights. William Carlos Williams has addressed this displacement going on when one reads the work of Marianne Moore.

> Miss Moore, using the same materials as all others before her, comes at it so effectively at a new angle as to throw out of fashion the classical conventional poetry to which one is used and puts her own and that about her in its place. The old stops are discarded. This must agonize many. Furthermore, there is a multiplication, a quickening, a burrowing through, a blasting aside, a dynamization, a flight over—it is modern, but the critic must show that this is only to reveal an essential poetry through the mass, as always, and with superlative effect in this case.[1]

Moore comes to her discourse "at a new angle." She thereby tends to throw old discourse out and discard the old stops, and as Williams says, such rejection of the expected can be agonizing. Frequently such agony is assauged by merely charging the new ideas with error—in Moore's case, to call her work nonpoetry or perhaps merely unenlightened verse.

One such aspect of Marianne Moore's discourse that has long troubled scholars and critics is her frequent use of unoriginal materials, many of which are not in the strict sense literary at all. In her book *The Poetry of Marianne Moore: A Study of Voice and Value*, Margaret Holley refers to Moore's "special art of quotation, . . . the visual reproduction of a found text."[2] Moore is certainly not the only one of her contemporaries to make use of allusions or quotations from previous texts, but she is distinctive in the choices she makes and in the ways she uses them. If T. S. Eliot sounded literary and mythical echoes from the past, he expected his readers to catch the reverberations, or at least to have enough of a poetic ear to sense the mood he was trying to establish. When Ezra Pound pulled evocations and stylistic devices from the past, he often recast them against his own experiences and his own perceptions of contemporary history. When William Carlos Williams chose nonliterary material from newspapers, magazines, letters, lists, and even verbal accounts, he was frequently trying to re-create the modern milieu without poetic disguise. Moore's use of what I am loosely choosing to call objets trouvés, or readymades, was really something quite original.

John Slatin argued that Moore's use of quotations operates in a larger context, that it is equated with a way of reading that does not rely on the vision of a single individual. I use this point in order to examine Moore's originality. Slatin senses that it is in the female ritual of visiting as opposed to the male ritual of setting boundaries (as described in Frost's "Mending Wall") that Moore often finds her voice. He moves further to suggest that by her unique choices, what one might call her "visiting," Moore eventually moved outside the male enclave—the authoritarian, canon-etched tradition—and thereby achieved her own ascendency.[3] Slatin is, I believe, on the right track when he perceives a definite choice of visiting on Moore's part, but he has not explored totally the motivations for her choice. In *Women's Ways of Knowing*, researchers Belenky, Clinchy, Goldberger, and Tarule devote a good deal of time to what they see as women's interest in visiting, what they call conversations. They offer an entire chapter entitled "Received Knowledge: Listening to the Voices of Others." "Women," they write, "are less inclined to see themselves as separate from [other] 'theys' than are men," which "may also be accounted for by women's rootedness in a sense of connection and men's emphasis on separation and autonomy."[4] Women understand and admit that they come to what they know through conversations, in the extended sense, with many people, texts, and ideologies. They seldom pretend that what they know are merely objective truths in which they profess absolute certainty.

As a very well-educated woman, Moore did place value on what one might call received knowledge, the voices from authority, especially early in her career. But because of her vast reading experience, she also found herself listening to and learning from the voices of many people from many times, and she came to respect those many voices, regardless of the authority (or lack of it) they might represent. This attention to other voices marks her work as different from that of many of her male contemporaries. I am choosing to call this difference—namely, Moore's tendency to incorporate the words and ideas of many other voices in her work—her special sense of found objects, or objets trouvés and readymades, although I can find no evidence that she made that direct linguistic connection herself.

An objet trouvé originally referred to the Cubist technique of gluing bits of real objects—newspaper clippings, dried flowers, pieces of music, bits of rope, strips of veneer—onto a picture. The result was a collage (a "glued" picture) or a montage, which featured elements from several different media superimposed one upon another. Marcel Duchamp introduced the concept of readymades. Ordinary objects—a bicycle wheel, a snow shovel, a rack for drying bottles—were displayed as art. Whether or not these objects were in themselves beautiful (and some certainly were), and although he frequently had not altered them in any way, Duchamp placed a new dimension on artistic creation by declaring objects "art" merely because they had been chosen by him, the artist. His readymades provoked lively discussion among artists, critics, and historians for two generations. Although I am not suggesting that Moore's use of borrowed materials was motivated by or even analogous to Cubist practice, a comparison of the two artistic techniques with Moore's discourse proves both useful and interesting.

Moore was asked frequently about her borrowed materials. In the 1961 Hall interview she responded: "I was just trying to be honorable and not to steal things. I've always felt that if a thing had been said in the *best* way, how can you say it better? If I wanted to say something and somebody had said it ideally, then I'd take it but give the person credit for it. That's all there is to it. If you are charmed by an author, I think it's a very strange and invalid imagination that doesn't long to share it."[5] Moore put the whole matter figuratively when she wrote: "'Why the many quotation marks?' I am asked. Pardon my saying more than once, When a thing has been said so well that it could not be said better, why para-phrase it? Hence my writing is, if not a cabinet of fossils, a kind of collection of flies in amber."[6]

Moore's use of the phrase "flies in amber" is indeed a helpful way of looking at her use of found objects, the raw materials for her verbal montages. She borrowed the phrase in her 1922 poem "Snakes, Mongooses, Snake-Charmers, and the Like" when describing a snake, that "plastic animal all of a piece from nose to tail," remarking that "one is compelled to look at it as at the shadows of the alps / imprisoning in their folds like flies in amber, the rhythms of the skating-rink." Note that Moore's use of both the phrase and the particulars of her analogies is anything but expected. Moore is making some very unusual connections. The comparison between the movement of a snake and shadows in the Alps which imprison in their folds the undulating rhythms of the skating rink all captured in time like flies in amber is scarcely a typical associa-tion. And one might assume that the connections did not occur to Moore all at one time but rather evolved slowly, probably over years of careful and even passionate rumination. Louise Bogan has used the term "passion wholly of the mind," and Moore herself wrote in her reading notebooks for 1923, "In the possibility of . . . intellectual emotion—the ethico-religious, for instance—lies the differentiation of Humanity from all else."[7] It is in that sense that one must speak of Moore's passion, her intensely intellectual game of connections that are indeed "supreme in their abnormality." Moore's phrases often mark, in Randall Jarrell's words, "a curious juxtaposition of curious particulars."[8] But if one gives the lines from a poem like "Snakes, Mongooses, Snake-Charmers, and the Like" a chance—and enough time—one begins to glimpse some-thing both musical and magical about the rhythms of three disparate undulations captured in nature: snakes, mountains, and skating move-ments.

Writing to Moore on 7 November 1944 about her new book of poems, *Nevertheless*, William Carlos Williams borrowed Moore's own phrase to describe her particular success in the poem "Elephants." Williams writes, "The Elephants are like flies in amber, there they stand perma-nently; this is something you do like no one else—with that modesty which is the hallmark of the artist."[9] The term "flies in amber," although originally scientific, certainly has poetic overtones. It refers to nature's own peculiar method of preserving once-living plants and animals from the past in a protective medium—actually an organic substance, the resin from certain pine trees, the "amber" of the phrase. Thus the magic of this semitransparent liquid, now hardened to a golden clarity, gives scientists a chance to view beautifully preserved specimens from another time. They are indeed fossils, but fossils preserved in peculiar clarity and detail, giving the present an excellent view of the past. (Williams's compliment to Moore's ability is expanded by the phrase, for he points out that Moore has found the capability of preserving not only mere flies but entire elephants in amber.)

From almost the very beginning of her career, Moore tended to incorporate "flies in amber" into her work. Sometimes she acknowledged such voices; at other times she did not. Sometimes she quoted the originals with painstaking care and acknowledgment; at other times she molded them to suit her own particular needs. Jarrell addresses this "abnormality" well in "Her Shield," noting that Moore "has a discriminating love of what others have seen and made and said, and has learned (like a burglar who marks everything that he has stolen with the owner's name, and then exhibits it in his stall in the marketplace) to make novel and beautiful use of such things in her own work, where they are sometimes set off by their surroundings, sometimes metamorphosed."[10]

Margaret Holley estimates that half of the poems of Moore's Carlisle period (1915–17) employ marked quotations. By the twenties, thirties, and the war years, two-thirds of the poems use quotations. In the fifties and the sixties, three-quarters of the poems demonstrate the use of borrowed materials. There is no increase in the quantity of material quoted; the practice simply appears in an increasing number of her poems, suggesting that it grows to be a strategy that is more and more reliable, even habitual.[11]

Moore's "conversations" with the world can be traced to several personal practices, beginning with her extraordinary reading habits. The range and sheer quantity of Moore's reading background is amazing. Few people could or would have read as voraciously and as carefully as she did. There simply would not have been time in their lives. But Moore was very jealous of her reading and study time, sacrificing other pleasures and even conveniences to allow enough time to read and to write. Helen Vendler notes that when the local librarian suggested to Mrs. Moore that Marianne might like to work in the library, since she was so often there (in 1918 Marianne and her mother moved across the street from the Hudson Branch of the New York Public Library, at 14 St. Luke's Place), Mrs. Moore said no—that if Marianne joined the staff, she would probably feel she had no time to read.[12] But Mrs. Moore came home and told her daughter of the offer. "I said, 'Why, certainly. Ideal. I'll tell her. Only I couldn't work more than half a day.' If I had worked all day and maybe evenings or overtime, like the mechanics, why, it would *not* have been ideal."[13] The half-day venture, if not ideal, proved stimulating for Moore—and she even had time to do more reading as part of the job. If the work sometimes took her outside her usual reading topics, the new subjects usually became interesting to her. Moore continued in this work for seven years until the *Dial* editorship.

Moore's mind was formidable for many reasons, but not the least for the astounding range of her reading interests. In his fictionalized autobiography *Troubadour*, Alfred Kreymborg wrote about Moore's expertise about almost everything. Both Kreymborg and William Carlos Williams, whom Kreymborg treated as characters in his book, held the mind of Marianne Moore in absolute admiration. What they lacked in intellectual stability was freely and unconsciously supplied by her. And her familiarity with books on every conceivable theme astonished them. "How she can spin words!" Kimmie would say, and Bill would add, "We're a pair of tongue-tied tyros by comparison." The two fictional characters endeavor to place Moore in a situation wherein she could not be an expert so as to have the pleasure at least once of stumping her. So on a Saturday afternoon, they took her to the Polo Grounds for a descent into the commonplace of a Cubs and Giants baseball game.

> Well, I got her safely to her seat and sat down beside her. Without so much as a glance toward the players at practice grabbing grounders and chasing fungos, she went on giving me her impression of the respective achievements of Mr. Pound and Mr. Aldington without missing a turn in the rhythm of her speech, until I, a little impatient, touched her arm and, indicating a man in the pitcher's box winding up with the movement Matty's so famous for, interrupted. "But Marianne, wait a moment, the game's about to begin. Don't you want to watch the first ball?" "Yes indeed," she said, stopped, blushed and leaned forward. . . . "Strike!" bawled Umpire Emslie. "Excellent," said Marianne.
>
> Delighted, I quickly turned to her with: "Do you happen to know the gentleman who threw that strike?"
>
> "I've never seen him before," she admitted, "but I take it it must be Mr. Mathewson."

I could only gasp, "Why?"

"I've read his instructive book on the art of pitching— . . .
and it's a pleasure" she continued imperturbably, "to note how
unerringly his execution supports his theories."[14]

The point of this anecdote is that Moore might find her literary raw
materials anywhere, and she made it a habit to read as far as her eyes
could take her. Those reading "conversations" went far beyond the usual
literary fare to art, science, travel literature, treatises on Christianity,
music, fables, translations, the Bible, Irish folklore, history, courtship,
biology, lapidary, baseball, horse racing, theater, dance, fashion, the
psychology of color, and theories of handwriting. She was particularly
interested in rare animals, saving numerous articles about and pictures
of them that she would work into her poetry. She could speak expertly on
the poetic theories of Chaucer, Shelley, Hardy, and Hopkins and dealt
insightfully with the work of contemporary poets and prose writers. Her
reading lists from her Bryn Mawr days on would stagger the most ardent
reader. The "Lectures on Literature" section of required freshman and
sophomore English at Bryn Mawr called for "Private Reading." Moore's
list of more than 170 items, with each item initialed when completed, is
enough to overwhelm the most intrepid undergraduate today.[15] In January 1925, she responded to an inquiry from P. Casper Harvey of the
Missouri Writers' Guild requesting information about her work for the
book page of the *Kansas City Journal-Post*. Moore responded by listing
biographical data, but also by writing:

> I feel that the impetus to produce as good work as I could, has
> come, first, from reading: from reading authors whose material
> and method afforded me perfect entertainment—Sir Francis
> Bacon, Chaucer, Spenser, Defoe, Bunyan, Sir Thomas Browne,
> Leigh Hunt, Burke, Dr. Johnson, Anthony Trollope, Hardy,
> Henry James, W. B. Yeats, W. H. Hudson, and Sidney's The
> Defense of Poesis [*sic*]. I have been entertained and instructed by
> advertisements, and book reviews in PUNCH, in the London
> SPECTATOR, in THE LONDON TIMES, by reviews in the fortnightly
> DIAL, the present DIAL, by reviews published in THE ENGLISH
> REVIEW during the years 1907–11; by Gordon Craig's books and
> other publications of his. And I have learned, I feel, from
> technical books, which, in addition to being instructive and
> entertaining, seem to me, aesthetically accomplished—John
> McGraw's "How to Play Baseball," Christy Mathewson's "Pitching

in a Pinch," Tilden's books on tennis, W. Rhend's "The
Earthenware Collector," Harold Bayne's manual on dogs
published by The National Geographic Magazine, articles
in THE JOURNAL OF NATURAL HISTORY.[16]

In 1951 she offered the following to the *New York Herald Tribune Book Review*: "My favorite authors, I think are Chaucer, Molière and Montaigne. I am attracted to Dr. Johnson; also like Xenophon, Hawthorne, Landor and Henry James. I take an interest in trade journals, books for children, and never tire of Beatrix Potter. My favorite reading is almost any form of biography—Ellen Terry, Cellini, Mr. Churchill's war memoirs, Capt. Corbett's *Man Eaters of Kumaon*, E. E. Cummings' *Eimi*, Wallace Fowlie's *Pantomime*, Sir Osbert Sitwell's *Escape with Me*."[17] In response to a 1965 inquiry "To what books published in the past ten years do you find yourself going back to most often?" Moore reported that Pound's translation of *The Analects of Confucius* was a frequent recent source of "new" materials from the past.[18] The *Dial* years urged her into even more areas of expertise, although the requirements of study and editing placed a temporary curtailment on her own writing. Moore's reading diaries serve as a record of her far-ranging reading and interests and help us to understand how she brought so many disparate ideas under one topic. She once characterized her own impetus to write in this way: "I think each time I write that it may be the last time; then I'm charmed by something and seem to have to say something. Everything I have written is the result of reading or of interest in people."[19]

Also in the Hall interview, Moore says, "A question I am often asked is: 'What work can I find that will enable me to spend my whole time writing?'" Using a convenient readymade, she replies, "Charles Ives, the composer, says, 'You cannot set art off in a corner and hope for it to have vitality, reality, and substance. The fabric weaves itself whole. My work in music helped my business [insurance] and my work in business helped my music.' I am like Charles Ives."[20]

So when Moore began a poem, she nearly always incorporated her fossils, her "flies in amber." Sometimes the found objects are the products of famous writers (or, as we have seen, painters or sculptors), but as often as not, the passages she has found and recorded in her amazing collection of fossils—her reading diaries, her personal library, and her amazingly retentive mind—are from sources the average reader, or even the above-average reader, would probably find obscure. The source and its historical or literary background usually remain unimportant to Moore. It is the exact phrase itself that she treasures. It is the excellence of the "fossil" she wishes to incorporate and her own desire to choose this ready-made object that are important. As a sensitive woman and a meticulous reader, she became a remarkable listener for other voices and was humble enough to incorporate those conversations into her own search for truth.

Holley makes a felicitous connection in this regard with a term from Lévi-Strauss, which sees the poet as "bricoleur," the maker of things from "odds and ends left over," as opposed to the engineer who tries to create from the wholly new.[21] Such a notion merges happily with Moore's own decision in "The Past Is the Present" that the poet's job is one of reverting to the past in order to interpret the present, and certainly to her notion in "Humility, Concentration, and Gusto" that "humility, indeed, is armor, for it realizes that it is impossible to be original, in the sense of doing something that has never been thought of before."[22] Certainly in "Novices," Moore takes great exception to "the supertadpoles of expression" who think it is not necessary to be associated with the past and its artifacts.

So when Scofield Thayer recommended in 1924 that Moore attach a set of notes about her references and quotations to the edition of her new book of poems, *Observations* (not unlike Eliot's notes to *The Waste Land*), Moore complied. These notes began a practice which she would continue throughout her career. Frequently the notes do little more than "put us on the scent" of the reference, a phrase from Moore's poem "Picking and Choosing." Often they do little to explain Moore's reasons for marshaling data on a particular theme. Jarrell suggests that Moore often leaves her jewels uncut but places them in "unimaginably complicated and difficult settings to sparkle under the Northern Lights of her continual irony."[23]

However, repeated inquiries about the notes and the use of quotations were finally met with "A Note on the Notes," appended to *Selected Poems*. A personage calling herself "M.M." or sometimes "M.C.M" wrote the following somewhat impatient disclaimer:

> A willingness to satisfy contradictory objections to one's manner
> of writing might turn one's work into the donkey that finally found
> itself being carried by its masters, since some readers suggest
> that quotation-marks are disruptive of pleasant progress; others,
> that notes to what should be complete are a pedantry or evidence

> of an insufficiently realized task. But since in anything I have
> written, there have been lines in which the chief interest is
> borrowed, and I have not yet been able to outgrow this hybrid
> method of composition, acknowledgements seem only honest.
> Perhaps those who are annoyed by provisos, detainments, and
> postscripts could be persuaded to take probity on faith and
> disregard the notes.[24]

Nonetheless the notes continued to appear at the end of the text and, with a few notable exceptions, generally shed very little light on why the text was chosen or how it is meant to add to the poem. It was simply the correct particular, the appropriate readymade, what seemed to Moore to be the right combination of "flies in amber." In "Nothing Will Cure the Sick Lion But to Eat an Ape," for example, the note reads simply, "Carlyle." (As late as 1977, the *Marianne Moore Newsletter* carried a query as to where in Carlyle that reference might be. The inquirer had searched the Carlyle *Letters*, at Moore's noted direction, to no avail.)[25] The Carlyle reference offers the reader little more than a beginning; whereas the note to "Kylin" from "Nine Nectarines" informs the reader that a Kylin is a Chinese unicorn, information gleaned from Frank Davis in the *Illustrated London News* for 7 March 1931. The note adds that a Kylin "has the body of a stag, with a single horn, the tail of a cow, horse's hoofs, a yellow belly, and hair of five colours." And the information provided about the Louis XV candelabra belonging to Lord Balfour added to the lines from the *New York Times Magazine*, "There is no water so still as the dead fountains of Versailles," are helpful in understanding "No Swan So Fine." Yet although tracing the sources of the twelve quotations in "Novices" does enrich the theme, it is not absolutely essential to interpreting the poem.

One might surmise, then, that Jarrell's point is well taken. It is not usually the source of a found object that interests Moore but instead the quality of its sparkle, the precision of the phrase itself. When, as Jarrell suggests, she "sets" the stone, the found object in the poem, it is meant merely to enhance a far larger and often unimaginably complicated and difficult setting. Tess Gallagher has a phrase for it, calling Moore "a true archaeologist of the spirit."[26]

Some have seen in Moore's constant quoting of others a sign of her unwillingness to accept responsibility for her own assertions. They prefer to see Moore as the shy librarian, hiding her own inadequacies be-

hind the "armor" of the experts. Stanley Lourdeaux, for example, asserts
that "if anyone were to object to statements in MM's poems, that critic
would first have to challenge nature's concrete details and other writers'
opinions. These techniques guarantee self-protectiveness."[27] Others,
particularly Randall Jarrell and Tess Gallagher, sense something entirely
different in Moore's personal "shield." Jarrell celebrates Moore's choices
of uncut stones set meticulously in the mosaic of a larger scheme. And
Gallagher sees the use of quotations as proof of Moore's ambition not to
write simply in the isolation of the ego but to write as if she were a team
or an orchestra,[28] a mode consonant with a woman's way of knowing. The
latter position puts Moore in touch with all of the great players, and
occasionally the not-so-great players, who have ever performed. And in
the very act of choosing from among the fossils, the objets trouvés and
readymades of the past, Moore orchestrates with confident master-
strokes. The quotations are not the act of a timid, inadequate poet at all,
but rather one who is confident enough to play the sorcerer, the magician, marshaling her phenomenal collection of fossils to her service, all
the while risking the chance that she may fool her audience by making
the trick look easy.

One who was not fooled by her sorcery was Geoffrey Hartman, who
wrote a set of notes for the Marianne Moore recording in the Yale Series
of Recorded Poets. Like so many of Moore's critics, Hartman fell naturally into the metaphor of magic.

> The mind, or rather Miss Moore's, is "an enchanting thing"; it
> takes us by its very irrelevancies. Here too everything is surface;
> she talks, so to say, from the top of her mind and represents
> herself as a gossip on the baroque scale. But secretly she is a
> magician, and distracts on purpose. While her message eludes
> us through understatement, the poem itself remains teasingly
> alive through overstatement of its many tactics, till we accept the
> conventional rabbit, glorified by prestidigitation. Yet the magic of
> language becomes intensely moral on further acquaintance and
> her crazy quilt of thoughts, quotations and sounds resolves into
> subtler units of meaning and rhythm. The free (but not formless)
> verse helps break up the automatic emphases of traditional
> syntax, and respects the more dynamic shifts of the inner, and
> not merely spoken voice. . . . Her technique is not uniform, not
> abstractly applied; it depends on the movement of the whole
> poem.[29]

As was noted earlier, examples of Moore's use of borrowed material can be found in nearly two-thirds of her published poems. But that use is certainly no better evidenced than in her masterpiece, "Marriage." As several critics have ventured to say, this poem is Moore's *The Waste Land*, a mosaic, a montage of fragments from Bacon, the *Scientific American*, Baxter's *Saint's Everlasting Rest*, Hazlitt on Burke, William Godwin, Trollope, *Hamlet*, *The Tempest*, a book on *The Syrian Christ*, the Bible, Ezra Pound, Daniel Webster (from an inscription on a statue), and about twenty other sources. Moore was frequently asked to explain several of her most enigmatic poems, and certainly "Marriage" was among them. In her notes to *The Complete Poems*, she wrote: "MARRIAGE: Statements that took my fancy which I tried to arrange plausibly." In a letter dated 25 May 1964, Moore admitted that she may seem "slow to reduce speculation to explicit statement." In the same letter she wrote, "MARRIAGE is not an expression of my philosophy—merely a little anthology of phrases that I did not want to lose."[30] She addressed "Marriage" again in the *Marianne Moore Reader*: "The thing (I would hardly call it a poem) is no philosophic precipitate; nor does it veil anything personal in the way of triumphs, entrapments, or dangerous colloquies. It is a little anthology of statements that took my fancy—phrasings that I liked."[31] It is, I would submit, a conversation.

The "anthology" had been long in the making. Moore's early diaries and notebooks demonstrate her keen interest in the subjects of love and marriage. But she was aware that courtship and marriage held complications for bright women. In January 1923, Moore compiled careful notes from W. L. George's *Art of Courtship*. She copied: "The usual principles do not apply to either emotional people, to artists, . . . or to the unduly intellectual. Such monsters must look after themselves in the lists of love." She also made note that "a certain amount of boasting is desirable. Probably the best form consiels [*sic*] in mock modesty." She added, "Today we must deal with a type of woman more intellectual . . . than the beautiful, selfish, revengeful idols represented by Shakespeare, Tennyson, Homer, Dante, etc."[32]

In the July notebook of 1923 Moore made the following note about D. H. Lawrence from Alyse Gregory's *New Republic* article "The Dilemma of Marriage": "No one has uncovered more searchingly those obscure poisoning enmities between men and women whose wills are crossed nor composed and executed such a rich heavy music of the emotions, the music of sex itself, which druggedly compels men and women into the still sharp death of each other's arms, only to let them part, thwarted, or ironically freed."[33]

By the time of "Marriage," Moore was ready to produce what was "superficially an outrageous collage but profoundly a poignant comic critique of every society's most sacred and tragic institution."[34] To highlight the "flies in amber" in this poem, the borrowed materials appear in bold, with lettered footnotes indicating the sources, as Moore gave them in her notes to the poem. (Although Moore carefully signaled most quoted materials with appropriate punctuation, she did not use bold type.)

Marriage

This institution,
perhaps one should say enterprise
out of respect for which
one says one need not change one's mind
about a thing one has believed in,
requiring public promises
of one's intention
to fulfill a private obligation:
I wonder what Adam and Eve
think of it by this time,
this fire-gilt steel
alive with goldenness;
how bright it shows—
**"of circular traditions and impostures,
committing many spoils"**,[a]
requiring all one's criminal ingenuity
to avoid!
Psychology which explains everything
explains nothing,
and we are still in doubt.
Eve: beautiful woman—
I have seen her
when she was so handsome
she gave me a start,
able to write simultaneously
in three languages—
English, German and French—

a. Francis Bacon.

and talk in the meantime;[b]
equally positive in demanding a commotion
and in stipulating quiet:
"*I* should like to be alone";
to which the visitor replies,
"I should like to be alone;
why not be alone together?"
Below the incandescent stars
below the incandescent fruit,
the strange experience of beauty;
its existence is too much;
it tears one to pieces
and each fresh wave of consciousness
is poison.
"See her, see her in this common world,"[c]
the central flaw
in that first crystal-fine experiment,
this amalgamation which can never be more
than an interesting impossibility,
describing it
as **"that strange paradise**
unlike flesh, stones,
gold or stately buildings,
the choicest piece of my life:
the heart rising
in its estate of peace
as a boat rises
with the rising of the water";[d]
constrained in speaking of the serpent—
shed snakeskin in the history of politeness
not to be returned to again—
that invaluable accident
exonerating Adam.
And he has beauty also;
it's distressing—the O thou
to whom from whom,
without whom nothing—Adam;
"something feline,

b. "Multiple Consciousness or Reflex Action of Unaccustomed Range," *Scientific American*, January 1922.
c. "George Shock."
d. Richard Baxter, *The Saints' Everlasting Rest*.

something colubrine"[e]—how true!
a crouching mythological monster
in that Persian miniature of emerald mines,
raw silk—ivory white, snow white,
oyster white and six others—
that paddock full of leopards and giraffes—
long lemon-yellow bodies
sown with trapezoids of blue.
Alive with words,
vibrating like a cymbal
touched before it has been struck,
he has prophesied correctly—
the industrious waterfall,
"the speedy stream
which violently bears all before it,
at one time silent as the air
and now as powerful as the wind."
"Treading chasms
on the uncertain footing of a spear,"[f]
forgetting that there is in woman
a quality of mind
which as an instinctive manifestation
is ˈunsafe,
he goes on speaking
in a formal customary strain,
of **"past states, the present state,**
seals, promises,
the evil one suffered,
the good one enjoys,
hell, heaven,
everything convenient
to promote one's joy."[g]
In him a state of mind
perceives what it was not
intended that he should;
"he experiences a solemn joy
in seeing that he has become an idol."[h]

e. Philip Littell, reviewing Santayana's *Poems* in *The New Republic*, March 21, 1923.
f. Hazlitt: "Essay on Burke's Style."
g. Richard Baxter.
h. *"A Travers Champs,"* by Anatole France in *Filles et Garçons* (Hachette).

Plagued by the nightingale
in the new leaves,
with its silence—
not its silence but its silences,
he says of it:
"It clothes me with a shirt of fire."[i]
"He dares not clap his hands
to make it go on
lest it should fly off;
if he does nothing, it will sleep;
if he cries out, it will not understand."[j]
Unnerved by the nightingale
and dazzled by the apple,
impelled by "the **illusion of a fire**
effectual to extinguish fire,"[k]
compared with which
the shining of the earth
is but deformity—a fire
"as high as deep
as bright as broad
as long as life itself,"[k]
he stumbles over marriage,
"a very trivial object indeed"[l]
to have destroyed the attitude
in which he stood—
the ease of the philosopher
unfathered by a woman.
Unhelpful Hymen!
a kind of overgrown cupid
reduced to insignificance
by the mechanical advertising
parading as involuntary comment,
by that experiment of Adam's
with ways out but no way in—
the ritual of marriage,
augmenting all its lavishness;
its fiddle-head ferns,

i. Hagop Boghossian in a poem, "The Nightingale."
j. Edward Thomas, *Feminine Influence on the Poets* (Martin Secker, 1910).
k. Richard Baxter.
l. [William] Godwin.

lotus flowers, opuntias, white dromedaries,
its hippopotamus—
nose and mouth combined
in one magnificent hopper—,
its snake and the potent apple.
He tells us
that **"for love that will**
gaze an eagle blind,
that is with Hercules
climbing the trees
in the garden of the Hesperides,
from forty-five to seventy
is the best age,"[m]
commending it
as a fine art, as an experiment,
a duty or as merely recreation.
One must not call him ruffian
nor friction a calamity—
the fight to be affectionate:
"no truth can be fully known
until it has been tried
by the tooth of disputation."[n]
The blue panther with black eyes,
the basalt panther with blue eyes,
entirely graceful—
one must give them the path—
the black obsidian Diana
who **"darkeneth her countenance**
as a bear doth,"[o]
the spiked hand
that has an affection for one
and proves it to the bone,
impatient to assure you
that impatience is the mark of independence,
not of bondage.
"Married people often look that way"[p]—
"seldom and cold, up and down,

m. Anthony Trollope, *Barchester Towers*.
n. Robert of Sorbonne.
o. Ecclesiasticus.
p. C. Bertram Hartmann.

**mixed and malarial
with a good day and a bad."**[q]
We occidentals are so unemotional,
we quarrel as we feed;
self lost, the irony preserved
in **"the Ahasuerus *tête-à-tête* banquet"**[r]
with its small orchids like snakes' tongues,
with its **"good monster, lead the way,"**[s]
with little laughter
and munificence of humour
in that quixotic atmosphere of frankness
in which **"four o'clock does not exist,
but at five o'clock
the ladies in their imperious humility
are ready to receive you";**[t]
in which experience attests
that men have power
and sometimes one is made to feel it.
He says **"What monarch would not blush
to have a wife
with hair like a shaving-brush?"**[u]
The fact of woman
is **"not the sound of the flute
but very poison."**[v]
She says, **"Men are monopolists
of 'stars, garters, buttons
and other shining baubles'—
unfit to be the guardians
of another person's happiness."**[w]
He says, **"These mummies
must be handled carefully—
'the crumbs from a lion's meal,
a couple of shins and the bit of an ear';**[x]

q. Richard Baxter.
r. George Adam Smith, *Expositor's Bible.*
s. *The Tempest.*
t. Comtesse de Noailles, "Le Thé," *Femina,* December 1921.
u. From "The Rape of the Lock," a parody by Mary Frances Nearing, with suggestions by M. Moore.
v. A. Mitram Rihbany, *The Syrian Christ* (Houghton, Mifflin, 1916).
w. Miss M. Carey Thomas, Founder's address, Mount Holyoke, 1921.
x. Amos iii, 12. Translation by George Adam Smith, *Expositor's Bible.*

turn to the letter **M**
and you will find
that 'a wife is a coffin,'[y]
that severe object
with the pleasing geometry
stipulating space not people,
refusing to be buried
and uniquely disappointing,
revengefully wrought in the attitude
of an adoring child
to a distinguished parent."
She says, "This butterfly,
this waterfly, this nomad
that has 'proposed
to settle on my hand for life'[z]—
What can one do with it?
There must have been more time
in Shakespeare's day
to sit and watch a play.
You know so many artists who are fools."
He says, "You know so many fools
who are not artists."
The fact forgot
that "some have merely rights
while some have obligations,"[aa]
he loves himself so much
he can permit himself
no rival in that love.
She loves herself so much,
She cannot see herself enough—
a statuette of ivory on ivory,
the logical last touch
to an expansive splendour
earned as wages for work done:
one is not rich but poor
when one can always seem so right.
What can one do for them—
these savages

y. Ezra Pound.
z. Charles Reade, *Christie Johnston.*
aa. Edmund Burke.

condemned to disaffect
all those who are not visionaries
alert to undertake the silly task
of making people noble?
The model of petrine fidelity
who **"leaves her peaceful husband
only because she has seen enough of him"**[bb]—
that orator reminding you,
"I am yours to command."
**"Everything to do with love is mystery;
it is more than a day's work
to investigate this science."**[cc]
One sees that it is rare—
that striking grasp of opposites
opposed each to the other, not to unity,
which in cycloid inclusiveness
has dwarfed the demonstration
of Columbus with the egg—
a triumph of simplicity—
that charitive Euroclydon
of frightening disinterestedness
which the world hates,
admitting:

> **"I am such a cow,
> if I had a sorrow
> I should feel it a long time;
> I am not one of those
> who have a great sorrow
> in the morning
> and a great joy at noon"**;

which says: **"I have encountered it
among those unpretentious
protégés of wisdom,
where seeming to parade
as the debater and the Roman,
the statesmanship**

---

bb. Simone Puget, advertisement entitled "Change of Fashion," *English Review*, June 1914.
cc. F. C. Tilney, *Fables of La Fontaine*, "Love and Folly," Book XII, No. 14.

of an archaic Daniel Webster
persists to their simplicity of temper
as the essence of the matter:

'Liberty and union
now and forever';[dd]

the Book on the writing-table;
the hand in the breast-pocket."

dd. Daniel Webster (statue with inscription, Central Park, New York City).

After a careful first reading, most readers can follow what Hartman described as Moore's "gossip on the baroque scale." She does indeed seem to have "arranged plausibly" in a kind of conversation almost everything one has always wanted to know about marriage, capsuling her collection of phrases with the disclaimer,

> Everything to do with love is a mystery;
> it is more than a day's work
> to investigate this science.

At first the catalogue of 289 lines seems random, only vaguely associative, but in fact, the dialectic is meticulously woven. Moore frequently claimed that she despised connectives, at least connectives in the obvious sense. In order to see this montage as a whole, the reader must learn to participate in and to enjoy the anthology—without the connecting links most poets provide. One idea merely melts into another, without transitions. (Moore once wrote, "I myself . . . would rather be told too little than too much.")[35] In "Marriage" Moore is assuming that the discriminating reader shares her predilection.

Once again, it is William Carlos Williams who offers a useful critical tool for dealing with the text. In "A Novelette and Other Prose, 1921–1931," Williams wrote of Moore:

> A course in mathematics would not be wasted on a poet, or a
> reader of poetry, if he remember no more from it than the
> intersection of loci: from all angles lines converging and crossing
> establish points. He might carry it further and say in his

imagination that apprehension perforates at places, through to understanding—as white is at the intersection of blue and green and yellow and red. It is this white light that is the background of all good work. . . . The intensification of desire toward this purity is the modern variant. It is that which interests me most and seems most solid among the qualities I witness in my contemporaries; it is a quality present in much or even all that Miss Moore does.[36]

Later, in 1948 in the *Quarterly Review of Literature*, he reiterates that point: "Therefore Miss Moore has taken recourse to the mathematics of art. Picasso does no different: a portrait is a stratagem singularly related to a movement among the means of the craft."[37]

Williams also calls Moore's "Marriage" an "anthology of transit,"[38] meaning that one must allow all of Moore's directions, insights, tones, quotations, and epigrams—her "crazy quilt," in Hartman's parlance—to move and to intersect. Through the intersection of ideas, one comes to appreciate the profound complexity of one of life's great enigmas, the interaction of one human being with another in the enterprise called marriage. The poem does not precisely "mean" anything. It is instead a conversation, a comprehensive dialectic based upon some of the greatest myths, motifs, symbols, visions, and commentaries on the subject of marriage. It passes no judgment, solves no problems. If, as Doris Lessing has said, people are "hungry for answers, not hungry for ways of thinking toward problems," they will be disappointed.[39] If they are willing to search for truths in the interstices, in the intersections of loci, they will learn a great deal from Moore's "little anthology of phrases [she] did not want to lose."

In "Feeling and Precision," Moore wrote, "Feeling at its deepest—as we all have reason to know—tends to be inarticulate."[40] And that is an important "mathematical" principle in "Marriage." Although the poem is replete with the deepest of human emotions, the intersections of emotional loci occur with such disarming precision that the reader must remain attentive to find them. Taffy Martin has argued that the voice here and in other poems remains deadpan, that it does not seem to convey grand emotions. In such a stance, Martin feels, Moore creates a music particularly suitable for the twentieth century.[41] One might argue instead that there are *many* voices in the poem and that they are not all deadpan. Sometimes the voice is that of the poet summarizing or synthesizing, but many times the voices are anonymous presenters of information, much of it ready-made from the past. In the intersection of the many voices, which speak but do not always hear, lies real poignancy and intense emotion, but emotion so deep that it tends to seem inarticulate.

In the poem "Silence," Moore observes that "the deepest feeling always shows itself in silence; / not in silence, but restraint." (The phrase is itself an objet trouvé, borrowed from a friend, Miss A. M. Homans's father.) Perhaps the real intensity lies in the reader's final awareness that although human words attempt to communicate logic and feeling, people seldom really touch each other. Communication is a difficult thing, especially when what is to be communicated is shaded by intense feelings like those of love and desire. The following lines suggest the need for personal uniqueness and privacy in tension with the antithetical desire for intimacy:

> "*I* should like to be alone";
> to which the visitor replies,
> "I should like to be alone;
> why not be alone together?"

Moore returns to the same idea late in the poem when she writes:

> One sees that it is rare—
> that striking grasp of opposites
> opposed each to the other, not to unity.

There are actually so many voices in "Marriage" that the poem is orchestrated like a great piece of choral music, a polyphonic, one verging on cacophony but held in place by Moore's own subtle harmonies. It is a kind of chorus where various voices deliver brief soliloquies which are not heard by the other characters. Some of the speeches are comic, some are serious; and one point of view tends to be layered upon another. It is the reader who must sense the tangential quality of the many male and female viewpoints and find where those tangents eventually cross and where they sadly never touch at all. In a chapter entitled "The Principle of Accommodation: Moore, Eliot, and the Search for Community," John Slatin argues convincingly that Moore was affected by many of Eliot's poetic theories and strategies.[42] One must grant that "Marriage" is a response to some of the strategies of *The Waste Land*, particularly the use of many voices. But the choices—the particular found objects and readymades that create the many voices—are of Moore's own design.

Consider, for example, Moore's leitmotif, which establishes a theme with variations that is echoed in the voices. Her repeated pattern here is not the syllabic line or the repeated stanza. There certainly is not a pattern as obvious as a refrain. The unifying figure is the circle, or perhaps more accurately, what Moore calls the cycloid, structures resembling the circle but overlapping, like scales on a fish or waves of sound. The pattern is repeated with many variations. There is first of all the wedding ring, that "fire-gilt steel / alive with goldenness." It is symbolic of "circular traditions" that have developed around the peculiar enterprise called marriage, itself a union of two intersecting circles. There is the "incandescent fruit," the apple, the visual representation of Eve's (and Adam's) demise. And there is the undulating snake and the colubrine (i.e., snakelike Adam); there is a circular enclosure, a paddock, full of leopards and giraffes, animals whose bodies are marked by circular designs. There is a cymbal that sounds before it is touched. There are stars, garters, buttons. Hercules pursues the labor of finding the Golden Apples of the Hesperides. There is a reference to Columbus's trick of making an egg stand on end by breaking the shell. There are the eyes of a panther and the Euroclydon, the Greek explanation for the wave. Everything in the poem about marriage is thematically circular—except that the circles are not concentric. They may intertwine, intersect, pass in and out of each other, overlap, but they are always cycloids, separate circles seeking unity but finding instead the tension of opposites. So the first intersection of loci is visual and circular, a reechoing leitmotif in the poem.

Moore undertakes separate discussions of women and men, not only Eve and Adam, but also of characters that are a montage of many layers of femaleness and maleness. First she responds to Eve's beauty. She is so handsome that "she gave me a start." But she is also intelligent in an oddly funny kind of way, for she is "able to write simultaneously / in three languages" and can "talk in the meantime." (As the note suggests, Moore had actually read of this remarkable ability in the *Scientific American.*) It seems probable that such praise of a woman's linguistic ability as well as of her propensity for conversation struck Moore as amusing, but rather typical of the world's praise of an intelligent woman's mind: it was merely side-show material.

And Adam too is beautiful, but there is also something distinctly sinister about him as he moves with catlike, snakelike movements, crouching like a mythological monster in a Persian miniature. He is "alive" with words, the namer of things, with his voice like "the industrious waterfall," violently bearing all before it. He goes on speaking like the grand master of

> past states, the present state,
> seals, promises,
> . . . .
> everything convenient
> to promote one's joy.

In his own mind, he has become an idol. The amazing story of the serpent in the garden, which has been recast in the modern idiom and has now "shed snakeskin in the history of politeness / not to be returned to again," that "invaluable accident," has exonerated Adam. Whether in the old tradition or the new, the fall from grace was fortunate for Adam in that a way has been found to attribute the cosmic mistake to Eve. But having passed the blame to Eve, he has nobly chosen to stand beside her. And the world has come to

> ". . . see her in this common world,"
> the central flaw
> in that first crystal-fine experiment.

Next Moore expands her "Adam and Eve" into more voices, some of them telling great classical stories of complex marriages. There is the story of Hercules, who killed his own children and his beloved Megara in a fit of mindless rage and then did penance through twelve prodigious labors. And the tale appears of Ahasuerus, who cast off his beautiful wife, Vashti, at the urging of his advisers because she caused him to lose face. Her lack of instant obedience at a banquet might, his advisers said, threaten the obedience of all the women in Persia. And so Ahasuerus commissioned a gathering of virgins, which he dutifully deflowered every night for a year, until he came upon Esther, a beautiful Jewess (incognito, of course), one who was worthy of his discriminating tastes, whom he took as his special concubine. And then it was Esther, who, with her kinsman Mordecai, manipulated Ahasuerus and his adviser Haman at the tête-à-tête banquet until she successfully prevented a pogrom of her people and caused the ignominious end of the evil Haman.

Another voice offers a reference to Diana, the virgin-huntress of Greek mythology, who would not marry at all. From ancient times she was honored by a strange cult in which her votaries dressed as bears. She was sometimes identified with Hecate, the dismal goddess of the darkness of the lower world. In this poem, one myth intersects with another, as we meet the

> black obsidian Diana
> who "darkeneth her countenance
> as a bear doth."

This Diana is

> impatient to assure you
> that impatience is the mark of independence,
> not of bondage.

Moore carefully offers a note about that darkened countenance: "Ecclesiasticus." A major problem for modern readers in this controversial book of the Bible (which Protestants relegate to the Apocrypha but Catholics classify as deuterocanonical) is that the writer, Jesus, son of Sirach, characterizes the wickedness of women as the highest of all evils. In the passage to which Moore refers, he writes: "It will be more agreeable to abide with a lion and a dragon, than to dwell with a wicked woman. The wickedness of a woman changeth her face: and she darkeneth her countenance as a bear" (Ecclus. 25:23–24, DR). He also writes, "For from garments cometh a moth: and from a woman the iniquity of a man" (42:13, DR). But perhaps the most disturbing lines read, "Follow close if her eyes are bold, and be not surprised if she betray you: As a thirsty traveler with eager mouth drinks from any water that he finds, so she settles down before every tent peg and opens her quiver for every arrow" (26:11–12, NAB).

There is no question that Moore was a most fastidious woman and poet. Her only arguments with William Carlos Williams were over matters of good taste. And although she willingly printed stories and poems by D. H. Lawrence in the *Dial*, she did not hesitate to reject his work when she considered it less than tasteful. And yet her discreet reference to Ecclesiasticus seems to suggest that she wishes to remind the reader that some cultures have found women innately vile. This intersection of voices seems to be suggesting that one should not be surprised to find that some women will always be impatient with such characterization and the bondage it allows; some have a flair for independence.

But the voices are not all such serious ones. The poet-narrator offers some delightful lines, including the suggestion that the fire-gilt steel symbolizing marriage requires "all one's criminal ingenuity / to avoid!" Marriage is so endemic that only a criminal few can manage to escape its snares. There is great charm too in introducing Adam and Eve as spectators to the whole debacle, not unlike the readers of the poem. One does wonder what the "originals" think of marriage by this time. (In a recording of Moore reading "Marriage," there is no doubt that she means to amuse, particularly in the early lines.) She also directs a bit of levity toward Freud, asserting that

> psychology which explains everything
> explains nothing,
> and we are still in doubt.

And the poignant lines quoted earlier have a discordantly futile brand of humor:

> "*I* should like to be alone";
> to which the visitor replies,
> "I should like to be alone;
> why not be alone together?"

The lines beginning "Unhelpful Hymen!" call up a disintegrating panorama from the Greek wedding song and the god of the wedding to something akin to a tawdry cupid on a modern mechanized billboard display.

> Unhelpful Hymen!
> a kind of overgrown cupid
> reduced to insignificance
> by the mechanical advertising
> parading as involuntary comment,
> by that experiment of Adam's.

The world has gone from magical mythology to a mechanical caricature, something in movable cardboard, one might presume. The speaker also calls up a light and comic voice from a parody of "The Rape of the Lock" (to which Moore herself had contributed) which counters with

> . . . What monarch would not blush
> to have a wife
> with hair like a shaving-brush?

But serious issues persist. Like a discordant counterpoint, "he" and "she" begin to exchange lists of stereotypical charges, although they do not really listen to one another's complaints, or so it seems, if we identify the speakers thus:

HE: four o'clock does not exist
but at five o'clock
the ladies in their imperious humility
are ready to receive you.

SHE: . . . experience attests
that men have power
and sometimes one is made to feel it.

HE: The fact of woman
is "not the sound of the flute
but very poison."

SHE: Men are monopolists
of "stars, garters, buttons
. . . .
unfit to be the guardians
of another person's happiness."

HE: These mummies
must be handled carefully—

SHE: revengefully wrought in the attitude
of an adoring child
to a distinguished parent.

HE: turn to the letter M
and you will find
that "a wife is a coffin."

SHE: This butterfly
this waterfly . . .
that has "proposed
to settle on my hand for life"—
What can one do with it?

HE: The fact forgot
that "some have merely rights
while some have obligations."

SHE: he loves himself so much
he can permit himself
no rival in that love.

But all of these differences do not explain what happens "below the incandescent stars / below the incandescent fruit." "Incandescent" can mean "aglow with ardor." That ardor is the great unknown that the poet describes as "the choicest piece of my life," that which starts

the heart rising
in its estate of peace
as a boat rises
with the rising of the water.

One does not need stars or apples or snakes to explain the incandescence of love and desire that overwhelmingly attracts what sometimes seem the most alien of creatures. (Note Moore's note cited above about D. H. Lawrence: "The music of sex itself, which druggedly compels men and women into the still sharp death of each other's arms.") Adam is "plagued by the nightingale / in the new leaves." He says of it, "It clothes me with a shirt of fire." He is afraid to drive the temptation off and yet equally afraid to call it to him. He is "unnerved by the nightingale" and, at the same time,

. . . dazzled by the apple,
impelled by "the illusion of a fire
effectual to extinguish fire."

Adam is overwhelmed by his desire. But then so is Eve:

. . . O thou
to whom from whom
without whom nothing—Adam.

The "strange experience of beauty" is "too much; / it tears one to pieces." So the pair stumble upon the solution of marriage, which

William Godwin, the pragmatic philosopher and challenger of institutions, had called "a very trivial object indeed." Until he knew this primal urge, Adam had known "the ease of a philosopher / unfathered by a woman." Now he is reduced from both ease and philosophy by his desire. "Unhelpful Hymen!" a voice cries out.

And so men and women marry, although one observes that

> Married people often look that way—
> seldom and cold, up and down,
> mixed and malarial,
> with a good day and a bad.

Some commend marriage "as a fine art, as an experiment, / a duty or as merely recreation." Whichever the institution is, it continues, fueled by a commodity so mysterious it can only be envisioned by the imagination. As the voices cease, the speaker asks:

> What can one do for them—
> these savages
> condemned to disaffect
> all those who are not visionaries
> alert to undertake the silly task
> of making people noble?

How does one civilize a primal urge? How does one focus on the nobility of that "noble savage," the human animal? One way is by augmenting marriage with ritual lavishness. But adding mere "fiddle-head ferns, / lotus flowers, opuntias" to the marriage ceremony does not hide "its snake and the potent apple." And so the impossible experiment, "this amalgamation which can never be more / than an interesting impossibility," continues. One encounters it everywhere, "among those unpretentious / protégés of wisdom" and those "seeming to parade / as the debater and the Roman." With the simplicity of the inscription on Daniel Webster's statue, the impossibly circular quest goes on: "Liberty and union / now and forever." That "striking grasp of opposites / opposed each to the other, not to unity" billows forth in the Euroclydon, with wave after futilely overlapping wave.

The poem ends with a visual image, a photograph, the classic wedding picture: "the Book on the writing table; / the hand in the breast-pocket."

And all of the Adams and Eves of all time continue their hopeless search for liberty and for union, two antithetical states of being. As D. H. Lawrence had perceived, there are strange enmities between men and women whose wills are crossed. But moved by the mysterious magic of "the incandescent stars" and "the incandescent fruit," the heavy music of the emotions, the music of sex itself, men and women repeat their inevitable cycloid patterns.

"Marriage" is a very effective poem, at least for those readers who, as T. S. Eliot had suggested, "are willing and accustomed to take a little trouble over poetry." Moore's success in "Marriage" occurs in part because she has turned to her cabinet of fossils, her "flies in amber," to pull off the shelves of her prodigious memory many different perceptions about the complexities of marriage. Sometimes the found objects, the objets trouvés, are lines that caught her fancy merely because of what they said or the way they said it. Some references carry the baggage of their stories (Diana, Ecclesiasticus, Ahasuerus, Hercules), while others are treasured primarily for their unique beauty ("something feline, / something colubrine," or "treading chasms / on the uncertain footing of a spear"). Perhaps reflecting some of the theories of Marcel Duchamp, Moore is suggesting that the important thing about a phrase is not that it is original but instead that she, as artist, chose it and placed it in a setting of her making. For the poem occurs, as William Carlos Williams has suggested, not in the originality of the materials but instead in what Moore does with them as she moves ideas and images along lines that will intersect and come alive in polyphonic conversations in the reader's mind. Sometimes the intersection produces laughter; sometimes it offers the most profound sadness. But it is this multiplication, this quickening, this burrowing through and blasting aside in which the poem happens. It is at the intersection of images and ideas that the white light of freshness and new insight really occurs. Moore was confident enough, and humble enough, to understand that she had to use the same materials as others before her. There was no need for pretense. Originality lay in edging ideas against one another in brilliantly novel ways.

There is far more magic to be discovered in "Marriage": the use of color, (the poem is cast primarily in various shades of white, with accents of blue, yellow and black), the use of internal rhyme to create harmony, and her experiments with "thought rhyme" as the Adams and Eves respond in their chorus. By noting her special use of borrowed materials, however, her objets trouvés and readymades in this complex poem, the reader has a useful key to her poetic method. It is possible once again to envision Moore as the imagnifico, the poet humble enough to understand that "the past is the present" and to acknowledge her place in the continuous order of creation, and yet brave enough to dynamite old combinations of ideas and strategies and to set them into new relationships.

Perhaps the following lines from Moore's own poem "The Frigate Pelican" address her predilection for borrowing as well as any other critical explanation:

> Rapidly cruising are lying on air there is a bird
>   that realizes Rasselas's friend's project
>   of wings uniting levity with strength. This
>   hell-diver, frigate-bird, hurricane-
> bird; unless swift is the proper word
>   for him, the storm omen when
>   he flies close to the waves, should be seen
>   fishing, although oftener
>   he appears to prefer
> to take, on the wing, from industrious crude-winged species,
>   the fish they have caught, and is seldom successless.
>   A marvel of grace, no matter how fast his
>   victim may fly. . . .

Like the frigate pelican, Moore rapidly cruised vast oceans of information. She recognized the delight of uniting levity and strength. But she exhibited a marked preference to "take, on the wing, from industrious crude-winged species, / the fish they have caught." She is "a marvel of grace" as she incorporates her catch into her own work. Like the "unconfiding frigate-bird," Moore hides "in the height and in the majestic / display of [her] art." "*Festina lente.* Be gay / civilly," she concludes. "If I do well I am blessed / whether any bless me or not."

In a review of a draft of *XXX Cantos* by Ezra Pound, Moore added, "Great poets, Mr. Pound says, seldom make bricks without straw. They pile up all the excellences they can beg, borrow or steal from their predecessors or contemporaries and then set their own inimitable light atop the mountain."[43] With her unique objets trouvés and readymades, Moore has indeed set her own inimitable light atop the mountain, a light marked by the addition of a woman's epistemology to the realities that poetry can tap.

CHAPTER 4

Kaleidoscope

On 24 May 1936, William Carlos Williams wrote the following to Marianne Moore: "You are an amazing person. For at the end of the narrowing horn I see a spot of sunlight toward which you are conducting us. . . . Everything is getting smaller but seems moving, always, to some—the same—climax as always. But what it is I cannot say."[1] Moore's natural acceptance of many voices, her willingness to include precise choices from among the vastness of her reading background and from her personal experience, can be jarring at times. Her very inclusiveness leads her readers to ask new questions as frequently as they find comfortable answers. One is sometimes so startled by the unfolding and complex images that her discourse provides that the ultimate insight to which she is leading us is in some danger of becoming fragmented.

Although many writers by their very nature tend to superimpose order on the universe—generally a male characteristic—Moore often demonstrates that the truth, or perhaps more accurately the truths, cannot be pinned down and viewed like butterflies on an examining tray. They are alive, organic, unfolding, and wonderful. They must be examined with great care and patience, turning their precise images patiently, all the while respecting their reality as they point to that "spot of sunlight" upon which she is focusing.

Thus there are almost never any obvious readings of Marianne Moore's poems. Even her best critics disagree about final interpretations. It is common for Moore scholars to explicate sections of long poems with real insight, only to fall away from other sections that present seemingly insurmountable problems of interpretation. Seldom is a critic able to pull all of the pieces into anything like a unified, manageable whole. The sensation of slipping the last puzzle piece into place and experiencing a satisfied "Aha!" seldom occurs. Many of Moore's critics eventually admit that at least some lines remain, for them, enigmatic. And yet we know that Moore did not mean to be obscure, although her work was during her lifetime, and is today, frequently called difficult. She had, what she called in her essay "Idiosyncrasy and Technique," a "mania for straight writing—however circuitous I may be in what I myself say of plants, animals, or places."[2] One of her favorite anecdotes regarding complaints about her complexity is retold in her 1966 essay "A Burning Desire to Be Explicit." She describes a "strikingly well-dressed member of the audience with a strikingly positive manner who inquired, 'What *is* metaphysical newmown hay?'" Moore replied, "Oh, something like a sudden whiff of fragrance in contrast with the doggedly continuous opposition to spontaneous conversation that had gone before. 'Then why don't you say so,' the impressive lady rejoined."[3] Moore was always trying "to say so," but doing it precisely and accurately—magically—with as much freshness as metaphysical newmown hay.

As a student at Bryn Mawr, Moore was told repeatedly by her instructors that her writing "was not clear," that she had failed to "make her point."[4] Another teacher wrote, "I presume you had an idea if one could find out what it is."[5] Moore wrote to her mother, "Miss Fullerton said on my weekly "you have narrative and descriptive ability . . . but you must pay attention to the requirements . . . you are incoherent and have no idea how to manage situations." Moore added: "I don't know why I am so possessed to write. I know it is not because of what nice things people say and it's not for the doing itself, for I cannot express myself."[6]

In "In the Days of Prismatic Color" (1919), Moore explained:

> . . . complexity is not a crime, but carry
>   it to the point of murkiness
>   and nothing is plain. Complexity,
> moreover, that has been committed to darkness, instead of

> granting itself to be the pestilence that it is, moves all a-
>   bout as if to bewilder us with the dismal

fallacy that insistence
   is the measure of achievement and that all
truth must be dark.

But later in her life she was to write phrases such as, "I have a very special fondness for writing that is obscure, that does not quite succeed, because of the author's intuitive restraint. All that I can say is that one must be as clear as one's natural reticence allows one to be."[7] And at Bryn Mawr in 1952, in a series of commentaries on selected contemporary poets,[8] she quoted Pound's "Salvationists," "Come, my songs, let us speak of perfection— / We shall get ourselves rather disliked."[9] She frequently rephrased the second line: "We shall get ourselves *very much* disliked."[10] In defense of her own precise use of language and her unusual juxtaposition of ideas, which others saw only as complexity, she remembered Eliot's words about another writer, "Pound's greatest contribution to the work of other poets is his insistence upon the immensity of conscious labor to be performed by the poet."[11]

Moore's work does not operate at the surface of even the most educated listener's mind. It requires real effort, persistence, an interest in language, and an understanding of the effects of prosody. And the results do not come in single leaps of knowledge. Instead, the reader is led through consistent formulations of sound, color, tempo, and ideas that fall into place in many patterns of beauty, patterns not unlike the turning of a kaleidoscope, which results in an ever-changing display of beautiful designs. If readers persist in attention and patience, they will see magnificent and magical combinations that deal with the enigmas of human experience. If they allow even larger combinations to come into focus, they will come to see a dimension of the world found only in the realm of the intuition, what Bergson had described as the highest stage in the evolution of human understanding and what Williams described as "a spot of sunlight." In intuition, knowledge is universal, immediate, reaching by sympathy to the heart. In the sense of her poetic intuition as a *kaleidoscope* I would like to look at some of the most puzzling of Moore's poems. I will use the term metaphorically in two senses: (1) to describe the development of Moore's discourse as an instrument for reflecting continuously changing but related forms, and (2) to demonstrate the difficulty implicit in interpreting such a purposely refractive discourse.

If one recalls Moore's acquaintance with Cubist art with its multiplicity of viewpoints, then her own method of refraction and her almost perverse pleasure in creating oblique ways of looking at things begins to make sense. In Moore's own words (in "When I Buy Pictures"), her ultimate goal was to look for "piercing glances into the life of things," the places where ideas intersect to create experience. Truth and beauty lie, then, not on the surfaces but in the cracks, the interstices wherein the precise details of her poems bring surprising new meanings.

Again, William Carlos Williams seemed instinctively to have understood his friend and colleague's intent, and at the same time the problems her work presented for her readers, when he wrote:

> If one come with Miss Moore's work to some wary friend and say,
> "Everything is worthless but the best and this is the best,"
> adding, "only with difficulty discerned," will he see anything, if
> he be at all well read, but destruction? From my experience he
> will be shocked and bewildered. He will perceive absolutely
> nothing except that his whole preconceived scheme of values has
> been ruined. And this is exactly what he should see, a break
> through all preconception of poetic form and mood and pace, a
> flaw, a crack in the bowl. It is this that one means when he says
> destruction and creation are simultaneous.[12]

To illustrate the principle of Moore's kaleidoscopic effect, and to accept Eliot's suggestion to put on the difficult stuff at once, consider Moore's poem "The Mind Is an Enchanting Thing," published in 1943.

The Mind Is an Enchanting Thing

is an enchanted thing
    like the glaze on a
katydid-wing
        subdivided by sun
        till the nettings are legion.
Like Gieseking playing Scarlatti;

like the apteryx-awl
    as a beak, or the
kiwi's rain-shawl
        of haired feathers, the mind
        feeling its way as though blind,
walks along with its eyes on the ground.

It has memory's ear
    that can hear without
having to hear.
        Like the gyroscope's fall,
        truly unequivocal
because trued by regnant certainty,

it is a power of
    strong enchantment. It
is like the dove-
        neck animated by
        sun; it is memory's eye;
it's conscientious inconsistency.

It tears off the veil; tears
    the temptation, the
mist the heart wears,
        from its eyes—if the heart
        has a face; it takes apart
dejection. It's fire in the dove-neck's

iridescence; in the
    inconsistencies
of Scarlatti.
        Unconfusion submits
        its confusion to proof; it's
not a Herod's oath that cannot change.

There is a dazzling quality to this poem; it is beautiful in its language, its images, its sounds, and its communication. There is a sonatalike stateliness to the verses with their exact syllabic pattern of 6, 5, 4, 6, 7, 9. Its rhyme scheme (*a b a c c d*) is heard only subtly. It is even beautiful visually upon the page, located in space with great precision and done according to Moore's instructions. It is also lovely to recite aloud, allowing the sounds to echo upon themselves as one reads to the controlling punctuation. Sometimes thoughts and sounds reverberate from one stanza to the next. And there are spectacular words: "Gieseking," "Scarlatti," "apteryx," "kiwi," "gyroscope," "unequivocal," "regnant," "iridescence." An attentive child could hear their musicality, whether or not the words are understood.

But Moore's intent in the poem is "only with difficulty discerned," for it does not merely say in Pope's words, "What oft was thought, but ne'er so well express'd." The mind, Moore suggests is capable of magic, both enchanting and enchanted. But that magic is quite delicate and ephemeral, like the glaze on a katydid wing, something which certainly exists, but whose delicate and complicated beauties are seldom seen by the mind's eye because they are not sufficiently illuminated. If they were to be "subdivided by the sun," the nettings revealed would be legion—numerous beyond belief, like the notes of the sonatas of the great Italian keyboard composer Domenico Scarlatti when they are played by the brilliant Walter Gieseking, an accomplished German pianist of great renown. (The katydid's music, sounding shrill on a midsummer afternoon, may also be composed of legions of notes like those written by Scarlatti, if the human ear and mind could slow them down sufficiently to hear them.)

If the mind is like the sounds of the katydid and Scarlatti, it is visually like the apteryx, a strange genus of birds of which the kiwi is an example. With underdeveloped wings, this ungainly, hairy ball of feathers must pick its way along with its awl-like beak, as though blind to all that goes on above and beyond it. To some degree the human mind picks its way along like the strange bird except that it has been blessed with the magic of memory, the ability to image, to imagine, and to store that data, to be able to hear without having to hear again. Like scientific, mechanical devices—a gyroscope, for example—the mind can come to some clear, unambiguous decisions because some things can indeed be calibrated against reality.

But given these bedrock principles the mind can depend upon, it can come into the greater power of strong enchantment; it can come to that truth which lies beyond precision—illusion. Once that happens, it can tear off the veil, tear off temptation, even emotion, the mist the heart wears. It can see with the eyes of magic, the "fire in the dove-neck's / iridescence." And with a sudden turn of the kaleidoscope, "Unconfusion submits / its confusion to proof." Unlike Herod's oath to kill the Baptist, an oath he could not break, even though he had foolishly given his word, the mind *can* change. The double mention of the dove as the poem "refracts" at its ending suggests yet another turning of the kaleidoscope. If one allows the mind to work beyond the limitations of the "gyroscope," to enter the world of intuition, one may find the Dove, the Spirit of God. In the dazzling complexities of the world's beauty, one may have to change one's mind about many things and perhaps find God—even in a "scientific" universe.

It seems clear here that Moore is also dealing with what has often been declared a woman's flaw: the propensity to change her mind. Moore, however, features that flaw as actually a woman's glory. Unlike the unyielding male (Herod, for example), she is willing to change her mind; she can find new perspectives; she can learn new ways of looking at things, new ways of seeing the world's beauty. That ability of bringing kaleidoscopic vision is one gift that a woman's way of knowing can bring to the knowledge of the human race.

To illustrate the point another way, consider a much earlier (1915) and much easier Moore poem.

Diligence Is to Magic As Progress Is to Flight

With an elephant to ride upon—"with rings on her fingers and
                                                bells on her toes,"
  she shall outdistance calamity anywhere she goes.
Speed is not in her mind inseparable from carpets. Locomotion
                                                                arose
    in the shape of an elephant; she clambered up and chose
to travel laboriously. So far as magic carpets are concerned, she
                                                                knows
    that although the semblance of speed may attach to scarecrows
of aesthetic procedure, the substance of it is embodied in such of
                                                                those
    tough-grained animals as have outstripped man's whim to
                                                                suppose
them ephemera, and have earned that fruit of their ability to
                                                                endure blows,
which dubs them prosaic necessities—not curios.

Observations

Like Williams's hypothetical friend, one must first be made to believe that there is excellence here, that this is indeed "the best." Similarly, audiences who first viewed the work of abstract painters like Matisse and Cézanne called it fauvism, the work of wild beasts, or who first heard the "barbarous style" of Bartok, Stravinsky, or Prokofiev where shocked and bewildered at their lack of harmony. These works did not follow the rules; they challenged existing order; they seemed more bent on destruction than on creation. And what one first sees in Moore's poem may ruin one's preconceived set of rhythms and values. It instead marks that flaw, that crack in the bowl, that Williams described. But the very breaking down of the expected becomes itself a creation. If ever there was an example of the style Moore herself called "a kind of pleasing jerky progress," it is obvious in "Diligence."[13]

Moore begins the poem by sounding lines from old nursery rhymes, "with elephants to ride upon," "with rings on her fingers and bells on her toes," but she surprises both the ear and the memory by fracturing our expectations. One should be riding on magic carpets, not elephants. And she with the rings on her fingers and bells on her toes should have music wherever she goes. But this female outdistances "calamity anywhere she goes," a marked departure from both the rhyme and the intent of the original. (The line also celebrates Moore's own predilection for that "pleasing jerky progress.") Instead of riding some kind of magic carpet, the writer of this bit of pseudodoggerel "clambered up and chose / to travel laboriously." (The poem is actually meticulously crafted; every line ends with a rhyme, and lines alternate in syllabic counts of 20 and 14, yet neither the rhyme scheme nor the strict syllabic count is obvious to the reader.) This poet's magic is no poetic flight of fancy; it comes the hard way, by diligence. For she knows that some purport to travel by "magic carpet" and that some "semblance of speed" may attach to what she calls "scarecrows / of aesthetic procedure," but she is putting her money, and her future, on the substantial, tough-grained, cumbersome elephant, who has learned to endure blows and has proven itself a "prosaic necessity," not merely a curio.

So even at a first careful reading, the meaning of the poem begins to emerge, given an analogical clue from the title. But turn the kaleidoscope ever so slightly, and a whole new picture comes into view. What are these "scarecrows / of aesthetic procedure" to which the semblance of speed may attach? A scarecrow is anything that frightens one but is actually not harmful. A scarecrow of aesthetic procedure calls up in the mind those defenders of the aesthetic, the poetic status quo, who try desperately to frighten off new artistic theorists by suggesting that they are only flashes-in-the-pan, ephemera, curios. Works like Moore's were dubbed "prosaic necessities," dull, uninteresting, unpoetic—all of which may at first seem true, up to a point (the "prose / with a kind of heightened consciousness" from "The Past Is the Present"). But what such scarecrows/critics do not understand is that just as diligence is the real secret behind magic, so it is steady progress that makes real flight. And elephants are remarkable at progress, being quite impervious to continual blows of criticism, or to almost anything else that gets in their way. They may not at first seem beautiful, but they are effective. Moore also uses the elephant metaphor to insist on the "immensity of conscious labor" on the part of the poet.

In 1977, John Slatin suggested in the "Replies" section of the *Marianne Moore Newsletter* that Moore was probably using the scarecrow reference to deal with such critics as Harold Monro and later Harriet Monroe and Louis Untermeyer in their discussions of Moore's own work. In his review of *Some Imagist Poets*, Harold Monro argued that much of the new work was merely "statements of fact, not poetry." And in her "Symposium on Marianne Moore," written well after the composition of "Diligence," Harriet Monroe suggests that "Miss Moore's steely and recondite art has long been a rallying-point for the radicals." She questions whether the author of "the geometrical verse-designs which frame these cryptic observations" is really a poet. Marian Strobel, an associate editor of *Poetry*, adds, "Because we are conscious that she has brains, that she is exceedingly well-informed, we are the more irritated that she has not learned simplicity." Another poet-critic, Pearl Andelson, says, "Marianne Moore has much of the Emily Dickinson type of mind, but where Emily Dickinson's not infrequent obscurities arise out of an authentic mysticism, Marianne Moore's are more likely the result of a relentless discipline in the subtler 'ologies' and 'osophies' . . . [some of her poems] are hybrids of a flagrantly prosy origin."[14] One cannot argue for Moore's ability to see into the future, but one can suggest that she understood the nature of her own work and could assess the reactions of her critics. She could predict the problems she would encounter among the scholarly and critical status quo, the scarecrows of aesthetic procedure.

The poem may also make reference to Mary Warner Moore, Marianne's own mother, whom she sometimes called Mole in her notebooks and in her letters to her brother. And she usually called herself Rat, for the poet in Kenneth Graham's *Wind in the Willows*. (Her brother, Warner, was sometimes Badger or Toad.) In her Conversation Notebook, someone named Mole advises Rat to change her style before trying to publish her work in a book. Rat exclaims, "Huh! Then you would omit all these things I prize so much?" Mole replies, "Yes, they're ephemeral."[15] The word "ephemera" in the poem may also reflect Moore's struggle with a "scarecrow of aesthetic procedure" much closer to home.[16] The point here is that "Diligence" is Moore's statement of her refusal to mold her developing style to any standard of "aesthetic procedure" then in existence. The world could call her poems ephemera or curios, but she would be proceeding in her own cumbersome and laborious mode nonetheless. The elephant, which looks as ponderous and clumsy as the long lines of this poem, is the perfect figure for Moore's perception of her work. (She would write several more "elephant" poems, as dissimilar to each other as her poems on time are, yet all deriving from the metaphorical figure she created here nonetheless.) Her poems may seem prosaic—turning the kaleidoscope from dull and uninteresting to "like prose"—but that is her intent, not an unfortunate accident. Her poems might not have looked and sounded the way a poem supposedly should, but they were conjuries that endure, magic far more durable than any romantic ride taken on an antique magic carpet from a worn-out era. She would "outdistance calamity," regardless of the criticism of the competition.

Thus, by fracturing the expected and forcing the reader to reassess old expectations, Moore succeeds in establishing her philosophy that magic is made of diligence, that poetry is prose "with a kind of heightened consciousness," and that she will not be frightened away by scarecrow critics who might declare her work merely a tedious curiosity. At the same time she speaks of progress by elephant, she demonstrates it, with ponderous lines almost humorously attached with tails linked to trunks by the repeated rhyme of "-ose" (toes, goes, arose, chose, knows, crows, those, suppose, blows, and curios), a rhyme that is scarcely heard in the "pleasing jerky progress" of the text.

An even more sophisticated example of Moore's use of the kaleidoscope is the 1917 poem "Roses Only." Again Moore's objective seems to be to create the intentional flaw, the crack in the bowl, which successfully challenges the expected.

Roses Only

You do not seem to realise that beauty is a liability rather than
    an asset—that in view of the fact that spirit creates form we
        are justified in supposing
   that you must have brains. For you, a symbol of the unit,
        stiff and sharp,
  conscious of surpassing by dint of native superiority and liking
        for everything

self-dependent, anything an

ambitious civilisation might produce: for you, unaided to attempt
                                                    through sheer
    reserve, to confute presumptions resulting from observation, is
                                        idle. You cannot make us
        think you a delightful happen-so. But rose, if you are
                                                    brilliant, it
        is not because your petals are the without-which-nothing of
                                pre-eminence. You would, minus thorns
    look like a what-is-this, a mere

peculiarity. They are not proof against a worm, the elements or
                                                    mildew
        but what about the predatory hand? What is brilliance without
                                co-ordination? Guarding the
            infinitesimal pieces of your mind, compelling audience to
            the remark that it is better to be forgotten than to be
                                        remembered too violently,
        your thorns are the best part of you.

Observations

In *Marianne Moore: The Cage and the Animal*, Donald Hall makes an
interesting observation relative to Moore's poem "Marriage." He remarks
that

> Because of its method of swift, verbally unconnected transition
> from thought to thought . . . the effort required of the reader to
> follow the sense of the poem through these transitions accounts
> in part for the poem's effectiveness. Loss of focus does not occur
> because nothing is held too long *in* focus. As one cannot look too
> long at a picture without beginning not to see it, so one cannot
> dwell too long on an idea without its beginning to lose its first
> power. [17]

The same kind of change of focus occurs in "Roses Only." In order to
allow the reader to learn something new about roses, Moore turns the
kaleidoscope with steady regularity, until she is successful in overturn-
ing the convention by which the rose is prized for its delicacy and unthinking beauty. Not every critic understands her intent. The writer for
the *Times Literary Supplement* who reviewed "Roses Only" in 1921

wrote, "She seems 'entirely ignorant' of all previous writing."[18] Nothing could be further from the truth.

Moore was very much aware of the historical and literary tradition of the rose and very familiar with traditional "rose" poetry. The rose was the flower of Aphrodite, and the flower of Venus as well. In the odes of poets and the lays of balladeers, the rose stood for womanly perfection and the mysteries of love. Although the rose was shunned by early Christians, who linked it with pagan excesses, by the Middle Ages the rose had become the symbol of the purity of the Virgin Mary and the model for stained-glass windows; Christ was at the center surrounded by interlacing petals, suggesting the twelve apostles and the church in sacred unity, a kind of eternal marriage. Centuries later, the rose became the symbol of decadence, of art for art's sake, of the notion that art existed merely to be admired; it could not—should not—be in any way useful. From literature Moore would probably have known "Le Roman de la Rose," Robert Herrick's "Gather Ye Rosebuds While Ye May," John Fletcher's "Bridal Song," Edmund Waller's "Goe, Lovely Rose," Oscar Wilde's "Roses and Rue," and a thousand other poems in the rose tradition. There is even something of the metaphysical conceit in Moore's "Roses." But one might expect such an approach from a student who was already studying seventeenth-century writers with Georgiana Goddard King at Bryn Mawr in 1909. (T. S. Eliot's rediscovery of the Metaphysical Poets did not appear until 1921. His essays on seventeenth-century prose writers appeared still later.) Moore understood the history of the symbol; her efforts lay in reexamining its validity in the modern world. In her poem, the sense of "rose" changes with alterations in focus as the poem unfolds.

Moore assumes the conceit of addressing the rose as an entity, perhaps even a person. "You" need to realize that by its very nature beauty is a liability rather than an asset, for it tends to attract admiration in the form of a desire to pluck the flower and make it the admirer's own. The principle is true of both roses—and women. The urge to "deflower" the beautiful in nature is a strong one; perhaps ultimately part of nature's plan.

But Moore turns the focus of her kaleidoscope only a fraction to make another point. If one accepts the principle that spirit creates form, something like the good produces the beautiful, one must confess that "roses" must have brains. That logic is evidenced in many ways. Most obviously, roses are wise enough to produce thorns, "stiff and sharp" as some form of protection against plucking. Second, roses (and others too) recognize the rose's own superiority. Such recognition is not bred of an inflated ego, but of reality. Roses are "conscious of surpassing by dint of native superiority" anything even "an ambitious civilisation might produce." Because of their complex and unmatched formation of as many as sixty petals, roses have become the symbol of unity, of the many in one, the paragon among flowers.

Although roses offer no explanation, do not try to confute the presumptions of excellence resulting from observation (and evidently, according to Moore, they could speak if they chose to), such effort would be idle waste anyway. "You" could never convince observers that the rose is just one of nature's accidents, "a delightful happen-so." It is entirely too spectacular.

Again the kaleidoscope turns: the poet addresses the rose, for the first time by its name rather than as "you," suggesting that it is not the petals that make this flower so remarkable, the "without-which-nothing of pre-eminence"; minus thorns, the rose would be a "what-is-this, a mere / peculiarity." Granted, thorns are not a perfect protection. They do not protect against a worm, the elements, or mildew, but they do discourage "the predatory hand."

Another change of focus: "What is brilliance without co-ordination?" Using the word "brilliance" to mean bright, beautiful, and at the same time intelligent, Moore suggests that such a quality must be coordinated, that is to say, placed in proper order or put in a harmonious relation. With brilliance comes the obligation to guard the infinitesimal pieces of your mind" and to remember "that it is better to be forgotten than to be remembered too violently." Again, a slight shift of focus: after all is said and done, "your thorns are the best part of you," for they are the most original, the truly unique quality that "Roses Only" possess. Only a flower that has brains could have designed such a clever protection against the "predatory hand."

But somewhere in the final turn of the kaleidoscope, Moore's choice of words—"the infinitesimal pieces of your mind," "better to be forgotten than to be remembered too violently"—urges the reader to consider almost an allegorical reading of the poem, to make the logical leap from roses to people, which the Symbolist tradition has so long encouraged. Generally the rose has been associated with the beauty of women and the mystical quality of their attraction. But a rose without the protection of thorns is a vulnerable creature indeed, one that is burdened by the liability of its own attractiveness. The poem may be suggesting that a woman's mind can easily be turned by the flowery (i.e., traditional) language of love that frequently "blinds us all to the violence with which both the flower and the woman are actually treated."[19] Poets of the past have made certain predictable assumptions about the submissive position of women—and the rights of their admirers. Robert Herrick, for example, advised:

> Then be not coy, but use your time,
>   And, while ye may, go marry;
> For, having lost but once your prime,
>   You may forever tarry.[20]

And Andrew Marvell intensified that idea with:

> . . . then worms shall try
> that long preserved virginity,
> And your quaint honor turn to dust,
> And into ashes all my lust.[21]

The "worms" and "dust" of Herrick's and Marvell's famous lines seem to be echoed by the worm, the elements, and the mildew of "Roses Only," against which thorns offer no protection. Mortality is not mitigated by thorns; only the predatory hand is prevented.

Again Moore changes focus and, in doing so, effectively challenges the status quo by suggesting to women that sometimes "it is better to be forgotten than to be remembered too violently." Perhaps independence and self-dependence are more desirable than submission. There must be valid ways to admire women and roses without doing them violent injury. Perhaps a woman's thorns, the prickly parts of her mind and her personality (those various scalpels?), are the best part of her. That is not to negate beauty but instead to put it into perspective, to execute "coordination." Six years later in "Marriage," Moore would write:

> the strange experience of beauty;
> its existence is too much;
> it tears one to pieces
> and each fresh wave of consciousness
> is poison.

Beauty alone, unprotected, uncontrolled, uncoordinated is a dangerous commodity, a poison. There is great need for what Moore has called "that weapon, self-protectiveness" (in her poem "In This Age of Hard Trying, Nonchalance Is Good And"). One could learn a great deal from roses; they understand the value of thorns.

But Moore's intellectual fine-tuning is still not complete. For if spirit creates form and if the form, the beautiful, exists, so must the spirit. And there is much evidence in the poem to suggest that this poem is also about excellence of the spirit, perhaps of the intellectual kind, what the poet calls "brains," "brilliance," "superiority," "pre-eminence," "the infinitesimal pieces of [the] mind." Anything in existence that is beyond the ordinary must learn to produce thorns by very "dint of its native superiority and liking for everything / self-dependent." Something in nature likes what is average, what is ordinary, and tries to pull all things to the center. So the extraordinary, the preeminent, is endangered and must be protected. Excellence of the "infinitesimal pieces of your mind" must be guarded at all costs, even at the risk that it is "better to be forgotten than to be remembered too violently." Thus there is a place, a need for "that weapon, self-protectiveness," for (as in "Black Earth," in *Observations*)

> this elephant skin
> which I inhabit, fibred over like the shell of
> the cocoanut.

One needs the "scale / lapping scale" of the pangolin. They are all forms of thorns, which "Roses Only" must develop as a guard against mediocrity.

Which of the focuses, or readings, of "Roses Only" is correct? Knowing Marianne Moore, I would say probably all three, and several more I have missed. For example, it is clear that the poem operates from an overpowering sibilance, always a clue to Moore's meanings; there are forty-seven "s" sounds in the work, with a marked change in the pattern in the final five lines, which have only eight. Knowing Moore's interest in precision, one can assume that the change from the "s" sound, which may be read as "feminine," signals a change in emphasis to a more "masculine" kind of assertiveness. The change also causes the reader to hear the final five lines punctuated by hard consonants, particularly the "p," and to read at a slower pace, one that could easily be called adagio. Several lines are themselves prickly, like thorns, particularly the inverted, Latinate, "without-which-nothing of pre-eminence" and "look like a what-is-this a mere peculiarity." The syllabic count, although not really heard by the reader, is exact: 21, 24, 17, 24, 8, for all three stanzas. The poem may proceed with a "kind of pleasing jerky progress," but the effect is not wrought without an immensity of conscious labor on the part of the poet.[22]

To return to my main point, then, "Roses Only" is a poem of many dimensions, of myriad meanings. The work is not so much obscure as it is complex and demanding of the reader's attention. Perhaps some might argue that the poem is not successful because it lends itself to many interpretations. I suspect the complexity of meanings was precisely Moore's intent; for her, "one should be as clear as one's natural reticence allows one to be."[23] She always has "a burning desire to be explicit." It is just that the truth does not stand still. It turns like the changing patterns of a kaleidoscope.

Moore's poem "The Fish," written in 1918, is widely anthologized; it is also almost universally admired as a "beautiful" poem. However, at that point, critics rapidly part company. There are marked differences in interpretation given to this single poem. Moore made at least three major revisions of the text, and we have access to her original work notes on the piece from Chatham, so one can be fairly confident that she had some objective in mind and that she worked diligently toward that objective. Once again she was trying to be as clear as she could, given her natural reticence. In this poem particularly, one is reminded of Moore's own words in "Subject, Predicate, Object": "As for the hobgoblin obscurity, it need never entail compromise. It should mean that one may fail and start again, never mutilate a suspicious premise. The object is architecture, not demolition."[24] What follows is the text as she prepared it for the 1924 edition of her poems called *Observations*.

The Fish

Wade
through black jade
   Of the crow-blue mussel shells, one
     keeps
      adjusting the ash heaps;
    opening and shutting itself like
an
injured fan.

The barnacles which encrust the
side
of the wave, cannot hide
there for the submerged shafts of the

sun, split like spun
glass, moved themselves with spotlight swift-
ness
into the crevices—
in and out, illuminating

the
turquoise sea
of bodies. The water drives a
wedge
of iron through the iron edge
of the cliff, whereupon the stars,

pink
rice grains, ink
bespattered jelly-fish, crabs like
green
lilies and submarine
toadstools, slide each on the other.

All
external
marks of abuse are present on
this
defiant edifice—
all the physical features of

ac-
cident—lack
of cornice, dynamite grooves, burns
and
hatchet strokes, these things stand
out on it; the chasm side is

dead.
Repeated
evidence has proved that it can

live
on what cannot revive
its youth. The sea grows old in it.

Observations

    The poem does indeed have a haunting, almost eerie beauty. It takes the reader into an undersea world seldom actually experienced by human beings, at least not in 1918. All the action occurs in an ethereal, surrealistic kind of slow motion, a movement suggested both by the undulations of the sea world and by the rhythm of the lines themselves, which operate in a peculiar and repeated cycloid pattern. There are eight stanzas with syllabic lines of 1, 3, 8, 1, 6, 8 and an exact rhyme scheme of *a a b c c d*; the stanzas themselves are a carefully contrived repetition of waves of sound. But at that point, anything obvious falls apart, as good critics devise very different explanations of Moore's intent.

    Wallace Stevens was among the first to recognize the poem's accomplishments. In a 1935 review of Moore's *Selected Poems*, he wrote: "In 'The Fish' for instance, the lines move waving to and fro under water with the rhythm of sea-fans. They are lines of exquisite propriety." Sensitive to the scrupulous craftsmanship of the poem, Stevens also applauds Moore's daring in managing to incorporate what might seem to be aesthetically inappropriate language (e.g., "external / marks of abuse") and diverse subjects ("defiant edifice") into a clearly effective representation of the sounds and sights of the sea. He demonstrates how Moore's light rhyme, predictable rhythms, and visual word placement give pleasure to the reader.[25]

    Sue Renick deals with both interpretation and aesthetics when she suggests that the poem's unity comes from a "central consciousness that identifies itself with the movement of the sea." She reads the poem as representative of the paradox of destruction and endurance. The movement of the sea has the power to destroy both small fish and, at the same time, the surprisingly vulnerable cliff. Yet that very movement also grants survival to both the fish and the cliff. And ironically, the powerful sea grows old in it; that is to say, the primeval sea actually grows old before the ever-enduring cliff. She senses in the structures of Moore's lines an attempt to capture the throb of the ocean current and in the rhyme "the organic sound of the sea as it might be heard by fish."[26]

    Donald Hall agrees that the subject of the poem is probably the sea and its power and potential for injury, but he, like Stevens, prefers to stress aesthetics over meaning, arguing that the poem exhibits "some of the loveliest images in all poetry." He admits that he does not "fully understand the poem" and that he finds the last lines particularly moving, without being able to penetrate them.[27]

Bonnie Costello comments that "The Fish" has been justly admired by critics for the precision of its images (William Pratt included it in his anthology *The Imagist Poem*), for its skillful ordering of sounds and syllables (which Hugh Kenner has discussed at length),[28] and for its poignant theme of defiance and endurance (which Bernard Engel elaborates in a close reading).[29] Costello maintains, as Stevens had long before, that our experience is sensuous long before it is intellectual or moral. She reads the shells as the fans, the piled up mussels as the ash heaps, and offers the additional insight that the predictable rhyme and rhythm of the verse offer stability in a world of flux.[30]

Hugh Kenner, always fascinated by Moore's poetics, finds the poem "primarily visible," a poem for the eye, one meticulously arranged on the page. He feels sure that the poem is "like a mosaic which has no point of beginning." He clearly understands Moore's fascination with the visual.[31]

Laurence Stapleton argues against complexity in the poem, feeling sure that "The Fish" cannot be said to be complex in the usual sense of that word, "although it fuses image and idea with fine disregard for open statement."[32] (She does not, however, offer to explicate these "uncomplicated" stanzas.)

Grace Schulman sees "the sea, sun, and rock set in opposition to one another, acting and acted upon as they are watched by an unobtrusive perceiver." The rays of the sun penetrate the sea and are fractured (i.e., refracted); the fish must wade, they cannot swim freely; the water "drives a wedge of iron through the iron edge of the cliff." "Only the rock, scarred though it is by the sea and by the other elements, does not deteriorate because it can survive 'on what cannot revive its youth.'"[33]

John Slatin, noticing the publication of "The Fish" beside "Reinforcements" in *Observations*, feels sure that "The Fish" is a war poem prompted by the assignment of Moore's brother, Warner, a Navy chaplain, to the North Atlantic in 1917. Slatin builds a case for a horror poem wherein a "strange, ominously silent landscape filled with ruins" suggests that "we are moving in a sea of bodies" and recalling some terrible wartime disaster, or perhaps a tragedy symbolic of all disasters at sea. There is no cliff at all, but rather "the iron hull of a ship which looms

clifflike above the surface."[34] The concussion caused by a torpedo has
sent the undersea world into a ghastly chaos,

> . . . whereupon the stars,
> pink
> rice grains, ink
>> bespattered jelly-fish, crabs like
>>> green
>>> lilies and submarine
>> toadstools, slide each on the other.

Margaret Holley argues that the poem's power is the water itself, with
its colored delicacies and the verbs of motion, which

> . . . drives a
>> wedge
>> of iron through the iron edge
> of the cliff.

Holley notes that while "we may allegorize the subject, the poet has
refrained from doing so."[35]

Which turn of the critical kaleidoscope is correct? Is there something
valid in each of them? How can a poem be complex and not complex;
meticulously crafted and yet a mosaic with no point of beginning; primarily about the power of the sea and about the observations of fish; a
war poem and a beautiful portrait of peace; violent and terrifying and
also serene and enobling; a communication about endurance and a portrait of despair; allegorical and literal? (One is reminded of the famous
tale of the blind men and the elephant. Each has a sensitive hand on a
part of the animal and is describing his perception accurately, but none
can report the nature of the whole.)

In her paper on Marianne Moore entitled "The Machinery of Grace,"
Elizabeth Bradburn has suggested that too many of Moore's critics feel
such satisfaction when they decode an enigmatic line or two in a poem
that they then gloss over other lines, even entire passages, reading them
as somehow obvious to the reader when they are not obvious at all.[36] (I
think Schulman's line "Only the rock, scarred though it is by the sea and
by the other elements does not deteriorate because it can survive 'on
what cannot revive its youth'" is in precisely that category. Schulman
makes the assumption that the phrase "on what cannot revive / its

youth" is somehow obvious to the reader, when, in fact, it is not at all. What is it that cannot revive its youth? The sea? time? endurance? steadfastness? faith?) Similar assumptions occur in the various interpretations of "The Fish" presented here. The critics' readings are not necessarily incorrect or bad; they are merely partial.

Margaret Holley offers a useful idea when she suggests that many readers rush too quickly into allegorical readings of the poem, while Moore herself carefully refrains from doing so. The critical kaleidoscope must be turned with greater care. It may also be helpful to know that Moore was a great admirer of T. S. Eliot's work as well as his personal friend; she frequently referred to him as a trout. In "English Literature since 1914" Moore wrote: "The sheen upon T. S. Eliot's poems, the facile troutlike passage of his mind, through a multiplicity of foreign objects recalls the 'Spic torrent' in Wallace Stevens's Pecksniffenia. Mr. Eliot does not mar his subject by overdoing it and he does not bring too heavy a touch to bear upon it. His nonchalance together with his power of implication make him one of the definite spirits of our time."[37] (One recalls also Moore's 1916 poem "In This Age of Hard Trying Nonchalance Is Good." According to Lane's *Concordance*, Moore used the word "nonchalance" only once in her poetry, giving some support to the notion that Eliot's figure as a representative poet remained in Moore's mind.) I do not mean to suggest that this is a poem about T. S. Eliot, but it is important to remember that the poem is entitled "The Fish" and that Moore may well be associating the job of the poet with a "troutlike passage . . . through a multiplicity of . . . objects." And that is a good way to approach the text. It is essential to keep Moore's title and her subject, "fish," uppermost in mind as one moves toward assessing her meaning. Moore associates fish, like elephants and roses, with certain characteristics of the poet, or for that matter, of any artist.

At face value, the poem is about fish moving through the greenish black (black jade) sea and along the sea bottom. On the sea floor they find various objects, including a mussel shell, opening and shutting itself like an injured fan. Nothing in the darkened undersea world is entirely hidden because shafts of sunlight "split like spun / glass" move themselves like spotlights down to the ocean floor,

> . . . illuminating
> the
> turquoise sea
> of bodies.

The phrase "split like spun / glass" is so similar to "split like a glass against a wall" in this "precipitate of dazzling impressions" (in "Novices") as to invite comparison. Many critics have pointed out Moore's use of the sea as a metaphor for facing innermost terror. In "The Fish," she is doing precisely that, placing herself—and analogously, her readers—directly into a grave where both she and they must wrestle with life's deepest fears. Yet on the very edge of terror one also encounters life's heights, for even the deepest sea is lit by the

> sun,
> split like spun
> glass.

The light is refracted but still moving "with spotlight swift- / ness." Even in the depths, the light is always there, illuminating the frightening darkness and making it appear surprisingly beautiful, comprehensible, and safe. All that is foreign and alarming—barnacles, crevices, the turquoise sea of bodies, the eerie sea creatures (all characters from childhood nightmares and even adult dreams)—are clarified and identified for what they are: merely mussel shells, jellyfish, and crabs. And regardless of what damage the sea is capable of doing to the earth, it cannot totally destroy the cliff, the permanence of land. It can wreak terrible—and oddly beautiful—damage to the civilizations that earth has nurtured, damage identified by lack of cornices, dynamite grooves, burns, and hatchet strokes. The destruction can be so dreadful that "the chasm side is / dead." But the cliff—solidity, earth—

> . . . can
> live
> on what cannot revive
> its youth.

It does endure. And "fish" can observe that.

Whether the forms at the bottom of the sea are Slatin's human bodies or merely the multiplicity of objects on the ocean floor, the fish "see" them there in the muted turquoise gloom. Because the way is lit by rays of sunlight, the fish glimpse "pink / rice grains" (sea anemones?), jellyfish that are "ink / bespattered," (suggesting perhaps that they appear to be inked over with shadows, or more probably that their air bladders are marked by a curious purple inklike dye), crabs like green lilies, moving eerily in the murky water, and sea toadstools, all giving the impression of oozing against one another and undulating onto each other in the sea currents.

Although the water may seem an amorphous and disarmingly innocuous commodity, once one actually "wades through black jade," one discovers that it is still powerful; it drives an iron wedge "through the iron edge / of the cliff." Through the power of natural persistence, the apparently formless and harmless water eventually erodes its way even through the rocks of a cliff, the edifice characterized by its "iron edge." The cliff has seen and has weathered great adversity, all the external "marks of abuse" that humans and nature can provide. Yet the great rock persists; it lives in the sea, that which "cannot revive / its youth." The sea can slowly provide destruction, erosion, but it cannot reverse the process and make the cliff young and unmarked again. And yet the sea grows old *in it*—while at the same time the rock continues to be battered by the power of the sea. The two are locked in a mutually nurturing and mutually destructive embrace.

If one keeps the poem "underwater," these are the images one sees. Moore demands no more. But it is obvious that critics instinctively move toward possible layers of meaning, and then the kaleidoscope begins its turn. One can use the data of the poem to argue convincingly, as Renick has, for a statement about the paradox of destruction and endurance. The movements of the sea—perhaps of human history, or perhaps of time—both grant life and destroy it at the same instant. As Costello has suggested, the very structure of the poem, the predictable rhymes and rhythms, themselves marking "time" in another sense, offer stability in a world of flux. And Schulman's notion that there is a resistance in all of life against which all must push, fracture, wade, and drive (the sea against the cliff, the cliff against the sea) contributes further to understanding the poem's intuition about the importance of struggle. And even Slatin's mental leap to an undersea world of destruction may work as well. Certainly Moore's own treatment of the sea in "A Grave" offers mute testimony to the possibility of his reading (note there "the sea has nothing to give but a well excavated grave" and "men lower nets, unconscious of the fact that they are desecrating a grave").

Once again, Moore seems to lead her readers to ambiguity. Like the abstract painter, she demands that her audience participate in the lines, turning them slowly until meaning takes shape within the parameters of her images. In the poem entitled "Charity Overcoming Envy" (1963),

Moore addresses her own design, using again the metaphor of the poet as elephant.

> The elephant, at no time borne down by self-pity,
>   convinces the victim
> that Destiny is not devising a plot.
>
> The problem is mastered—insupportably
> tiring when it was impending.
> Deliverance accounts for what sounds like an axiom.
>
> The Gordian knot need not be cut.

It is not the poet's business to "devise a plot." And as eager as the reader may be to be delivered by something that "sounds like an axiom," that is also not the poet's concern. What does begin to emerge is a poem that is indeed beautiful, that does give pleasure; it appeals to the sensual before the intellectual and the moral. It is a poem that is visual, both as it appears on the page and in the images it evokes. Its sounds and rhythms capture the life force of the sea. Through the poet's power to strike "piercing glances into the life of things," one is offered some momentary insight into the fragile tension of life, caught always between endurance and destruction, but life which is real and precious nonetheless. The poet's power to swim with "troutlike passage . . . through a multiplicity of . . . objects" offers an illumination of propriety, accuracy, beauty, and insight into the fragile tension and rhythms of existence.

Some critics have argued that Moore's later poetry is far less difficult for her reader, that she tired of her private enigmas and became more committed to public concerns and to public understanding. To argue in that direction is to overlook a significant body of the poet's later work. Poems such as "Voracities and Verities Sometimes Are Interacting" (1947), "Armor's Undermining Modesty" (1950), "O to Be a Dragon" (1957), "Charity Overcoming Envy" (1963), or "The Mind, Intractable Thing" (1965) can scarcely be categorized as lightweight.

For sheer intricacy it is difficult to outdo "Logic and 'The Magic Flute,'" written in 1956. This poem may be shorter than earlier works such as "Marriage" (1923), "The Octopus" (1924), or the transitional poem "The Pangolin" (1936), but it is by no means a simple poem; it demands its own kind of critical kaleidoscope.

Logic and "The Magic Flute"

Up winding stair,
here, where, in what theater lost?
was I seeing a ghost—
a reminder at least
    of a sunbeam or moonbeam
that has not a waist?
    By hasty hop
    or accomplished mishap,
the magic flute and harp
somehow confused themselves
    with China's precious wentletrap.

Near Life and Time
in their peculiar catacomb,
abalonean gloom
and an intrusive hum
    pervaded the mammoth cast's
small audience-room.
    Then out of doors,
    where interlacing pairs
of skaters raced from rink
to ramp, a demon roared
    as if down flights of marble stairs:

"'What is love and
shall I ever have it?'" The truth
is simple. Banish sloth,
fetter-feigning uncouth
    fraud. Trapper Love with noble
noise, the magic sleuth,
    as bird-notes prove—
    first telecolor-trove—
illogically wove
what logic can't unweave:
    one need not shoulder, need not shove.

Moore offered notes to this poem, suggesting perhaps that she wanted
to be sure her readers understood her starting place: *"The Magic Flute.*
Colorcast by NBC Opera Theater, January 15, 1956." On "precious
wentletrap" in line 11 she wrote, "*n.* [D *wenteltrap* a winding staircase;

cf. G. *wendeltreppe.*] The shell of *E. pretiosa*, of the genus *Epitonium.*— *Webster's New International Dictionary.*" There is even a sketch of the wentletrap shell, presumably by Moore's own hand.

Moore's great friend and younger colleague Elizabeth Bishop was very interested in her mentor's intent in "Logic and 'The Magic Flute.'" She found the poem "wonderful. I'm grateful for the word *wentletrap* and shall do my best to see that it passes into common usage. But the beginning is so good and so Mozartian, too—that light, direct attack. . . . I do admire it! 'peculiar catacomb, / abalonean gloom' is also perfectly Mozartian too—his glooms could be so abalonean, I should think. Without ever saying red or blue, it is colored."[38] Bishop's notion that the poem is Mozartian in style is interesting. Its pace is rapid, traveling in motifs of threes, offering chords of harmonic sounds. Those chords of sound occur in its rhyme scheme, one accomplished with a touch as light as any notes on a magic flute. Note the echoes of

> stair here, where;
> lost, ghost, least, waist;
> sunbeam, moonbeam;
> hap, mishap, harp;
> themselves, wentletrap;
> catacomb, abalonean, gloom, room;
> rink, ramp, roared;
> pairs, stairs;
> truth, sloth, uncouth, sleuth;
> prove, trove, wove;
> unweave, need.

It is no wonder Eliot declared Moore the greatest living master of light rhyme.[39] Only Mozart's touch falls as lightly.

Moore says that she was moved by a color telecast of Mozart's "Magic Flute" on NBC television in January 1956 and thus came to write this poem. At first readers may feel as confused ("here, where, in what theater lost?") as if they had suddenly awakened in Sarastro's court, as had Mozart's Oriental hero, Tamino. With the poet (and perhaps with Tamino), we are all lost in some magic kingdom where wondrous things are happening, although we cannot quite tell how. What ought to be produced in a theater and performed by some "mammoth cast" is happening just up the stairs, here, in one's own living room. "[Am] I seeing a ghost?" the speaker asks,

> a reminder at least
> of a sunbeam or moonbeam
> that has not a waist?

People have waists, sunbeams and moonbeams do not; are television signals some kind of ghostly beams? or do they represent some work of the human animal, the beam with a waist, after all? Is this incredible performance, this "telecolor-trove" (punning on treasure trove) the result of some "hasty hop / or accomplished mishap?" This indeed is magic.

As if to pinch herself to test reality, the poet looks down beside her television set "Near Life and Time / in their peculiar catacomb." The capitalized words "Life" "Time" at first suggest some great symbolic truths, until one realizes that the speaker may merely be looking at her magazines, her *Life* and *Time* in their appropriate space, mute testaments to the reality that she is merely in her own home. The "intrusive hum" of the performance fills the "mammoth cast's / small audience-room," the speaker's own living room, where the television set is playing in the shimmering darkness, the abalonean gloom. Meanwhile, quite ordinary activities go on out of doors,

> where interlacing pairs
> of skaters raced from rink
> to ramp.

But on the television performance, someone, perhaps the Queen of Night, appears in a tremendous crash of thunder and lightning, screaming out in her terrible fury and pointing her shining dagger at the evil Moor, Monostatos, who is attacking her daughter ("a demon roared / as if down flights of marble stairs").

The last stanza could well be a statement of some of the major themes of Mozart's *Magic Flute*. Both Tamino and his comic companion, Papageno (who is, incidentally dressed in a motley costume of feathers and who is loaded down with bird cages), ask and sing the all-consuming human question, "What is love and / shall I ever have it?" And the same might be said for the objects of their quest, Pamina and Papagena. The answer to that question is, "The truth / is simple." In the Temple of Wisdom the heroes discover that they must learn to banish sloth and "fetter-feigning uncouth / fraud." And they must undergo the three great trials of silence, of fire, and of water, the magical trio of all great fantasies.

Overcoming any quest, any trial, is possible because the two heroes possess magic—the magic of the flute awarded to Tamino and the wonderful glockenspiel belonging to Papageno. With the aid of such magic, and a little good sense, their success is ensured. Both search for love "with noble / noise"—Tamino, by the "bird-notes" on his flute, and Papageno, who is himself dressed as a bird, plays "bird-notes" on his glockenspiel.

One does not waste time looking for logic in a fantasy world so perfectly woven by an artist like Mozart; he has produced what logic cannot unweave. It is again Bergson's intuition, the highest stage in the evolution of human understanding. There is no need to shoulder, no need to shove; given the miracle of television, the magic of music conveys its message to audiences of perhaps millions, each in the privacy of one's own "precious wentletrap." The wentletrap can refer to a winding stairway, but it can also mean a tiny shell, one which gives its possessor access to the mystical message of the sea. In the modern world, anyone can see a magnificent production on television and hold the wentletrap to one's ear and hear the magic of Mozart, one of the most intuitive composers of all time. Now it is not even necessary to shoulder one's way through a theater crowd to have access to one of the most remarkable productions ever imagined by the human mind. There is the magic of image and the imagination everywhere in Mozart, which through television reproduces the greatest magic known to humankind.

But just as the possibility—even the probability—of this reading comes into focus, Moore turns the kaleidoscope again to demand a larger, more comprehensive picture. In one sense, the wentletrap is like a tiny shell, the receiver, the "television set" which transmits a performance of Mozart to a human audience. Yet in another sense, that receiver, as complicated and as magical as it may be, is nothing by comparison with the next receiver, the wentletrap that is a winding staircase, the spiral upon spiral of the human mind and soul that receives data and performs the real magic of understanding, of intuiting for itself the unspoken message of the human spirit the first receiver conveys. Music is a universal language, a language without words, that speaks a logic—as if by magic—directly to the psyche.

And yet when one perceives a feeling or a truth about the human condition from great music, that glimpse is so fragmentary as to leave only a flash of insight into the reality it signals. It is like the beautiful and fleeting notes of the flute or the harp. Once sounded, they can be recalled only imperfectly. But to have experienced such a flash of insight and beauty is to have reached the height of human experience, to have made the ultimate human connection. How does one define the magic— or the logical method—of Mozart, the creator of such magnificent music? Or how does one celebrate the varied and mysterious whorls of the human mind that receive his music, each with one's own special wentletrap? There is no logic capable of explaining this mystery. It is "illogically wove[en]" and is "what logic can't unweave." There is no pushing or shoving capable of forcing this incredible enchantment.

Again, a slight twist of focus, and one comes to understand something about the mysterious communion between the artist, whether a musician, a dancer, a painter, a playwright, or a poet, and the artist's audience. At the right moment, illusion is more precise than precision. The audience becomes one with the artist in a direct leap of intuition about "Life" and "Time" from one "instrument" to another. But that connection does not come without perfection on the part of the artist and concentration on the part of the audience. Reaching for what Williams called that "spot of sunlight" toward which Marianne Moore is conducting us takes effort and concentration, and a readiness for unexpected turns in the images, sounds, and experiences we perceive. One must learn to cultivate in oneself Moore's "special fondness for writing that is obscure, that does not quite succeed"[40] and also learn to enjoy her ever-changing kaleidoscope of voices, color, sound, rhythm and insight. One must develop a taste for "butterflies" that are alive, organic, unfolding, and wonderful. Unlike Herod, we may also have to learn to change our minds, for minds are enchanting and enchanted things.

CHAPTER 5

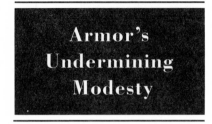

Armor's
Undermining
Modesty

Like many people who risk the public eye, Marianne Moore was an intensely sensitive person. From the hindsight of her success, it is easy to applaud her daring, her honest originality, and her idiosyncrasy, what she herself called the "courage of her peculiarities." Now we recognize the value of her technical and thematic innovations; they have become so commonplace in the latter half of the twentieth century that sometimes only contemporary technicians, poets themselves, are aware that she was their source. Furthermore, Moore made the artistic choice to work at some distance from emotion, sensuality, depravity, and despair, at a time when most of her colleagues were making far different choices; she did not join the literary mainstream. But whatever is original in any generation is usually slow to win acceptance. The status quo fights back, as it were, and tries to pull things toward itself. If the work is difficult for the average audience, there is a tendency to declare it obscure and to favor a more comfortable mediocrity. (A favorite stance of many early modern critics was merely to declare Moore's work "non poetry," frequently suggesting that it was all artificial form and no substance.) As noted earlier, among Moore's early critics of precisely that kind of formal control was Harriet Monroe. In 1922, Monroe first offered faint praise by saying "unquestionably there is a poet within the hard, deliberately patterned crust" but then countered with:

> Moore's forms impose themselves arbitrarily upon word-structure
> and sentence structure instead of accepting happily the

> limitations of the art's materials which naturally reject it. . . .
> And as she takes her own way in these details of style, so she
> gives little heed to the more general laws of shapeliness; each
> poem begins as it ends and ends as it begins—a coruscating
> succession of ideas, with little curve of growth or climax. . . .
> The grim and haughty humor of this lady strikes deep, so deep
> as to absorb her dreams and possess her soul. . . . may even
> grief soften a heart of brass?[1]

Charges of stiff geometrical intellectuality and grim and haughty humor
are the very blows that might eventually drive any writer behind armor.

Moore's poetry is, undeniably, difficult and somewhat off-putting.
From the beginning Moore was, as John Slatin puts it, "fiercely ambitious" and "stubbornly determined" to make a significant place for
herself in the artistic community of her time.[2] But venturing into new
territory, the avant-garde, is always difficult, especially when one ven-
tures in, for all practical purposes, alone. In order to maintain her own
difference, her idiosyncrasy, it was necessary to develop a thick skin,
thorns, overlapping scales, a persona—to become "another armored animal." Without some protection, without some kind of armor, one's vulnerability is too great; any artist runs the risk of annihilation.

Moore was always different in many respects. She was a woman in an
artistic world that tended to value the work of men and to discount the
writing of women unless it seemed to mirror "a man's way of thinking."
She was not part of the cosmopolitan world of Yeats, Pound, Eliot, Stein,
H.D., and Bryher, nor did she have the American sophistication of Wallace Stevens and William Carlos Williams. She must have seemed very
fastidious with her part-time librarian's job and her simple and austere
life with her mother in a small, lower-level apartment at St. Luke's Place
in New York City. While others, like Williams, Kreymborg, and Mina
Loy, enjoyed parties, sensual pleasures, gossip, and innuendo, Moore
remained upright. Williams once described her as so "out of place . . .
like a red berry still hanging to the jaded rose bush." Elsewhere he
called her "our saint—if we had one—in whom we all instinctively felt
our purpose come together to form a stream."[3] His use of the word
"saint" here marks another example of Moore's difference. Her religious
faith—and the expectations of what it meant to be a Presbyterian Christian—may have seemed strangely old-fashioned to her modernist
friends. But it goes a long way toward explaining her humility, while
paradoxically accounting for her supreme self-confidence that her spe-

cial gift was a grace from God that could not be hidden under a bushel, whatever her personal temptations to anonymity. She must reflect the kingdom of God by her excellence.

After she had achieved success, many would remember her as the animal poet, or the dear old lady who was the Brooklyn Dodgers fan, or the strange lady-poet who almost named the Edsel, or that eccentric old lady in the black cape and tricorne hat whom one passed on the streets of New York or met at the Gotham Book Mart. Although certainly all part of the Marianne Moore facade, none of those descriptions gets past externals. In 1964, an old *Dial* cohort, Alyse Gregory, offered an insightful glimpse into the personal qualities behind the magazine photos of the white-haired poet visiting the zoo or strolling through Washington Park.

> What did most continually and penetratingly come home to me was the rarity, the utter unimpressiveness of our Marianne . . . what a combination of total outgoing, almost heedless naturalness and most delicate and minute observation. . . . She says no one will believe how naive she is or how torpid—but what remains as my final impression is one of a combination of extreme fragility and vulnerability, combined with a firmness and fineness of texture and an intrepidity of spirit and generosity of heart that I found deeply moving.[4]

Moore understood the price of her own vulnerability; she also understood the nature of the poetic revolution she was attempting. While Moore frequently pursued a theme of self-protection, of armoring, she did so not from personal inadequacy but from the position of an artist who wishes to explore the issue of self-protection from many perspectives. In "Her Shield," Randall Jarrell points out that "a good deal of Moore's poetry is specifically (and changingly) about armour, weapons, protection, places to hide; and she is not only conscious that this is so, but after a while writes poems about the fact that it is so."[5] Jarrell makes two key points here: (1) Moore's explorations of the subject of armoring are not static, they are always changing, and (2) she was perfectly honest and comfortable about her shield and everybody else's. There is no mysterious, Freudian component to her interest in armoring.

Any artist takes a terrible risk each time he or she dares to place a performance before the tribunal of public opinion and dares to reveal what he or she really is and believes in, particularly if that belief ranges well outside public taste. Some form of armor against rejection becomes essential. Moore donned this kind of armor when she thanked T. S. Eliot for his support in a letter dated 18 January 1934: "An array of appreciators is so unessential if one is valued by five or even two, that I cannot see why Ezra Pound exhausts himself trying to engender intelligence in the whole world."[6] The very act of writing is a public act, and it requires personal determination to keep the process going if one is not always well received. There is perhaps something of the literary zealot seeking to change the world in any poet. In "Humility, Concentration, and Gusto" (an address to the Grolier Club on 21 December 1948), Moore addressed the need for a shield against rejection as well as a shield against overweening self-importance when she wrote the following about humility: "With what shall the artist arm himself save with his humility? Humility, indeed, is armor, for it realizes that it is impossible to be original, in the sense of doing something that has never been thought of before. Originality is in any case a by-product of sincerity; that is to say, of feeling that is honest and accordingly rejects anything that might cloud the impression."[7]

Humility is not a popular word today, particularly among some women critics. In her book *Naked and Fiery Forms: Modern American Poetry by Women: A New Tradition*, Suzanne Juhasz "continues the tradition of beating Moore over the head, Moore being without Emily Dickinson's range and passion."[8] The thought of anyone—particularly a woman—assuming realistic modesty about her own gift seems to some abhorrent. But for Moore, humility was simply connected with what might be called a genuine sense of grace, a peculiar brand of honesty about her gift, which she saw as a sacred trust. She had no real doubt about her brilliance and her accomplishments; but she always attributed their source to something larger than herself. As Gallagher sees it, she was "fully prepared for what Grace would deliver."[9] She knew her work was of the highest quality; she also recognized that not everyone would understand it. One has only to peruse her archive at the Rosenbach Museum in Philadelphia to know that she valued her work and left a careful record of both the work and its method so that others might learn from them. Taffy Martin has even dubbed her a "subversive modernist," although one wonders how subversive Moore ever was about her modernist intent. It seems clear that Marianne Moore understood that her success came from more than the mere audacity of her will. In an essay on Anna Pavlova, she wrote, "Genius is a trust concerning which vanity would be impossible."[10] This genius, this imagnifico, had little vanity and wrought her magic by taking delight in years of study and painstakingly thorough work, what she called in her essay, "humility, concentration, and gusto." Perhaps it might be more accurate to call Marianne Moore honest rather than humble, although "humility" is the word she herself used to describe her armor.

But it is important to look carefully at what Moore means by armor and armoring. As is evident in the poem "Roses Only," Moore understands that anything or anybody out of the ordinary must create some thorns to protect itself against the "predatory hand." And Moore was and wished to be out of the ordinary. It is interesting that she always delighted in extraordinary excellence and the self-confidence it took to declare it. She reported Anna Pavlova's describing herself as:

> **ANNA PAVLOVA**
> **THE INCOMPARABLE**
> **PRIMA BALLERINA ABSOLUTA.**[11]

She noted Cassius Clay's declaring "I Am the Greatest" on a record album cover in 1963.[12] And in "The Mind, Intractable Thing," Moore addressed herself,

> O imagnifico,
> wizard in words—poet, was it, as
> Alfredo Panzini defined you?

Moore always expressed an extraordinary affection for Anna Pavlova, writing one of her most moving essays some years after Pavlova's death. Nowhere else in Moore's prose does one come upon such pure, although carefully controlled, emotion. Pavlova seems to have been almost an alter ego, certainly a fellow performer, whom Moore admired beyond measure. Perhaps it was Pavlova's ability to create illusion that Moore admired so much; it may also have been her humility. Moore wrote: "It is the uncontaminated innocence of her fervor that is really the portrait of her pose. . . . [Her] truthful hands, the most sincere, the least greedy imaginable, indeed like priests, a sacerdotal gravity impressed upon their features; yet, as noticed by Cyril Beaumont, they 'were a little large for her arms, and the fingers inclined to be thick; so the illusion of grace, though not accidental, must have been a concomitant to her subconscious fire.'" Nor were Pavlova's feet dainty, but "remarkable for the power of the ankle, their high arch and toes of steel made her *pizzicati* on tiptoe and steadily held pauses possible." Moore also admired Pavlova's "utter straightness of spirit . . . matched by an incapacity for subterfuge that is all but spectacular; when speaking of stage fright she admitted that each time before an appearance she was subject to it, and 'this emotion,' she said, 'instead of decreasing with time, becomes stronger and stronger. For I am increasingly conscious of . . . my responsibilities.'"[13] Even the "Incomparable / Prima Ballerina Absolute" assumed the armor of an improbable title both to protect herself and to project herself.

Moore too worried about her large hands and big feet, both literally and figuratively. She praised photographers who made her hands look small and elegant. On 5 December 1936, Elizabeth Bishop wrote the following to Moore after a poetry reading: "You looked so nice down there on the platform: the black velvet is overwhelmingly becoming, and you should not have apologized for the shoes, they looked extremely small."[14] And she too had stage fright until the end, worrying over every text and revising relentlessly. Like Pavlova, Moore took her artistic responsibilities very seriously.

In her essay on Ezra Pound, Moore also instinctively reaches out to him as "another armored animal." She writes:

> There is no easy way if you are to be a great artist; and the nature of one, in achieving his art, is different from the nature of another.
> Mr. Pound, in the prose that he writes, has formulated his own commentary upon the Cantos. They are an armorial coat of attitudes to things that have happened in books and in life; they are not a shield but a coat worn by a man, as in the days when heraldry was beginning. . . . "Ordinary people," he says, in his turtle poem, "touch me not." His art is his turtle-shell or animal house; it is all one animal moving together.[15]

And Pound had declared, to Moore's delight, "Come my songs, let us speak of perfection— / We shall get ourselves rather disliked."[16] Armor is not what one wears as a shield; it is part of oneself, a coat of excellence, an aura of perfection. As Moore says in "The Pangolin," "armor [only] seems extra." (In "To a Snail" she reminds us that style may be no more than "the curious phenomenon of your occipital horn," the natural oddity of one's peculiar armorial coat, worn proudly, like a coat of arms.)

In a review of *The Necessary Angel* in 1952, Moore also wrote, "Wallace Stevens . . . puts his finger on this thing poetry, it seems to me, where he refers to 'a violence within that protects us from a violence without.'"[17] It is "armor" that creates protection against violence to one's own ideas and one's own style, and yet that paradoxically allows inner violence to be expressed. This is the tension that makes the struggle we call art possible. But it is an armor based on honesty, humility, and the knowledge that the artist's gift is a sacred trust. At the same time there is in Moore a sense of exhilaration, of true ego in the most positive sense, of honest celebration of what one can do—in the magic one's precision can perform. The term she used to express that exhilaration was "gusto." Anything less than gusto, than concentration on the excellence of performance according to one's own high standards, would be unthinkable. But at the same time, in a practical sense, it is necessary to develop a tough hide along the way, one that becomes an armorial coat to guard against the "predatory hand" as well as to announce one's own artistic identity. But one must beware of "armor's undermining modesty," of starting to confuse the armorial coat with the fragile "life under the mechanism."

Among Moore's first significant poems about armoring, poems which included "Diligence Is to Magic As Progress Is to Flight" and "Roses Only," was the 1918 poem "Black Earth." She reworked the poem in 1956, giving it a new name, "Melanchthon." The new title may refer to Philipp Melanchthon, a German humanist and colleague of Martin Luther who was an evangelical reformer and first systematic theologian of the Protestant Reformation; the Greek word *melanchthōn* also means "black earth."

Black Earth

Openly, yes
    with the naturalness
of the hippopotamus or the alligator
when it climbs out on the bank to experience the

sun, I do these
things which I do, which please
        no one but myself. Now I breathe and now I am sub-
            merged; the blemishes stand up and shout when the object

in view was a
renaissance; shall I say

the contrary? The sediment of the river which
encrusts my joints, makes me very gray but I am used

to it, it may
remain there; do away
    with it and I am myself done away with, for the
    patina of circumstance can but enrich what was

there to begin
with. This elephant skin
    which I inhabit, fibred over like the shell of
    the cocoanut, this piece of black glass through which no light

can filter—cut
into checkers by rut
    upon rut of unpreventable experience—
    it is a manual for the peanut-tongued and the

hairy toed. Black
but beautiful, my back
    is full of the history of power. Of power? What
    is powerful and what is not? My soul shall never

be cut into
by a wooden spear; through-
    out childhood to the present time, the unity of
    life and death has been expressed by the circumference

described by my
trunk; nevertheless, I
    perceive feats of strength to be inexplicable after
    all; and I am on my guard; external poise, it

has its centre
well nurtured—we know
    where—in pride, but spiritual poise, it has its centre where?
    My ears are sensitized to more than the sound of

the wind. I see
and I hear, unlike the
    wandlike body of which one hears so much, which was made
    to see and not to see; to hear and not to hear;

that tree trunk without
roots, accustomed to shout
    its own thoughts to itself like a shell, maintained intact
    by one who knows what strange pressure of the atmosphere;
                                                       that

spiritual
brother to the coral
    plant, absorbed into which, the equable sapphire light
    becomes a nebulous green. The I of each is to

the I of each,
a kind of fretful speech
    which sets a limit on itself; the elephant is?
    Black earth preceded by a tendril? It is to that

phenomenon
the above formation,
    translucent like the atmosphere—a cortex merely—
    that on which darts cannot strike decisively the first

time, a substance
needful as an instance
    of the indestructibility of matter; it
    has looked at the electricity and at the earth-

quake and is still
here; the name means thick. Will
    depth be depth, thick skin be thick, to one who can see no
    beautiful element of unreason under it?

                                   Observations

Moore's opening stanza has an amusing element of understatement. With the "naturalness / of the hippopotamus or the alligator," two of nature's most truly "armored animals," the speaker, presumably an elephant, "climbs out on the bank to experience the / sun." Proud of its immense size and tough hide, the animal smugly reports,

    . . . I do these
  things which I do, which please
    no one but myself.

Not many creatures can claim such confidence, but then not many creatures would venture to attack an alligator, a hippopotamus, or an elephant. Everything about them is off-putting. They are huge, ugly, primordial (in a manner of speaking, they are the last vestiges of dinosaurs and dragons, and dragons certainly are one of Moore's favorite armored animals: witness "O to Be a Dragon"); they inhabit slimy and inaccessible places; their hides are thick; and their very ungainliness makes them hazardous. In fact, full-grown members of the three species have no natural enemies except human beings; they are anomalies.

The poem itself is an anomaly among Moore's works because it is written in the first person in a voice which presents itself as something other than the poet's own. By line 18 the speaker admits that it inhabits an elephant skin, and that skin, that cortex, and its relationship to the elephant's soul is the major subject of the poem. That skin is made gray by the "sediment of the river which / encrusts my joints," but the creature is quite comfortable living in skin that is "fibred over like the shell of / the cocoanut." Both skin and sediment provide protection, an armor. The skin is also described as a "piece of black glass through which no light / can filter." One cannot see inside it, but at the same time, nothing from outside can penetrate it; it cannot learn from the experience of others. And whatever is inside cannot see out, at least not through the armor of the skin. The hide also serves as a record of the animal's existence because it is

> . . . cut
> into checkers by rut
> upon rut of unpreventable experience.

In fact, the very ruts have become a manual—at least for the peanut-tongued and hairy toed. Others of its species have learned to read the effects its life's experience have had upon it.

But the concrete externals about the animal, so meticulously described by the poet, suddenly recede in stanza 7 when the elephant begins to speak of abstract realities: power, the soul, the unity of life and death. Actually several phrases from earlier stanzas have alerted the reader to the fact that the writer is dealing with more than elephants:

> . . . the blemishes stand up and shout
> when the object

in view was a
renaissance.

Note also "the / patina of circumstance" and "unpreventable experience."

The elephant, fretful over life's enigmas in spite of the strong statement of self-assurance at the poem's beginning, continues to assuage its
own doubts. "What / is powerful and what is not?" it asks. After all, the
elephant is the largest animal in the jungle—and its

> . . . soul shall never
> be cut into
> by a wooden spear.

If its tough body, its external skin, should ever prove vulnerable, its
spirit is infinitely tougher because it is immortal. But the dialectic is not
that easily resolved. What is the relationship between one's body—one's
"armor," as it were—and one's spirit?

John Slatin makes an important contribution to any consideration of
this poem when he connects the crux of this argument with a similar
argument broached by Henry James in *The Portrait of a Lady*. Knowing
Moore's deep familiarity with James's work, the argument is surely connected to "Black Earth," whether Moore is making that connection consciously or unconsciously.[18] The sophisticated Madame Merle has one
view of the world, and her protégée, Isabel Archer, quite another.
Madame Merle suggests that

> when you've lived as long as I you'll see that every human being
> has its shell and that you must take the shell into account. By
> the shell I mean the whole envelope of circumstances. There's no
> such thing as an isolated man or woman; we're each of us made
> up of some cluster of appurtenances. What shall we call our
> "self"? Where does it begin? Where does it end? It overflows
> into everything that belongs to us—and then it flows back again.
> I know a large part of myself is in the clothes I choose to wear.
> I've a great respect for *things*! One's self—for other people—is
> one's expression of oneself; and one's house, one's furniture, one's
> garments, the books one reads, the company one keeps—these
> things are all expressive.

But the young and idealistic Isabel cannot agree. "I think just the other way," she responds. "I don't know whether I succeed in expressing myself, but I know that nothing else expresses me. Nothing that belongs to me is any measure of me; everything's on the contrary a limit, a barrier, and a perfectly arbitrary one."[19]

Close to the mind of Isabel Archer is the initial statement in "Black Earth" of complete independence.

> . . . I do these
> things which I do, which please
> no one but myself.

(Isabel defends her choice of a husband by saying, "Whatever I do, I do with reason.")[20] But like Madame Merle, the elephant also understands that he or she inhabits a skin "fibered over like the shell of / the cocoanut" and that

> . . . the unity of
> life and death has been expressed by the circumference
> described by my
> trunk.

As Slatin suggests, the two positions, "far from being mutually exclusive, shade constantly into one another, overflowing and then flowing back again."[21] An equilibrium, a poise between what is body and what is spirit, what is armor and what is not, is a fragile thing to achieve. One is fooling oneself to think otherwise.

The elephant undertakes a discussion of poise.

> . . . External poise, it
> has its centre
> well nurtured—we know
>   where—in pride, but spiritual poise, it has its centre where?

This question is essential to the poem and is the source of great uneasiness for the speaker; "I am on my guard," the elephant declares. Interestingly, that is also the place in the poem where Moore's formal structure loses its poise. Stanzas 1–8 are consistent in their rhyme scheme of *a a b c* and syllabic pattern of 4, 6, 13, 13. But at stanza 9, the one which contains the discussion of external versus spiritual poise, the rhyme scheme fails; "centre" does not rhyme with "know." The exact syllabic pattern also fails, beginning at stanza 8, where the discussion of poise is initiated. The pattern becomes erratic: 4, 6, 14, 12; in stanza 9 it is 4, 5, 15, 11, and then in stanza 10 we have 4, 6, 13, 12; finally in stanza 11, the pattern is 5, 6, 13, 14. A resolution is made in stanza 12, and the poem regains its poise for the final five stanzas. Knowing Moore's precision, one can safely assume that she is deliberately disrupting the poise of the poetic form to reflect the disruption in the poem's argument and, more to the point, in the elephant's self-assurance.

In a chapter entitled "The Forms of Resistance," Slatin envisions the elephant of this poem as "fretful, self-aggrandizing, and so vastly proud of the figure it cuts."[22] It may indeed not be far from Moore's own image of herself as a poet in her 1915 poem involving another elephant, "Diligence Is to Magic As Progress Is to Flight." In that poem Moore argued for the necessity of developing a thick skin, one that could "endure blows" from the "scarecrows of aesthetic procedure," critics that sought to destroy new work by belittling it. In "Diligence," Moore pictured herself as having chosen to "travel laboriously." She "clambered up" the cumbersome elephant which would serve as her magic carpet, the vehicle for her own artistic journey.

In "Black Earth," she has placed herself inside the elephant skin, where the elephant becomes her persona. It becomes a tragicomic mask through which she can both laugh and cry at elements of her own and, I would suggest, every sensitive person's image of himself or herself. She is "black / but beautiful," "peanut-tongued," and "hairy toed." But she also boasts of power.

> . . . I do these
> things which I do, which please
> no one but myself.

She also wonders "what / is powerful and what is not?" The thick skin, her armor—"a cortex merely"—does protect from "darts [that] cannot strike decisively the first / time," but is that kind of power really all the elephant needs? (When Moore identifies with the elephant, she also assumes an identity with the reader. The reader joins the persona as Moore's sensitive fellow traveler, included in the perception.) She has tried to be successful in making herself impervious both to criticism and to the influence of other writers, but is that the best course of action? Is

that honesty? Her equilibrium, her poise and pride, are at least tem-
porarily shaken. Perhaps the true source of spiritual poise, the poem
implies, is the opposite of pride: humility.

And in spite of her thick skin, there are parts of her that are still
sensititve to things outside herself. "My ears are sensitized to more than
the sound of / the wind." Also, the elephant skin is cut "into checkers
by rut / upon rut of unpreventable experience." Even within the armor of
the elephant skin, the speaker is not totally impervious to experience
beyond her own, and that experience disturbs the poise so carefully
centered in pride and signaled by the consciously crafted forms of the
early part of the poem. Unlike the "wandlike body" of one that was made
"to see and not to see; to hear and not to hear," this elephant does see
and does hear that "strange pressure of the atmosphere." It might be
"accustomed to shout / its own thoughts to itself, like a shell," but it is
becoming increasingly obvious that that is not entirely desirable.

> The I of each is to
> the I of each,
> a kind of fretful speech
>   which sets a limit on itself.

What is an elephant? the poet asks. "Black earth preceded by a tendril?" The term "tendril" is effectively used here, for it suggests new
growth, a seedling, a progression out of the "black earth" that has been
its home. In one sense, the black earth is the cortex, the enclosure, a
blemished object encrusted by the sediment (again "black earth") of the
river which will grant life to its oddity, its "occipital horn," the tendril of
a trunk, the first tentative and hopeful reaching toward a new maturity. In
another sense the skin forms a case for the spirit, the "phenomenon,"
something "translucent like the atmosphere." Must matter exist for spirit
to be known, or does spirit inform matter? Which is it that

> has looked at the electricity and at the earth-
> quake and is still
> here?

The answer to the poem's rhetorical question is probably both, for one cannot be complete without the other. And perhaps most important, is it possible for skin, obscurity, armoring to be too thick so that one cannot see the spirit, the "beautiful element of unreason under it"? The questions are rhetorical, but they are important considerations for any "elephant." (Once again, if one is hungry for answers rather than hungry for ways of thinking about problems, one will be disappointed.) Moore's use of the term "unreason" here harkens back to Bergson and the theory that the highest level of human understanding is not logic but intuition, beautiful unreason, the language of the soul and, one would assume, the ultimate goal of poetry.

So this poem ends with the hope that the sensitive reader and critic will not let "depth be depth" (i.e., profundity to be obscurity) or "thick skin be thick" (armor to get in the way); the person must remain sensitive enough to intuit "the beautiful element of unreason" under it. But the reverse is also true; the poet must let neither profundity nor armor get in the way of learning the truth or of the poet's expression of it. So one must beware of one's armor because it can be harmful and limiting. It *is* the skin one inhabits, however; it is a part of one's persona; one must learn to know it well, both from the inside and from the outside. The physical and the spiritual are an integral combination.

We find here, then, a different view of armoring than that expressed by the very young poet in "Diligence Is to Magic As Progress Is to Flight" or in "Roses Only." Like Isabel Archer and the elephant, she still has confidence in her own ideas and her own forms, which "please no one but myself." But with maturity has come new insight about her own armor, insight not unlike that expressed by Madame Merle in James's *Portrait of a Lady*. One must come to deal with the relationship between one's spirit and its armorial coat.

One of Moore's poems about armoring, "The Pangolin," may well be one of the most important poems of the twentieth century, but it is, unfortunately, more often praised than read. It is a difficult poem, but one well worth the reader's time and concentration. Moore first heard about pangolins in 1927, when she wrote to her brother, then on tour with the navy: "I want you to tell me if you see a pangolin. It looks like an artichoke, has a tail about a foot long and lives on ants (is in fact an armoured ant-eater)."[23] Some nine years later she published a poem named for this unusual animal.

The Pangolin

Another armored animal—scale
    lapping scale with spruce-cone regularity until they
form the uninterrupted central
    tail row! This near artichoke with head and legs and grit-
                    equipped gizzard,
    the night miniature artist engineer is,
        yes, Leonardo da Vinci's replica—
            impressive animal and toiler of whom we seldom hear.
    Armor seems extra. But for him,
        the closing ear-ridge—
            or bare ear lacking even this small
            eminence and similarly safe

contracting nose and eye apertures
    impenetrably closable, are not;—a true ant-eater,
not cockroach-eater, who endures
    exhausting solitary trips through unfamiliar ground at night,
    returning before sunrise; stepping in the moonlight,
        on the moonlight peculiarly, that the outside
            edges of his hands may bear the weight and save the
                              claws

    for digging. Serpentined about
        the tree, he draws
            away from danger unpugnaciously,
            with no sound but a harmless hiss; keeping

the fragile grace of the Thomas-
    of-Leighton Buzzard Westminster Abbey wrought-iron vine,
                                     or

rolls himself into a ball that has
    power to defy all effort to unroll it; strongly intailed, neat
    head for core, on neck not breaking off, with curled-in-feet.
        Nevertheless he has sting-proof scales; and nest
            of rocks closed with earth from inside, which he can
                            thus darken.
        Sun and moon and day and night and man and beast
            each with a splendor
                which man in all his vileness cannot
                set aside; each with an excellence!

"Fearful yet to be feared," the armored
    ant-eater met by the driver-ant does not turn back, but
engulfs what he can, the flattened sword-
    edged leafpoints on the tail and artichoke set leg- and body-
                              plates
    quivering violently when it retaliates
        and swarms on him. Compact like the furled fringed frill
           on the hat-brim of Gargallo's hollow iron head of a
        matador, he will drop and will
           then walk away
              unhurt, although if unintruded on,
              he cautiously works down the tree, helped

by his tail. The giant-pangolin-
    tail, graceful tool, as prop or hand or broom or ax, tipped
                                   like
an elephant's trunk with special skin,
    is not lost on this ant- and stone-swallowing uninjurable
    artichoke which simpletons thought a living fable
        whom the stones had nourished, whereas ants had done
          so. Pangolins are not aggressive animals; between
        dusk and day they have not the unchain-like machine-
                                  like
        form and frictionless creep of a thing
        made graceful by adversities, con-

versities. To explain grace requires
    a curious hand. If that which is at all were not forever,
why would those who graced the spires
    with animals and gathered there to rest, on cold luxurious
    low stone seats—a monk and monk and monk—between the
                                 thus
        ingenious roof-supports, have slaved to confuse
          grace with a kindly manner, time in which to pay a
                               debt,
        the cure for sins, a graceful use
          of what are yet
             approved stone mullions branching out across
             the perpendiculars? A sailboat

was the first machine. Pangolins, made
    for moving quietly also, are models of exactness,

on four legs; on hind feet plantigrade,
  with certain postures of a man. Beneath sun and moon, man
                                              slaving
  to make his life more sweet, leaves half the flowers worth
                                              having,
      needing to choose wisely how to use his strength;
        a paper-maker like the wasp; a tractor of foodstuffs,
      like the ant; spidering a length
      of web from bluffs
          above a stream; in fighting, mechanicked
          like the pangolin; capsizing in

disheartenment. Bedizened or stark
    naked, man, the self, the being we call human, writing-
master to this world, griffons a dark
  "Like does not like like that is obnoxious"; and writes error
                                              with four
  r's. Among animals, *one* has a sense of humor.
      Humor saves a few steps, it saves years. Unignorant,
        modest and unemotional, and all emotion,
      he has everlasting vigor,
        power to grow,
            though there are few creatures who can make one
            breathe faster and make one erecter.

Not afraid of anything is he,
    and then goes cowering forth, tread paced to meet an
                                              obstacle
at every step. Consistent with the
    formula—warm blood, no gills, two pairs of hands and a few
                                              hairs—that
  is a mammal; there he sits in his own habitat,
      serge-clad, strong-shod. The prey of fear, he, always
        curtailed, extinguished, thwarted by the dusk, work
                                              partly done,
      says to the alternating blaze,
        "Again the sun!
          anew each day; and new and new and new,
          that comes into and steadies my soul."

  Everything about "The Pangolin" is complicated. Many critics pass it
off as interesting but too lengthy and disjointed for explication, prolong-

ing the misconception that it is merely a collection of clever, but only vaguely related, parts. Its title creates in some critics the notion that it is merely a poem which celebrates one of nature's rare animals, a poem precisely crafted in its detailed description of a natural oddity, but not really of much value beyond that. Few venture toward interpretation. Careful reading finds two distinct parts of the poem: one about the pangolin, the other about "another armored animal"—human beings and their relationship to something larger. The challenge is in discovering the connection between the two parts.

This poem about armoring was written in 1936, a transitional time in Moore's career. She had completed her editorship of the *Dial* in 1929 and had returned to her own work. *Selected Poems*, published in 1935, had brought Moore's poetry to the attention of a public larger than the literary circle that had all along admired her work. She was awarded the Ernest Hartsock Memorial Prize for *Selected Poems* in 1935. At long last she had begun to receive real literary recognition. Donald Hall feels that *The Pangolin and Other Verse* marked another change as well. He writes that the work

> gives evidence of a return to the outside world. . . . War and threats of war were unavoidably foremost in the minds of everyone in the years between 1935 and 1941. Man lived in a dangerous world. The emotional threats, the metaphysical dangers that haunted Miss Moore's earlier poems are now objectified in the reality of a world on the edge of war. . . . The armoring recommended in the poems of the forties is no longer a withdrawal into an inexplicit and rather aristocratic reticence. It is instead an inward armoring of self which includes the courage to participate actively in the affairs of man.[24]

Margaret Holley lists "The Pangolin" among Moore's "Animiles," a word Moore herself coined in a letter to T. S. Eliot about the order of poems in the publication of her *Selected Poems*. She writes, "Your congregation of animiles at the front is wily in the extreme."[25] The word means literally "pertaining to animals" but probably suggests the larger notion of a form of affinity, as in "Anglophile," because the poems were not all about animals.[26] One finds oneself playing with the word "similes" as well, poems of related subjects. (The "Animiles" include "The Steeple-Jack," "No Swan So Fine," "The Jerboa," "The Plumet Basilisk," "Camellia Sabina," "The Frigate Pelican," "Bird-Witted," and others.)

Technically "The Pangolin" is a wonder of architectural construction. Composed of nine stanzas of eleven lines each (with one notable exception; stanza 5 has only ten lines), each stanza operates with a predictable, although not identical, syllable count, as follows:

Line	Syllables	Line	Syllables
1	8–9	7	13–15
2	14–16	8	8–13
3	7–9	9	4–5
4	16–17	10	9–10
5	12–13	11	9–10
6	11–13		

The rhyme scheme is *a b a c c d e d f g*, although the rhyme is often more approximate than exact, somewhat akin to the harmonics of a stringed instrument (e.g., "scale/central," "gizzard/engineer is," "Thomas-/has," "nest/beast," "body-plates/retaliates," "pangolin/special skin"). And Moore's architectural forms do not impose themselves arbitrarily upon word structure and sentence structure. They are part of the very texture of the poem's meaning. As a matter of fact, neither the syllabic rhythm nor the rhyme is at all obvious to the reader. Even one sensitive to prosody must make an effort to hear it. The effect is gentle and unobtrusive, almost like background music, but its progress signals the feelings of the poem very much like the score of an opera or of a motion picture. The hypnotic rhythm is carefully orchestrated by the poet, an expertise long in Moore's repertoire.

In "Feeling and Precision" she echoed Bergson's theory of the poet's ability to "put to sleep the active or rather resistant powers of our personality, and thus bring us into a state of perfect responsiveness"[27] when she spoke of the poet's control of sound and rhythm operating as a kind of hypnosis. Moore wrote of her predilection for original rhythmic devices in a 1944 essay.

> My own fondess for the unaccented rhyme derives, I think, from an instinctive effort to insure naturalness. . . . One notices the wholesomeness of the uncapitalized beginnings of lines, and the gusto of invention, with climax proceeding out of climax, which is the mark of feeling.
>
> We call climax a device, but is it not the natural result of strong feeling? It is, moreover, a pyramid that can rest either on

its point or on its base. . . . Intentional anticlimax as a
department of surprise is a subject by itself; indeed, an art,
"bearing," as Longinus says, "the stamp of vehement emotion
like a ship before a veering wind," both as content and as sound;
but especially as sound, in the use of which the poet becomes a
kind of hypnotist—recalling Kenneth Burke's statement that "the
hypnotist has a way out and a way in."[28]

So from Moore's perspective, what at first might seem only prose cast
on the page in an imposed and artificial verse form is actually intricately
constructed and controlled verse made to read as natural speech ("when
I am as complete as I like to be, I seem unable to get an effect plain
enough")[29] Moore speaks of climax proceeding out of climax and intentional anticlimax, all blowing the reader along like a ship before a veering wind, and that is exactly what the formal rhythms of the poem
accomplish.

For example, as Elizabeth Bradburn points out in her brilliant essay
"The Machinery of Grace," the poem proceeds "climax out of climax,
rising and falling in tension as it moves forward. Furthermore, the rhyme
is not only concealed, but itself a form of climax."[30] The first climax
occurs at line 4 with the signal of an exclamation point at "tail row!"
Then it subsides into a more natural rhythm until it begins to rise again,
signaled by a series of strong monosyllables connected by a series of
repeated conjunctions, a form Moore uses several times in the poem to
punctuate the rhythm.

> with head and legs and grit-equipped gizzard (line 4)
> Sun and moon and day and night and man and beast (line 30)
> as prop or hand or broom or ax (line 46)
> a monk and monk and monk (line 59)
> warm blood, no gills, two pairs of hands and a few hairs (line 91)
> anew day day; and new and new and new (line 97)

There is also a rhythmic climax matching meaning in stanza 8.

> . . . Unignorant,
>   modest and unemotional, and all emotion,
> he has everlasting vigor,
>   power to grow,
>   though there are few creatures who can make one
>   breathe faster and make one erecter.

The rhythmic peak at "power to grow" shows that the lines themselves have power to grow and that these human creatures stimulate the poet, making her breathe faster and become more erect, that is, experience poetic growth and insight.[31]

The most important climactic moment in the poem is carefully prepared for in the poem's form. It is stanza 5, which has only ten lines, compared with eleven in all others. There is also a change in the rhyme scheme. A *d* rhyme closes the rhyme scheme, which until now has been left open. Breaking the rhythm and changing the rhyme scheme effectively breaks the pace and prepares the reader for the internal climax of the entire poem, the rhetorical question of lines 56–65, which begins: "If that which is at all were not forever." As Bradburn points out, that important question is poised between two shorter statements: "To explain grace requires / a curious hand" (lines 55–56) and "A sailboat / was the first machine" (lines 65–66). Bradburn calls the scheme of alternation in stanza 5 a "coiled spring" which triggers the theme of the poem: the "sprawling energetic question about grace."[32] This is what Moore means by "interiorized climax." (I return to the theme itself elsewhere in this discussion.)

Stylistically, stanza melts into stanza as lines flow across the barriers of stanza endings in elaborate enjambment. One is particularly struck in the maverick stanza 5, the ten-line stanza, by the verse ending with the hyphenated "con-" followed by "versities" to begin stanza 6. The reader is forced to read with greater concentration, guided by the rhythms of the poetry itself. The reader's senses are driven by that kind of "pleasing, jerky progress" that Moore relished.

But, I would argue further, the technical complexities complement the meaning of the poem itself, "climax proceeding out of climax." One almost senses here Moore's deliberate refutation of Monroe's charge that her work showed little curve of growth or climax. And her declaration that climax is really "the natural result of strong feeling" may respond to Monroe's declaration that Moore had only a "heart of brass." One wonders too if two lines from "The Pangolin"—"Among animals, *one* has a sense of humor. / Humor saves a few steps, it saves years"—just might be, in a subtle way, a firm stand against Monroe's old charge of "grim and haughty humor."

In order to clarify further the connections between form and meaning, one must first look for Moore's intent in "The Pangolin." The opening lines already provide a link.

Another armored animal—scale
　　lapping scale with spruce-cone regularity until they
form the uninterrupted central
　　　tail row.

The poem itself has a similar kind of armor made of words, line lapping line with real regularity until the poem's center, stanza 5, the "uninterrupted central / tail row."

The first half of the poem is a precise description of the pangolin, a creature which Moore calls "another armored animal." Many readings of this poem have centered on that opening phrase. Is this merely another in Moore's series of poems about armored animals? Or does Moore see in the creature a likeness to herself, a woman who feels safest when she places herself "behind armor," in a self-effacing and self-protective way? The answer, I would argue, is neither. As Bradburn has suggested, an alternative reading might well be that Moore compares herself to the pangolin, "not as an emotionally armored woman, but as an artist"[33] as I have suggested earlier, Moore shared the role of artist with all sensitive human beings.

Moore has collected a great deal of exact information about pangolins. In the notes she directs her reader to two good sources: Robert T. Hatt's *Natural History*, (December 1935), and Lyddeker's *Royal Natural History*, although the poetic text alone is rich with detail. If one has never seen a picture of a pangolin, her visual comparison with an artichoke is of great assistance. For the first half of the poem, Moore offers both visual close-ups and distance shots, as we note everything from the "closing ear-ridge" to a pangolin's serpentine position around a tree. We can even watch the creature's movement in the mind's eye, as it carefully walks on

　　　. . . the outside
　　　　edges of his hands . . . and save[s] the claws
　　　for digging.

The pangolin is always armored, for it can roll "himself into a ball that has / power to defy all effort to unroll it." We watch the creature's precision, "stepping in the moonlight, / on the moonlight" to be even more exact. Everything the pangolin does outside its nest happens at night; it is a nocturnal creature, a "night miniature artist engineer," a clue to which the reader will want to return.

Moore is always searching for perfect—and refreshing—means of comparison. For example, she notes that pangolins look like spruce cones and artichokes, and that the "fragile grace of the Thomas- / of-Leighton Buzzard Westminster Abbey wrought-iron vine" she had seen in a 1922 visit to Westminster Abbey was similar to the pangolin's scales. Each represented a delicately wrought armor. She included another work of art in wrought iron—"Picador," by Pablo Gargallo (1928), on display at the Museum of Modern Art—and remembered the gallant attitude of the matador as he "walk[ed] away / unhurt."

The precision and detail of everything are vivid and memorable. We see, for example, that

> . . . the flattened sword-
>   edged leafpoints on the tail and artichoke set leg- and body-
>   plates
>   quivering violently when it retaliates.

One even hears a "harmless hiss" as the pangolin draws away from danger. Like the visual artist, Moore offers exact details, what A. Kingsley Weatherhead describes as feeling expressed by concrete images.[34] Hugh Kenner's assessment of Moore's descriptive technique as "experience of the eye" is also generally correct.

> In her poems, things utter puns to the senses. These, registered
> in words, make odd corrugations on the linguistic surface. . . .
> This policy of accurate comparison . . . does not worry about
> congruousness, much as Braque did not worry about perspective,
> being intent on a different way of filling its elected spaces.
> Congruity, like perspective, deals in proportion with an overall
> view. Miss Moore's poems deal in many separate acts of attention
> all close up; optical puns, seen by snapshot, in a poetic normally
> governed by the eye, sometimes by the ears and fingers,
> ultimately by the moral sense.[35]

But Kenner errs, I believe, in one particular: although Moore's poems do deal with many separate acts of attention, many of them very close up, there is an overall view, a congruity; the poem is not nearly as depersonalized as it may at first appear. The separate acts of attention are related to one another and are working toward a general impression active in the mind of the poet.

In *The Edge of the Image*, A. Kingsley Weatherhead is one of the few critics who understands that "strong emotion is unquestionably present in [Moore's] poems," but he feels that the imagery is not a correlative for it in the sense of T. S. Eliot's objective correlative.[36] That is to suggest that the imagery, as Monroe had suggested about the form, is somehow outside of Moore's intent, existing of and for itself. Nothing could be further from the truth.

Both the imagery and the separate acts of attention contribute to the theme that Moore has so carefully pointed out with her formal devices: "To explain grace requires / a curious hand" and "If that which is at all were not forever." Recalling that with Moore words often operate in a kaleidoscope of meanings, one must begin to amplify both "grace" and "curious." Curious can mean odd, but it can also mean inquisitive. An archaic meaning, but one Moore surely would have intended is "made or prepared skillfully, done with painstaking accuracy or attention to detail." It is in all of these senses that Moore sends out her filaments of thought. "To explain grace requires a curious hand," whether one is describing the grace of a peculiar armored animal, a pangolin, or grace in its many meanings, several of which Moore includes later in the poem. The writer who would take the time to describe the grace of anything must be inquisitive, attentive to detail, and maybe even a little odd. ("Humor saves a few steps, it saves years.") The one who would create the "machinery"—the words, the rhythms, and the forms to describe grace—must have "a curious hand." Like the pangolin, that one must be an "artist engineer . . . Leonardo Da Vinci's replica," that "impressive animal and toiler of whom we seldom hear." (The nocturnal pangolin is a "night miniature artist engineer.") The pangolin and the man are Leonardo Da Vinci's replica not only in that they are both artists and engineers but also in that they are both described in precise detail, like Da Vinci's famous illustrations of the human body, an engineer's hand "explaining grace." Moore has done for the pangolin what Da Vinci did for the human being.[37] Thus Moore is clearly establishing threads of likeness and connection between the pangolin and the artist.

Actually, Moore is reaching even higher. She is trying to demonstrate the real likenesses and value of all creatures in a scheme far larger than the world of either pangolins or humans.

> Sun and moon and day and night and man and beast
> each with a splendor

which man in all his vileness cannot
set aside; each with an excellence!

This idea is an ancient concept of God's creation that has permeated
science and literature since the time of Plato: the Great Chain of Being.
The concept views all of creation from God to the lowest form of matter as
essentially good and as existing in a hierarchical and interconnected
system, with humankind occupying the middle rung. Nothing is vile,
although various human philosophical systems might have declared it so.
Thus whether one speaks of the sun and moon or man and beast, each
has a "splendor" and an "excellence" because it has come from God, the
Author of all that is good, all that is *grace-full.*
On the complex subject of grace, Moore asks a rhetorical question.

> . . . If that which is at all were not forever,
> why would those who graced the spires
> with animals and gathered there to rest, on cold luxurious
> low stone seats—a monk and monk and monk—

have slaved to pursue the many meanings of grace: a kindly manner, time
in which to pay a debt, the cure for sins, elegance, a graceful style of
architecture? What would be the use of knowing and describing what is
good and kind, efficient and beautiful if there were no ultimate good?
Moore raises us to the crest of a great climax with this question and
then surprises us with what might seem an illogical response: "A sailboat / was the first machine." "Pangolins," she adds,

> . . . made
> for moving quietly also, are models of exactness,
> on four legs; on hind feet plantigrade,
> with certain postures of a man.

The thought shifts suddenly from sailboats to pangolins to human beings,
who share a surprising number of traits with other creatures; the human
is:

> a paper-maker like the wasp; a tractor of foodstuffs,
> like the ant; spidering a length
> of web from bluffs

above a stream; in fighting, mechanicked
like the pangolin.

But humans do not usually like these kinds of comparisons. After all, they are superior beings, acting as the "writing- / master[s] to this world," even if they sometimes make silly mistakes like writing "error with four / r's." Moore's reminder of human frailty makes us laugh and brings back some realistic humility. Fortunately for humans, they do have risibility, a sense of humor about their own place in the universe—and "Humor saves a few steps, it saves years." Human beings are "unignorant / modest and unemotional, and all emotion." Most of all they have "everlasting vigor" and "power to grow"—potential, the possibility to be more than we already are; they have hope based on the faith that all there is, is forever.

Given the basic design, "warm blood, no gills, two pair of hands and a few hairs," the human sits "in his own habitat, / serge-clad, strongshod." (Note how Moore is establishing the same kind of objectivity about this armored animal that she has already exhibited toward the pangolin; but there is one vast difference: this creature has a mind and the gift of hope.) Although humans have enough intelligence to know fear and to become discouraged, they are also blessed in that they can say to the alternating blaze,

Again the sun!
anew each day; and new and new and new,
that comes into and steadies my soul.

The poem ends with a climax of grand proportions, a climax of hope bred of deep emotion, Harriet Monroe notwithstanding.

And the poem has also moved from darkness, the nocturnal world of the pangolin, "who endures / exhausting solitary trips through unfamiliar ground at night" and who lives in a "nest / of rocks closed with earth from inside," to a world wherein a human person greets the alternating blaze, "Again the sun!" If even pangolins are susceptible to happiness and theirs is a toil worked out in darkness, how much more is possible for humans, who are even closer to the Light.

But one must return for a moment to the odd line of response to the central rhetorical question about the possibility of eternity, "A sailboat / was the first machine." Taffy Martin points out that this "cryptic answer" seems to answer nothing at all.[38] But Martin's instincts about the importance of this line to the full meaning of the poem are correct. Moore uses the term "machine-like" earlier in the poem.

> . . . Pangolins are not aggressive animals; between
> dusk and day they have the not unchain-like machine-
> > like
> > > form and frictionless creep of a thing
> > > made graceful by adversities, con-
> versities.

(Recall too that she calls the pangolin an "artist engineer.") In Moore's value system, to be "machine-like" is a beautiful compliment, meaning well made, efficient, and graceful. Moore has a spiritual appreciation for that which is well engineered, like pangolins (designed by God) and sailboats (made by the first machine-makers) and meticulously crafted wrought-iron vines or even poetry (made by artist-engineers). The pangolin's "frictionless creep" foreshadows the graceful efficiency of the first machine, the sailboat, perhaps somewhat akin to what Longinus noted about "the stamp of vehement emotion [moved] like a ship before a veering wind."[39] Through the "machinery" of her poetry (which critics like Monroe had found so contrived), Moore has done a curious thing: she has described grace, that which is found in both pangolins and humans. She has also, in her gentle way, complimented the Author of all grace. The pangolin embodies many of the most important qualities of grace: quietness, compactness, orderliness, efficiency, exactness—the very qualities of Moore's own style of poetry, which she can "engineer"—by the grace of God.

In "The Pangolin" Moore has thus moved well beyond the examination of armor she had made in "Black Earth." She has made forays outside the elephant skin (although she connects with it in lines 45–47):

> . . . The giant-pangolin-
> > tail, graceful tool, as prop or hand or broom or ax, tipped
> > > like
> > an elephant's trunk with special skin.

She understands now that Madam Merle had a point, that "there's no such thing as an isolated man or woman; we're each of us made up of some cluster of appurtenances." "Armor [only] seems extra." And the poet's art *is* the poet's armor. According to Bradburn, "The poet obscures himself not as an effort to be objective, not out of personal morality with regard to the 'other,' but because to create at all is to build armor around oneself. This is not an erasure of self, but a kind of self-definition."[40] It is a projection, a feat of engineering; it is one's armorial coat. It is Pavlova's "Prima Ballerina Absoluta." The armor signals the presence, not the absence, of the self. In a manner of speaking, in making a piece of art, artists make themselves. But both the art and the act celebrate the grace that was given to complete the task.

There is no way one can deny Moore's deep faith in a power beyond herself. It is always there, from the very beginning. The articulation of that confidence, the power of that faith to signal order and reason over chaos, has always been difficult in the twentieth century. Unlike the faith-filled worlds of a Dante or a Milton, Moore lived in a world in which an intellectual had to proceed cautiously when talking about faith, but she did proceed. She did not see the world as a wasteland or vile or in need of ideas of order. As a good Presbyterian, she saw the entire universe as an expression of the kingdom of heaven in the world. And she saw sailboats and pangolins as part of that kingdom. Moore found the Deity's reflected beauty, order, and grace in everything, even in pangolins.

Moore again explored armoring in 1944 with "His Shield," a poem remarkable for its humor and for the undisguised use of the "I." She seems to delight in dealing with the very accusations of armoring she herself had received and to point in praise to "another armored animal" whom she had come to admire, Haile Selassie.

His Shield

The pin-swin or spine-swine
    (the edgehog miscalled hedgehog) with all his edges out,
  echidna and echinoderm in distressed-
pin-cushion thorn-fur coats, the spiny pig or porcupine,
    the rhino with horned snout—
everything is battle-dressed.

Pig-fur won't do, I'll wrap
    myself in salamander-skin like Presbyter John.
  A lizard in the midst of flames, a firebrand
that is life, asbestos-eyed asbestos-eared, with tattooed nap

and permanent pig on
the instep; he can withstand

fire and won't drown. In his
unconquerable country of unpompous gusto,
gold was so common none considered it; greed
and flattery were unknown. Though rubies large as tennis-
balls conjoined in streams so
that the mountain seemed to bleed,

the inextinguishable
salamander styled himself but presbyter. His shield
was his humility. In Carpasian
linen coat, flanked by his household lion-cubs and sable
retinue, he revealed
a formula safer than

an armorer's: the power of relinquishing
what one would keep; that is freedom. Become dinosaur-
skulled, quilled or salamander-wooled, more ironshod
and javelin-dressed than a hedgehog battalion of steel, but be
dull. Don't be envied or
armed with a measuring-rod.

There is little doubt that Moore enjoyed writing "His Shield." Her verbal acrobatics, what Kenner called her "optical puns," are a delight, particularly in stanza 1.[41] The very words bristle "with all [their] edges out." Moore had been collecting data about prickly animals for years. In the 1920s an echidna arrived at the Bronx Zoo from Australia. The spiny creature, which resembles a hedgehog, is called "porcupine-anteater" in Australia, according to an article Marianne Moore had clipped and saved from the *New York Times*. "The echidna . . . is one of the zoo-logical freaks that are found in that country. . . . Nellie is about seven-teen inches long . . . she looked very warlike when, on the approach of fancied danger, she dropped to the floor and rolled herself up like a hedgehog. The echidna has sharp spines. They are not only presented to the enemy but stuck in the ground, making it harder to lift the animal up."[42] The echinoderm, the spiny cucumber, and the rhino round out Moore's array of armored, "battle-dressed" characters. The optical pun of a "distressed- / pin-cushion thorn-fur coat" worn by this "spiny pig or porcupine" is a visual overstatement, an amusing exaggeration even for this poet, a longtime wearer of "body armor," or at least her critics have said so. But this kind of "pig-fur won't do." Instead, she will wrap herself "in salamander skin like Presbyter John."

Moore's interest in the legend of Presbyter John may have begun elsewhere but was certainly reaffirmed in a biography of Haile Selassie which Moore purchased in the 1930s. Moore marked several passages in the book, including the explanation that Presbyter John, "the King of All the Indies," became associated with Ethiopia through a historical error of long standing. She also marked passages describing the opulence of his court, including: "Do you ask why, though ruling in such magnificence, he styles himself only 'presbyter'? That is his humility."[43] Other passages described incredibly rich mines and a magic mountain out of which rivers of rubies flowed. This king "hunted not lions but dragons, protected from their breath by robes of salamander skin. In these he passed through fire to the amazement of all beholders."[44]

Presbyter John, an imaginary and benevolent ruler, shielded only by his humility and his salamander-skin coat, is in Moore's poem, "flanked by household lion cubs," like the real king of Ethiopia, Haile Selassie. At the time of the poem's conception, Haile Selassie had already regained power in Ethiopia during the ravages of World War II. On 20 January 1941, he returned to his country and reinstated his policy of operating under a written constitution and insisting that his people share in his power ("relinquishing / what one would keep"). Under his title "Conquering Lion of Judah," this diminutive emperor kept a dozen lions at his palace as symbols of his title and of his power ("flanked by household lion-cubs"). Moore seems always to have admired this young emperor's priorities: education, communication, and employment for all Ethiopians. She honored him in 1959 in yet another poem, "Leonardo Da Vinci's."[45]

So, Moore has at least four interrelated perceptions operating at once in this kaleidoscope: (1) a menagerie of rare armored animals, all naturally "battle-dressed"; (2) the legend of Presbyter John, who "armored" himself in his salamander skin and his humility; (3) Haile Selassie, who regained his power and promptly reinstituted his policy of sharing the government with the people; and (4) some words of advice for anyone who might have the "courage of his peculiarities."

She reminds the reader first that "everything is battle-dressed"; it is merely a matter of the nature of the armor. The "I" of the poem has chosen salamander skin, like Presbyter John, because it can withstand even the breath of fire-breathing dragons—and there are always fire-breathing dragons to contend with. And this legendary king "styled himself but presbyter. His shield / was his humility." Moore is perhaps smiling at herself in this poem because she has done exactly that and enclosed herself in all kinds of skins: elephant's, pangolin's, salamander's—maybe even one day in dragon skin, as she expressed in another poem.

O to Be a Dragon
If I, like Solomon, . . .
could have my wish—

my wish . . . O to be a dragon,
a symbol of the power of Heaven—of silkworm
size or immense; at times invisible.
Felicitous phenomenon!

Moore was, after all, born at the manse of the First Presbyterian Church on 15 November 1887, and she remained a lifelong Presbyterian. And she too tried to live in an "unconquerable country of unpompous gusto" in which "greed / and flattery were unknown." The stories of Moore's generosity in spite of her simple means are legend. T. S. Eliot requested and paid for an article by Moore which was never published. The remuneration was small, but when it became obvious to Moore that the article was not going to be used, she returned the payment. On 20 September 1935, T. S. Eliot wrote to Moore: "You are one of the strangest children I have ever had anything to do with. . . . I am almost speechless at meeting with such absence of avarice in any human being."[46] Although others deserted Ezra Pound after his incarceration at St. Elizabeth's, Moore did not. In a letter dated 31 July 1946 she wrote:

> Dear Ezra:
> Some months ago I wrote to you to say what goes without saying—that misfortune does not alter friendship. The money enclosed I hoped might procure something you might like to read, or eat, or wear.[47]

William Wasserstrom remembers meeting Moore at Schrafft's in 1958 and finding that she had arranged every detail of their luncheon with grace and concern, even to the point of telling him that "false vanity was not seemly, hence [he] must not quarrel with her for the bill."[48] Hugh Kenner remembers his own embarrassment, when the great lot of them shared a New York taxi, to discover that Marianne had already arranged to pay the fare.[49] As Randall Jarrell has pointed out, "Her Shield" was her humility. For she, like Haile Selassie, sought real freedom: "the power of relinquishing / what one would keep."

Life only offers two choices: one can become "dinosaur-skulled" and dull (the dinosaur skull and brain are proportionately smaller to the body than that of any other creature) or be prepared to don one's armor: "quilled or salamander-wooled, more ironshod / and javelin-dressed than a hedgehog batallion of steel." To risk excellence is to invite envy and to expect criticism; therefore, be "armed with a measuring-rod." Life does not come any other way. If one is unwilling to establish some kind of armor and proceed, the only other choice is to be dull.

Moore says it beautifully at the end of her essay "Humility, Concentration, and Gusto." "To summarize: Humility is an indispensable ally, enabling concentration to heighten gusto. There are always objecters, but we must not be sensitive about not being liked or not being printed. David Low, the cartoonist, when carped at, said, 'Ah, well—' But he has never compromised; he goes right on doing what idiosyncrasy tells him to do. The thing is to see the vision and not deny it; to care and admit that we do."[50] One must wear his or her own peculiar shield— must care about one's idiosyncrasies—"and admit we do."

On 25 February 1950, Moore published "Armor's Undermining Modesty" in the *Nation*. Although this would not be her final word on armoring, it was her last major and synthesizing exploration of the subject. Written from the perspective of maturity (Moore was sixty-two) and the perspective of success, this poem marked yet another in Moore's changing views about self-protection, but one which, surprisingly, harkens back to a perception about armor from her own youth. In many ways it is the most subtle and "unarmored" view of all.

Armor's Undermining Modesty

At first I thought a pest
Must have alighted on my wrist.
It was a moth almost an owl,
Its wings were furred so well,

with backgammon-board wedges interlacing
on the wing—

    like cloth of gold in a pattern
    of scales with a hair-seal Persian
    sheen. Once, self-determination
    made an ax of a stone
and hacked things out with hairy paws. The consequence—our
                           mis-set
alphabet.

    Arise, for it is day.
    Even gifted scholars lose their way
    through faulty etymology.
    No wonder we hate poetry,
and stars and harps and the new moon. If tributes cannot
be implicit,

    give me diatribes and the fragrance of iodine,
    the cork oak acorn grown in Spain;
    the pale-ale-eyed impersonal look
    which the sales-placard gives the bock beer buck.
What is more precise than precision? Illusion.
Knights we've known,

    like those familiar
    now unfamiliar knights who sought the Grail, were
    ducs in old Roman fashion
    without the addition
of wreaths and silver rods, and armor gilded
or inlaid.

    They did not let self bar
    their usefulness to others who were
    different. Though Mars is excessive
    in being preventive,
heroes need not write an ordinall of attributes to enumerate
what they hate.

    I should, I confess,
    like to have a talk with one of them about excess,
    and armor's undermining modesty

instead of innocent depravity.
A mirror-of-steel uninsistence should countenance
continence,

objectified and not by chance,
there in its frame of circumstance
of innocence and altitude
in an unhackneyed solitude.
There is the tarnish; and there, the imperishable wish.

Most critics seem confused by this poem, some arguing that it is a war poem, maybe even an antiwar poem, while others sense that it has something to do with art and the creation of poetry. Moore herself addressed the issue indirectly during a radio broadcast in 1951, when she remarked:

> Books, conversation, a remark, objects, circumstances,
> sometimes make an indelible impression on one, and a few
> words which occurred to one at the time the impression was
> made, remain associated with the original impression and suggest
> other words. Then, upon scrutiny, these words seem to have
> distorted the concept, so the effort to effect a record of what
> seemed valuable—say a testimony to the impression made, is
> abandoned perhaps, but remains dormant. Then perhaps the
> original impression reasserts itself with added associative detail
> and results in a suitable development. For instance, you see a
> suit of armor. The moveability suggests a wearer—there is life
> under the mechanism; you are reminded of an armadillo, say, or
> a crayfish, and recall the beauty of the ancient testudo, the
> shield laid on the shield of the Romans. Then perhaps the idea
> of conflict counteracts that of romance. Presently you see a live
> iguana and are startled by the paradox of its docility in
> connection with its horrific aspect. The idea of beauty outweighs
> the thought of painful self-protectiveness, and you have a
> developing theme.[51]

Moore's description of the inspirational process she used in producing a poem on the theme of how "beauty outweighs the thought of painful self-protectiveness" certainly parallels many of the ideas of "Armor's Undermining Modesty," written one year earlier. I find it even more amazing that many of the actual images used in the poem were already established, exactly as Moore described in the radio broadcast, in a vivid experience she had years before during her first European tour and recorded in a letter to her brother from Oxford, England, dated 5 July 1911.

> Dear Weaz,
> Oxford for fat rich olfactory impressions. I have never seen such a place. Its [*sic*] a Persian garden of modern student life. Everything we have seen is a rush of light in comparison . . . the peacocks make your hair stand on end. One spread his tail and tottered about a little before us, every feather perfect and the green on his neck enough to make you faint. And the portraits and statuary and the collection of arms in the house are very fine. I shan't be satisfied now till we have an armoury (if we have to sack Abbotsford to fit it out). The Roman swords were the only ones Ive [*sic*] seen and the chain mail was particularly fine. We had splendid coaching from Warwick to Kenilworth and also to Stratford. The private estates are beautiful. The Lucy estate was an eye opened. Millions of bunnies, playing around holes in the roots of trees and deer, brown and red, the descendents of the ones the Shakespeares poached.[52]

The essential connections are all in place. Evidently the experience had been so vivid for the impressionable young woman that the details remained interrelated and, in her own word, "dormant" until they became part of a poem published in 1950, precisely as Moore described the process in the radio broadcast interview in 1951.

On the basis of what Moore said in the interview, there need be no mystery about Moore's basic theme in "Armor's Undermining Modesty." It is "beauty outweighs the thought of painful self-protectiveness," and it is driven by the notion that "the idea of conflict counteracts that of romance," a notion simmering in Moore's consciousness for nearly forty years. One image from the European trip, that of the beautiful peacock from Oxford, was so vivid that it recurred again and again in Moore's poetry; it appeared in "The Steeple-Jack," "The Jerboa," "The Peacock of France," "Spenser's Ireland," and "People's Surroundings." In "Armor's Undermining Modesty," for reasons I will explore later, the peacock shrinks to moth-size. But it still echoes Moore's memory of a "Persian garden," for it looks

like cloth of gold in a pattern
of scales with a hair-seal Persian
sheen.

Having made the essential thematic and visual connection, one must
return to "Armor's Undermining Modesty" to watch what at first might
have seemed an odd kaleidoscope of images fall into their thematic
places, images expanded by nearly thirty-nine years of intervening experience. One senses in this poem perhaps more than in any other (with the
possible exception of "The Jerboa") glimpses of what Moore always
called her "gusto." Marianne Moore is having a wonderful time with this
poem and is, I would argue, operating almost without armor. She is daring to cast aside "her shield" and take a hard look at it. As she wrote in
"The Jerboa" (and like the jerboa itself), she dares to leap through time
and ideas "by fifths and sevenths," "like the uneven notes / of the Be-
douin flute," and to make "fern-seed / footprints with kangaroo speed."
One watches Moore's mind rushing with intuitive quickness that only the
most alert reader can follow. She is offering a glimpse of the problems
inherent in her own armoring—and everybody else's. The effect is exhilarating.

Donald Hall's instincts are sound when he writes: "The substance may
be feeling that cannot be reached directly. It may be perception best
expressed by indirection. . . . 'Armour's Undermining Modesty' grows
like a plant, one uncurling image at a time until it is all leafed out. The
images cohere to a central root, perhaps, but the root has been growing
underground, feeding the imagery without seeming to feed."[53] It is that
central root that Hall could not find, the one that had been so long been
"growing underground" in Moore's mind and feeding on imagery connected with the root memory of armor and Roman *ducs* and peacocks
preening.

The poem is replete with a wide array of changing images: a moth that
almost turns into an owl, Early Stone Age literary types hacking out the
first alphabet with hairy paws, stars, harps, moons, oak acorns, bock
beer advertisements, knights who search for the Holy Grail but are really
more like Roman *ducs*, and Mars, the god of war. The kaleidoscopic
images at first seem unrelated; and they do not remain static but seem to
change, from moths to owls and knights to *ducs* and mirror-of-steel armor
that reflects what it sees and at the same time camouflages its wearer.

That changeable quality of the imagery is an interesting technical motif in the poem as a whole.

This time the stanzas sound as though they follow an exact rhythmic count, but they do not. It is the rhyme scheme *a a b b c c* that drives the "carriage," while the rhythm is a thing of the ear, not of unyielding syllabic count. Moore teases us to attention by varying the first and last lines of various stanzas and then by incorporating the last two lines of the poem into one. (There is rhyme within the final line—"tarnish" and "wish"—but it occurs within the line, not between lines.) One sees the poem as patterned on the page, like the wings of the moth "with back-gammon-board wedges interlacing" and like the "cloth of gold in a pattern / of scales," but the patterns are not as regular as they appear. They flash in and out of focus just as the images themselves do. (Stanza 1, for example, has a syllabic pattern of 6, 8, 8, 6, 11, 3; the second stanza is 8, 8, 8, 6, 15, 3, while the third is 6, 8, 9, 8, 13, 4 and so on throughout the text.)

The poem opens very concretely when the speaker feels something on her wrist, probably a pest. But the pest turns out to be a moth of extraordinarily beautiful design, forming an intricate interlacing of wedges woven as beautifully as oriental cloth of gold. The moth is so magnificently designed, it seems to enlarge before the speaker's eyes, becoming "almost an owl." What does one do when one finds something beautiful, not in the usual sense—not as beautiful, say, as peacocks are—but something beautiful and important in its own right and deserving of one's attention and one's celebration nonetheless? The usual words and syntax will not work. Language is filled with limitations. As Moore puts it in the radio interview, "Upon scrutiny, [the] words seem to have distorted the concept, so the effort to effect a record of what seemed valuable . . . remains dormant." Perhaps the fault lies in our crude ancestors, who "hacked things out with hairy paws." All one has to work with is our "mis-set / alphabet." Even for the best writer words are rough-hewn commodities and always have been. And the situation is not much better in these enlightened times.

> Arise, for it is day.
> Even gifted scholars lose their way
> through faulty etymology.

The root meanings of words—words which must have started out closer to the reality they sought to represent—have become lost in hopeless intricacy and nuance and "armored" by "ordinalls of attributes." That is to say, they are submerged beneath the prescribed forms about what language, or more specifically, what poetry, should be. Poetry and poetic language have failed because they do not express the felt truth of intuition.[54]

The same poet who in 1919 wrote, "I, too, dislike it," in a poem called simply "Poetry," says again, "No wonder we hate poetry," and all the trite, cliché-ridden subjects with which it has become associated: "stars and harps and the new moon," and sometimes even peacocks. If one cannot get to the essence of the matter, what she calls in "Poetry" "the genuine," maybe one ought to reassess the efficacy of the entire process. After all, the quest is to "present / for inspection, imaginary gardens with real toads in them." The only thing that is more precise than precision is illusion—that is to say, the creation of those imaginary gardens, approaching intuitive truth by indirection. If one is not successful in expressing the genuine, one had better examine what might be getting in the way. Perhaps it is armor's undermining modesty.

As for Moore's own work, and in the work that she enjoys, she would rather have "diatribes and the fragrance of iodine" (the equivalent of ugly toads, one might suppose) than that which is artificial and "dragged into prominence by half poets."[55] Moore's reference to "the pale-ale-eyed impersonal look / which the sales-placard gives the bock beer buck" is another of her amusing "toads." The buck to which Moore refers is probably one of several "bock bucks" designed for beer cans and beer advertisements in the early fifties. Two excellent examples are Schaefer's Bock Beer and Ruppert Bock Beer, both featuring steely eyed buck rams. For the etymology of "bock" is merely "bukke" and the German *bock*. The two words represent the same male rite of spring, both driven by nature's magic change, one for bucks and another for beer. Both images place an exact "toad" in Moore's imaginary garden.[56]

But the subject is, after all, what gets in the way of valid communication, how "armor" of one kind or another ends up undermining modesty. As Moore says in the radio broadcast, "The idea of conflict counteracts that of romance." And in the poem, we are suddenly thrust into ultimate romance, the stories of knights in shining armor in quest of the Holy Grail:

> Knights we've known,
>> like those familiar
>> now unfamiliar knights who sought the Grail.

Our information about these knights, however, is really only romance, not reality. Real knights were far more like *ducs* in Roman fashion. The knights of our imagination, resplendent in shining armor, are far different from the real knights of the Grail stories. The "unfamiliar knights" wore the chain mail Moore had seen at England in 1911; they carried iron swords and fought shield laid on shield in the testudo formation. They did not have

> . . . the addition
>> of wreaths and silver rods, and armor gilded
>> or inlaid.

All of those "extras" about armor came later. The first knights, who were really more like *ducs*,

> . . . did not let self bar
>> their usefulness to others who were
>> different.

So, like early language, early knights may have been a bit rough-hewn, but they were real and not laden with layers of armor and decoration that got in the way of the job they were meant to do.

The persona of the poem would, she suggests, like to have a talk with these heroes (Moore often used the word "hero" to suggest the poet, but it would not be unreasonable to opt for "male poets" here), these "knights," about excess. How much armor is enough? "Mars is excessive / in being preventive." Mars, the god of war, certainly has gone to great lengths in the modes he has devised to protect against attack from his enemies. The Cold War may serve as a perfect example of that ironic reality, because, in order to protect itself from war, a country must nearly impoverish itself creating armor against attack—to the point where there is a delicate balance between what is being saved and how one is saving it. The armor becomes everything, "excessive / in being preventive," part of "armor's undermining modesty." The wearer of any kind of armor has to be careful; the armor may become so elaborate that one wearing it loses track of the reality it is meant to protect. Armor-wearers may well come to overestimate (or underestimate) themselves; they will lack true humility and modesty. They will lose track of the fact that "there is life under the mechanism." But then so will those who see them. Where does one draw the line with any kind of armor? Too much confuses the truth, the reality being protected. Use too little, however, and the creature is untenably vulnerable.

The same problem exists with poetry. The truth to be presented is sometimes so dazzling as to be blinding, and at the same time so fragile and vulnerable as to be easily destroyed. The only way to get at it is with a kind of armor, a "mirror-of-steel uninsistence" which reflects sufficiently to prevent dazzling and yet which protects sufficiently to keep the truth from crumbling. But the trick of accomplishing just that is never an easy one, unless one becomes the magician, operating with mirrors, the "mirror-of-steel uninsistence." Illusion is more precise than precision: too much, and "there is the tarnish," but at the same time, if the magic works, "there is the imperishable wish."

In this poem the last vestiges of armor as personal protection are cast aside. Moore speaks here largely of the work itself—which can never totally be separated from its creator. But one must not let armor undermine modesty, lest the goal she has stated in "O to Be a Dragon"—to be "a symbol of the power of heaven"—be lost. Whether one is silkworm size or immense—at times even invisible—one must not forget the reason for existence. (As she points out in "He 'Digesteth Harde Yron,'" "the power of the visible / is the invisible.") One is, after all, the spokesperson for the source of all grace, and for Moore, doing the job well is "the imperishable wish."

And that takes uninsistence, work that is precisely honed, work that is

> objectified and not by chance,
> there in its frame of circumstance
> of innocence and altitude
> in an unhackneyed solitude.

The artist is the pangolin again, the "night miniature artist engineer," the "toiler of whom we seldom hear," one for whom "armor seems extra but [is] not."

Alyse Gregory's words about Marianne Moore earlier in this chapter well summarize the dilemma of "armor's undermining modesty." She says Moore was a "combination of extreme fragility and vulnerability, com-

bined with firmness and fineness of texture and an intrepidity of spirit."
The magic is to produce a "mirror-of-steel" uninsistence that communi-
cates clarity without demeaning the truth; one must let let

> self bar
> . . . usefulness to others who [are]
> different.

One has the obligation to express beauty that is greater than even self-
preservation, and that is the essence of humility. So when a "pest" lights
on one's wrist and one discovers that it is something true and beautiful,
even if it is not a peacock, the obligation to be an artist-engineer super-
sedes the desire for self-protectiveness. One must never let one's armor
undermine one's modesty, for one must reflect the grace of God.

CHAPTER 6

Conjuries
That
Endure

Marianne Moore's *Selected Poems* appeared in April 1935, co-published in London by Faber & Faber and in New York by Macmillan. T. S. Eliot wrote the following introduction to this work, an assessment that marked a milestone in Moore's work.

We know very little about the value of the work of our contemporaries, almost as little as we know about our own. It may have merits which exist only for contemporary sensibility; it may have concealed virtues which will only become apparent with time. . . . The last thing, certainly, that we are likely to know about them is their "greatness", or their relative distinction or triviality in relation to the standard of "greatness". . . . But the *genuineness* of poetry is something which we have some warrant for believing that a small number, but only a small number, of contemporary readers can recognise. . . . And in asserting that what I call *genuineness* is a more important thing to recognise in a contemporary than *greatness*, I am distinguishing between his function while living and his function when dead. Living, the poet is carrying on that struggle for maintenance of a living language, for the maintenance of its strength, its subtlety, for the preservation of quality of feeling, which must be kept up in every generation; dead, he provides standards for those who take up the struggle after him. Miss Moore is, I believe, one of those few who have done the language some service in my lifetime.

This introduction was significant because it was strong praise from a respected contemporary, praise which gave Moore's work a second look in literary circles. But probably even more important was the fact that her personal joy in Eliot's carefully weighed evaluation gave her the courage to continue her work, as well as the satisfaction of finding a kindred spirit, one who really understood what she was about. Moore must have seen the introduction before its publication, because in a letter dated 23 October 1934, she wrote: "One could scarcely be human and not wish your *Introduction* might have the effect of a tidal wave, on the public, that it has had on me. The energy of thought that you bring to bear in behalf of this venture is the kind one summons in case of fire or flood, and is a generosity the most self-ministering could not hope or pray for.[1]

Not only did Eliot speak positively about her productions, but he understood them as perhaps no one had before. He had exerted what Moore called "energy of thought." When one looks back at Eliot's assessment in the introduction, one can appreciate his remarkable sensitivity as a critic. In the introduction he demonstrated that he understood the really important and original aspects of Moore's conjury. She was *geniune*; she had "saturated her mind in the perfections of *prose*"; she had a gift for *detailed observation*, for finding the exact words for some experience of the eye; she was certainly an *intellectual*; but for the sensitive reader, she always had intense, if restrained, *emotional value*. Eliot spoke of Moore's versification as "anything but 'free'" and spoke of *elegance* as one of her certain attributes. And perhaps most important of all, he was among the first to understand that the minute detail of her work was never an end in itself but always had "its service to perform for the whole."

Eliot's good opinion of Moore was of long standing. On 4 April 1921 he wrote: "I am writing to thank you for your review of my essays in *The Dial.* I have delayed writing to you since the 1917 'Others,' to tell you how much I admire your verse. It interests me, I think, more than that of anyone now writing in America. I wish you would make a book of it."[2] The opinion articulated in this letter never wavered. As Eliot wrote at the end of the introduction: "My conviction, for what it is worth, has remained unchanged for the last fourteen years: that Miss Moore's poems form part of the small body of durable poetry written in our time."[3]

By way of summarizing this study, I would like to offer support for Eliot's assessment that Moore's work is indeed part of the small body of durable poetry written in the twentieth century. I will do so in three ways: (1) by examining the judgments of her contemporaries; (2) by exploring the attitudes of more recent writers and critics, especially regarding the conscious and unconscious imitation of Moore by many poets today; and (3) by demonstrating Moore's expertise in the most convincing way of all: by a close examination of the poem I consider her masterpiece, "An Octopus." Like Eliot, then, I will look for the genuine, supporting the notion that "living, the poet is carrying on that struggle for the maintenance of a living language, for the maintenance of its strength, its subtlety, for the preservation of quality of feeling, which must be kept up in every generation." But I will argue further for Moore's greatness when as "dead, [s]he provides standards for those who take up the struggle after [her]." I will argue then, as Marianne Moore has done for Wallace Stevens, that her magic provided "conjuries that endure."

To be well received by one's contemporaries, especially those few whom one respects, is a particular gift. It makes one's "armor" fit more easily—and makes both personal growth and generosity to others possible. By 1920, Moore had begun to publish in the *Dial* and had come to know its editors, Scofield Thayer and James Sibley Watson. Their positive opinion of her work encouraged her to submit an ever-increasing number of poems for publication. And in the early twenties Richard Aldington proposed Moore's work to Harriet Monroe (then editor of *Poetry*) for an award, although she had not published in *Poetry* since 1915. Pound had mentioned Moore in a 1918 article in *Future* that was reprinted in *Instigations* in New York in 1920. Yvor Winters encouraged her to get together a book of her poems. And William Carlos Williams, impressed by her originality from the very first, introduced two of her poems in his new magazine, *Contact*, coedited by Robert McAlmon. It was two young women poets and friends, H.D. and Bryher, who published Moore's first collection of poems on 10 July 1921 without Moore's knowledge. (The project seems to have also been encouraged by Ezra Pound, who encouraged Harriet Shaw Weaver of the *Egoist* to publish a collection of Moore's rather than one of his.)[4] Publication was also encouraged by Robert McAlmon, then Bryher's husband, although publication costs were met entirely by Bryher.

It was at this point that Harriet Monroe's bitter "Symposium" on the poetry of Marianne Moore appeared in *Poetry*. Whatever her reasons, Monroe chose to present a critique of Moore with what were represented as a series of largely negative opinions voiced from many quarters. Some of the reviews, (that of Yvor Winters, for example) had been carefully edited. In the original letter from Winters to Monroe, he had used the phrase "a very great poet." That phrase never appeared in the *Poetry* symposium. In the margin of that letter, Monroe had written "Piffle." Other opinions, like that offered by Marion Strobel, an associate editor of *Poetry*, targeted Moore's obscurity: "because we are conscious that she has brains, that she is exceedingly well-informed, we are the more irritated that she has not learned to write simply." Monroe herself questions whether the author of "the geometrical verse-designs which frame these cryptic observations" is a poet.[5]

Such negative reviews of Moore's first book of poems might have been paralyzing, had it not been for support from other critics. McAlmon considered her poems "Picking and Choosing" and "Poetry" perfect expressions of the "modern movement." T. S. Eliot, in response to a request from Watson at the *Dial*, suggested that Moore already had imitators and that her work was "too good to be appreciated anywhere." Ezra Pound was corresponding with Moore by 1919 and had begun a long campaign to convince both Moore and William Carlos Williams to move to Europe. Although Moore always valued her European visits, she held in higher esteem what was "in the American grain." In a letter to Pound dated 10 May 1921, Moore wrote: "As for native material, I think we have it in Wallace Stevens, in Dr. Williams, and in E. E. Cummings as poets and, of course, we pride ourselves in H.D. Alfred Stieglitz in his published statements and early magazines is worth owning, and Scofield Thayer in his discernment and interplay of metaphor is very brilliant. . . . We pride ourselves also, on you and T. S. Eliot."[6] And one can only imagine Monroe's response when Pound wrote to her, nominating Moore for the Levinson Prize on the grounds that Moore's work was both American and modern. Meanwhile, Harold Latham of Macmillan suggested that Moore get together a manuscript for publication.[7]

By 1924, several of Moore's poems had already appeared in the *Dial*. After an offer from the Dial Press, a publisher connected with the magazine, Moore published *Observations* (1924). This book of fifty-six poems, arranged chronologically by date of publication, promptly won the *Dial* award for service to literature. (T. S. Eliot had won the same award in 1922; *The Waste Land* appeared in the *Dial* during that year.)

In that same year, Scofield Thayer approached Moore, whose work and opinions he had come to value highly, with the suggestion that she might join the *Dial* staff. (She was still quite happy working at the Hudson Branch of the New York Public Library.) But by 1925, Moore had become acting editor of the *Dial*, as Thayer withdrew to spend increasing amounts of time abroad. Patricia Willis puts it succinctly when she says that in "ten years, Moore had moved from bottom to top of the list of influential modernists. Last to be published, she became editor of them all."[8]

Andrew Kappel points out that Marianne Moore always made a stunning first impression.[9] This is true both of her person and of her work. In spite of her characteristic modesty, there was a sureness about her; she spoke with such insight, clarity, and confidence that one trusted her and valued her opinions. Mark Van Doren met her in about 1927 at the *Dial*; he describes his reaction: "I had encountered in one person the courtesy of a queen and the precision of a surgeon."[10] William Carlos Williams, quoting himself in a letter to Marianne Moore 7 December 1936, after they had both read poems at the Brooklyn Institute, said: "Marianne was BEAUTIFUL! I found myself drifting off into the trance which only beauty creates more than once. There is a quality there which is unspeakably elevating—through all her frail pretense of being this or that, by God she IS. The modern Andromeda."[11]

Among the earliest stories about Moore's particular ability to engender confidence is the following episode which is recorded in the actual letters of William Carlos Williams and Marianne Moore:

> January 21, 1917
> Dear Marianne Moore,
>   William Carlos Williams wants to call his new book AL QUE
> QUIERE! "to him who wants it"—but I like the spanish [*sic*]
> as I like a chinese [*sic*] image cut out of stone: it is decorative
> and has a certain integral charm. But such a title is not
> democratic—does not truly represent the contents of the book
> so I have added

A Book of Poems
AL QUE QUIERE!
or
THE PLEASURES OF DEMOCRACY

> Now I like this conglomerate title! It is nearly a perfect image of
> my own grinning mug (seen from the inside) but my publisher
> objects—and I shake and wobble. Help me O leading light of
> the Sex of the Future.

Moore responded:

Chatham
February 23, 1917

Dear Dr. Williams,

I'm glad to be asked to assist. . . . In my mind AL QUE QUIERE!
is the better title for the book. [It] . . . is succinct and beautiful
. . . but everyone does not know Spanish. . . . I cannot refrain
from giving you my mother's comments. She thinks that while it
is perfectly true that the average person will [not know Spanish,]
all the better, for its beauty attracts even when not a word of
Spanish is understood and involuntarily curiosity will lead people
to go further to find what the book is about.[12]

Williams called the book *AL QUE QUIERE!* and a well-worn copy
remained in Moore's possession for the rest of her life. In his probably
humorous reference to Moore as the "leading light of the Sex of the
Future," it seems that Williams once again intuits an important perception about Moore and her discourse: that she was a precursor, a leading
light not only for her own sex but also for a new ability to value the
contributions of both sexes to the total vision of the future. Moore was a
woman whose voice pointed to what Ann Douglas celebrates in the feminization of American culture, the inclusion of a woman's way of knowing
the world into the total epistemology of the twentieth century.

Nonetheless, this story and others like it illustrate the respect in
which Moore was held by her young modernist colleagues. In a tribute
entitled "She Taught Me to Blush," Kenneth Burke remembered working
with her at the *Dial* in the mid-twenties and suggested, "Many writers,
dented by dint of much striving, contrive to think up unusualness of one
sort or another. But Marianne Moore's interweaving of the aesthetic and
the ethical is so intrinsically unusual, she could be extraordinary even in
the attempt to be average. . . . I believe she could tame wild-beasts and
even the bomb-happy, if such organisms are at all susceptible to civilized
and civilizing poetic wiles."[13]

Communications from Ezra Pound, T. S. Eliot, Hilda Doolittle,
Scofield Thayer, and others demonstrate that Moore's special qualities
were recognized almost from the first. Certainly Moore's elevation to the
editorship of the *Dial,* a little magazine with a circulation of over eigh-

teen thousand, suggests that her colleagues held her opinions and her abilities in high esteem. And as editor of the *Dial*, in its time the country's most prestigious magazine of arts and letters, Moore became "arguably the most powerful arbiter of modernist poetry in the decade."[14]

Moore recalled the *Dial* years fondly. In *"The Dial*: A Retrospect" (1940), Moore wrote, "I think of the compacted pleasantness of those days at 152 West Thirteenth Street." She remembered a visiting editor's incredulity when she said, upon being asked if she did not find reading manuscripts tiresome, "To me it's a revel."[15] The years must have been incredibly busy ones as Moore wrote for and edited issues of the *Dial*. Her own poetry simply stopped during the years of her editorship. There are stories of Moore's fastidiousness and severity as editor, most of them apocryphal. Among the most famous is the story of Hart Crane's "Wine Menagerie," which Moore revised; the title was also changed to "Again." At the time of publication Crane was in dire financial straits and expressed only gratitude for Moore's assistance. In later years he complained bitterly about her treatment. In the Donald Hall interview, Moore was asked about the episode. She replied, "Hart Crane complains of me? Well, I complain of *him*." As Moore explained it, "We had an inflexible rule: do not ask changes of so much as a comma. Accept it or reject it. But in that instance I felt that in compassion I should disregard the rule."[16]

In general, Moore was quite broad-minded, artistically and technically, but drew the literary line at work that she considered tasteless. That included some sections of Joyce, some poetry by Yeats, and some of the work of D. H. Lawrence. She also pared down some of Gertrude Stein's *Long Gay Book*, with Stein's apparent approval. She published Bertrand Russell, Paul Valery, D. H. Lawrence, John Dos Passos, Hart Crane's "To Brooklyn Bridge," Pound's *Canto XXII*, Yeats's "Among School Children," and various poems by William Carlos Williams, Louis Zukofsky, and Stanley Kunitz. (Although Wallace Stevens received requests from her for work, he offered none at that time.)[17]

In spite of their lifelong mutual admiration, Moore and William Carlos Williams had private differences in matters of taste. Publicly, Moore wrote in praise of most of Williams's work, but privately, their letters reveal their differences. On 23 March 1921, Williams wrote: "Your gentleness too makes me stop and think. Perhaps you are right in your adverse view of my obstreperous objections to decorum. I must think more of that. But each must free himself from the bonds of banality as best he can; you or another may turn into a lively field of intelligent activity quite easily, but I being perhaps more timid and unstable at heart, must free myself by more violent methods."[18]

Years later, the argument continued. On 22 June 1951, Moore wrote to Williams regarding *Paterson*: "The trouble for me with your rough and ready girl, is that she does not seem to me part of something that is inescapably typical. That is to say, writing is not just virtuosity; but an interpretation of life—protest as you may in the style of our early arguments about the lily and the mud. (One as 'lovely' technically speaking, as the other!)"[19]

Moore frequently wrote the monthly "Comments" section and contributed often to "Briefer Mentions" in the *Dial*. She reviewed Eliot's *Sacred Wood*, George Moore, George Saintsbury, Thomas Hardy, E. E. Cummings, Wallace Stevens, William Carlos Williams, and Gertrude Stein. Like her poems, her criticisms sparkle with freshness and originality; some of the titles are themselves poetic: "Well Moused, Lion," a review of Stevens's *Harmonium*; "Memory's Immortal Gear," a review of *Human Shows, Far Phantasies, Songs and Trifles*, by Thomas Hardy; "Is the Real Actual?" about Alfeo Faggi's sculptures; and "A Poet of the Quattrocento," about William Carlos Williams. A 1926 essay entitled "'New' Poetry since 1912" is an amazingly compact and accurate assessment of the origins and early development of modernism. Moore's insight is remarkable both for its objectivity and its accuracy, even with the historical perspective we have attained today.

The *Dial* published its last issue in July 1929. The Thayer family was no longer willing to underwrite publication costs, and the economic world as a whole was rapidly plunging into the Great Depression. Within three years, Moore was again writing her own poetry, claiming always that the years at the *Dial*, like the years she would spend later translating LaFontaine, were of great benefit to her own development as a poet because they forced her to examine uses of language other than her own.

The work she published in the thirties, which included the trilogy "The Steeple-Jack," "The Hero," and "The Student," brought Moore's poetry back into prominence. From 1930 on, Moore supported herself and her mother by free-lance work: reviews for *Poetry* and a host of other magazines; poems accepted by the *Nation, Poetry*, and, after 1953, the *New Yorker*, among many others.[20] By 1935, Faber and Faber was ready to publish the British edition of *Selected Poems*, while Macmillan brought out the American edition.

Two shorter books of poems in the forties were followed by *Collected Poems* in 1951. This book brought Moore the Bollingen Award, the Pulitzer Prize, and the National Book Award (all of the major awards in poetry)—and eventually, fame as the poet of New York City, the remarkable eccentric in the tricorne hat and cape.

Some have called Marianne Moore a poet's poet, for she has always been held in the highest regard by other writers, even when she was not always a popular success. Most of her contemporaries found in her work that genuineness of which Eliot spoke. They also had to grant Moore real originality, for as Eliot explained, try as he would, he could not trace a direct influence for her poetry.[21] And as Donald Hall later expressed it, "Her poems had broken with tradition. They were examples of the sort of new poetry her contemporaries had envisioned, for although there was agreement among poets about what innovations were required to revitalize American poetry, writing the new thing was something else."[22] Ezra Pound had said, "Make it new," and Marianne Moore quietly had. (At one point, Pound thought he had discovered Moore's antecedents when he said, "Someone has been reading Laforgue, and French authors." Moore admitted that retroactively one might make some comparisons, but that she had not read them in preparation for her own work.)[23]

She was an original—except that she never saw it that way. Her real innovations, she thought, were in her hard work and precise methods of composition, because it is impossible to be truly original "in the sense of doing something that has never been thought of before."[24] She unabashedly listened to many voices, using quotations when they were useful and almost always frankly admitting their sources. She explained that she used the structure of Hebrew poetry as a model, as Pound had used Chinese models. There is no question that her work is modern, but it is modern in ways unexplored by her contemporaries. It was "patterned but non-accentual, rhymed but not obviously, and embracing subjects as far from conventional poetry as anything later found in Pound's *Cantos* or Williams's *Paterson*."[25] Amy Clampitt even suggests that although it is frequently Pound who is credited with the introduction of natural or prose tone into poetry, it is in the work of Marianne Moore that we find the real break with precedent.

There is no argument about the difficulty of Moore's work. It is always a challenge. As Pound perceived from the beginning, "You will never sell more than five hundred copies, as your work demands mental attention" (1918 letter). Or as Eliot had said about her genuineness, "We have some warrant for believing that a small number, but only a small number, of contemporary readers can recognise it."

On 14 November 1939, W. H. Auden wrote to Moore: "How much I admire your work. When I first came across it, I must confess, I was baffled, it seemed so strange to this foolish and undisciplined young man. . . . I have come to appreciate its depth and integrity. It illustrates very clearly that American writers have to accept isolation as a blessing. . . . Like Rilke, you really do 'praise.' "[26] Monroe Wheeler claimed that with typical candor, W. H. Auden later declared to Moore, "I have stolen from you more treasure that I can accurately assess."[27]

Moore and Wallace Stevens enjoyed an elegant and sensitive correspondence, although they saw the world from different perspectives: Moore, the ardent Christian, hoping to project the order that she believed was already there, and Stevens, the insistent pagan, trying to order a world he found in essential chaos. One thing they surely shared was a sense of grace, albeit one with different definitions. Moore reviewed Stevens's work frequently and with great sensitivity, sharing with him her own sense of the poet as conjurer. In a 1935 letter Moore wrote to Stevens: "Therefore encouragement takes on an air of miragelike illusion; though your matter-of-factness in counterfeiting the essential mirage is so factual one finds oneself perhaps permanently cheered. It is a delight to feel such legerdemain; . . . that is to say, that you never find the gossamer assuming the texture of the carpet."[28] Over the years Stevens replied with lovely missals of support featuring phrases such as "as we both know, being oneself is the most difficult thing in the world" and "you are genuine in every syllable."[29] There is a charming Western Union telegram in the Rosenbach collection from Stevens dated 29 January 1952: "I KNOCK THIS MORNING AT YOUR DOOR TO BOW AND SAY FOREVER MOORE." The two enjoyed an almost ethereal friendship, like a flight of eagles.

But the most remarkable poetic friendship was probably that between Moore and Ezra Pound. Moore was not the only poet to be drawn—or pushed—to excellence by the powerful catalyst of Ezra Pound. His remarkable genius directed the magic of most of the great modernists, if not positively, then negatively. Andrew Kappel argues that it is with Pound that Moore had the greatest affinities. To her mind, his work embodied all the strengths of her other contemporaries, but none of their weaknesses. For although Moore admired much about Williams's work, particularly his desire to experience a close encounter with the world ("no ideas but in things"), she never quite forgave his failure to order his materials or his persistence in what she considered unredeemed secularism. And although she loved and respected T. S. Eliot, his "retreat from life," his Anglican predilection for "passionate waiting," unnerved her active Presbyterianism. Moore wanted—and expected—triumphs, no matter how hard the struggle; in Eliot she too frequently found failures and retreats. Stevens always received high praise from Moore, but his imagination remained a pagan one, a series of acts of collective imagination. Moore would have "recognized this as the disarming sophistry of the devil."[30] She understood the apparent chaos of this world as a continuous test in which one demonstrates one's commitment to good over evil, so she could celebrate the very chaos of existence (as she stated in "The Steeple-Jack," "it is a privilege to see so / much confusion").

But Pound never gave up his quest for some kind of order, even when the unmanageableness of reality overwhelmed him. He documented his journey, his commitment to struggle, in *The Cantos*. He was determined to find an ordering principle, although he expected it to be a secular one. When at the end of his life he still could not prove his "extraordinarily simple assumption that the world was of a piece," he continued to believe it anyway. "It coheres all right," he wrote at the end of *The Cantos*, "even if my notes do not cohere."[31] So the two shared a sense of struggle and an unshakable faith in themselves and in some principle beyond themselves, albeit different principles.

Their correspondence is a delight. Many of their exchanges were of a technical nature, one sharing with the other the problems and solutions of the texts themselves. In a letter dated 9 January 1919, Moore wrote: "Any verse that I have written has been an arrangement of stanzas, each stanza being an exact duplicate of every other stanza. I have occasionally been at pains to make an arrangement of lines and rhymes that I liked repeat itself, but the form of the original stanza of anything I have written has been a matter of expediency hit upon as being approximately suitable to the subject."[32]

Moore sent a poem drafted in about 1918 and entitled "A Graveyard" to Pound for possible use in the *Little Review*. It was rhymed and arranged in syllabic meter in three stanzas. Pound sent the poem back with several technical suggestions: "Are you quite satisfied with the final ca-

dence and the graphic arrangement of same . . . ? Perhaps you will find
a more drastic change suits better. I do not offer an alternative as
dogma." Moore made some drastic changes, ending lines after a natural
phrase rather than ending in midword or midphrase. She thereby col-
lapsed her rhyme scheme, rendering it invisible. From 1921 to 1925 this
new precedent—free verse—governed her poems. After the *Dial* years
she returned to her earlier, self-devised verse patterns.[33] When Moore
found herself struggling with the translations of LaFontaine, she turned
again to Pound for technical advice. From his incarceration at St. Elizabeth's Hospital he wrote:

> May 26, 1948
> Yes, m'dr Marianna
>
> the least taint of quality and/or merit upsets these blighters
> . . . kick OUT this god damned french syntax with relative
> clauses. Write the sense in plain english PROSE, and then versify
> the SENSE of your prose.[34]

Evidently Moore did exactly that. Later when a guard praised Moore
for her faithful visits to Pound by saying, "Good of you to come to see
him," she responded, "Good? You have no idea how much he has done
for me, and others."[35] In *Pound as Wuz*, James Laughlin offers a touching anecdote about Pound's final visit to the United States. A courtly if
aged white-haired and bearded Pound attended a reception at the New
York Public Library. Seated in a chair at the end of a large room, he rose
to shake hands with each of the people who came up to speak with him,
but he said absolutely nothing. Finally Marianne Moore came up to greet
him, and Marie Bullock took them off to a side room, standing guard at
the door to give them privacy. Laughlin was amazed to catch a glimpse of
Ezra talking to Moore with real animation.[36] And Moore's promoter,
teacher, and instigator had the final word. Learning of Moore's death in
February 1972, Pound came out of the deep silence to which he had
confined himself for several years to arrange a memorial service for her at
the Protestant Church in Venice. As a tribute to his "dear Marianna," he
read not one of his own poems but one of hers, a poem about the struggle
with mortality and the triumph of eternity: "What Are Years?"[37]
Another particularly important and interesting personal and professional relationship developed between Marianne Moore and Elizabeth

Bishop, two poets of very different styles and of separate generations. (Bonnie Costello calls them the "gentlewoman and the seeker.") As one reads their correspondence, one watches the relationship move from admirer and admired, from protégée and mentor, from younger friend and older one, and finally from sister to sister. Bishop's letters progress from "Dear Miss Moore" to "Darling Marianna." Although the two had very different personalities and markedly different themes, they shared a love of precision and a habit of careful observation culminating in a delight in perfection. Because Moore was Bishop's elder by twenty-two years, there is a temptation to make assumptions about some kind of mother-daughter relationship between them, but such a conclusion, as Costello points out, is far too facile.[38] As Moore wrote to Bishop on 21 June 1959, "You have sometimes asked what I thought, Elizabeth, but even if you ever took my advice, did you ever get to sound like me? or I like you? You sound like Lope de Vega and I sound like Jacob Abbott or Peter Rabbit."[39]

One real difference between the two poets was that Moore's vision tended to focus on stability, optimism, and a vigorous enchantment, while Bishop's world was often seen through a darker, more tragic vision, focusing on "loss, on traces of decay, on mysterious resemblances to the human which the mind cannot dissect."[40] Sometimes Moore questioned Bishop's moral intentions, as she did in this 7 March 1935 letter: "I enclose the suggestions I spoke of, about THE LABORS OF HANNIBAL. Your things have the insidiousness of creativeness, in that the after impression is stronger than the impression while reading, but you are menaced by the goodness of your mechanics. One should, of course, have the feeling, this is ingeniously contrived; but a thing should make one feel after reading it, that one's life has been altered or added to."[41]

When Moore offered specific suggestions in 1940 about Bishop's war poem "Roosters," especially about the use of the phrase "water closet," Bishop replied: "What I'm about to say, I'm afraid, will sound like ELIZABETH KNOWS BEST. . . . However, I *have* changed to small initial letters! and I have made several other of your corrections and suggestions. . . . [but] I cherish my 'water-closet' and other sordidities because I want to emphasize the essential baseness of militarism."[42]

Although Bishop always valued Moore's opinions, she generally retained the "courage of her own peculiarities," and many differences between the two writers persist. Randall Jarrell was among the first to remark on Bishop's indebtedness to Moore in his review of Bishop's *North*

and South. "When you read Miss Bishop's 'Florida,' a poem whose first
sentence begins, 'The state with the prettiest name,'and whose last sentence begins, 'The alligator who has five distinct calls: friendliness, love,
mating, war, and warning' you don't need to be told that the poetry
of Marianne Moore was in the beginning an appropriately selected foundation for Miss Bishop's work." But he also noted that Bishop is "simpler,
milder, less driven to desperate straits or dens of innocence." While
Moore provides a dazzling, highly idiosyncratic poetry, picking and
choosing carefully from a vast array of reading and life experiences,
based always on a confidence in a moral order beyond her own, Bishop is
"a disarmed traveler rather than a collector pursu[ing] an elusive image
of stability with less confidence about the self protective value of art."[43]
"Less idiosyncratic and less magnificent," in Robert Lowell's words,
Bishop is also "softer, dreamier, more human and more personal."[44]

Bishop published an essay entitled "Efforts of Affection: A Memoir of
Marianne Moore." The title itself suggests something about the nature of
their relationship. The two poets continued their efforts of affection in
their correspondence—sometimes about the technicalities of their art,
sometimes about lovely commonplaces, like Bishop's cat, Minnow, or
circuses they had seen. In August 1969, Bishop wrote from South America, "I have been thinking of naming my house "Casa Mariana" in your
honor." She later reported to Moore from Kirkland House at Harvard, "I
have Ezra Pound's grandson in one of my classes—a very nice boy."[45]

The two poets lived very different but complementary lives. Bishop
found in Marianne Moore a source of "stability, vigorous enchantment,
optimism and dedication to craft. Moore found in Bishop a source of
vicarious adventure and mystery, but was also drawn to her personal and
artistic courage and to the promised continuation of many of her own
poetic values in an entirely different voice."[46]

The list of other poets and critics who admired Marianne Moore and
learned from her innovations reads like the index to a contemporary
literary anthology. For the poets of the younger generation have found in
Marianne Moore, in one way or another, a guide and a master. Robert
Lowell, for example, urged his students to read Marianne Moore "because she never said a commonplace thing in her life." She is, he suggested, the "inventor of a new kind of English poem, one that is able to
fix the splendor and variety of prose in very compressed spaces. She is
lavish and meticulous."[47]

Padraic Colum claimed that he liked to entertain himself with Moore's poetry. "No other poetry," he said, "gives me quite the same experience. The formal pattern is unlike anything else in English verse; the unexpected shape of the lines keeps me constantly on the alert."[48]

Allen Tate offered the interesting observation in 1964 (probably unutterable in the feminist eighties) that "women like Marianne Moore keep civilized intercourse alive not by demanding homage but by being what Marianne Moore is; and what she is is spontaneous, elegant, and upright. By expecting the best of people she usually gets it."[49] The truth of Tate's judgment rests on solid artistic merit and is not limited by sexual identity.

John Ashbery, whose work some critics compare with Marianne Moore's, wrote to Moore on 20 November 1960, "It was thrilling for me to know that you, one of my favorite poets, enjoyed some of my poems."[50] He is quoted on the book jacket to the *Complete Poems* as saying that "more than any modern poet, she gives us the feeling that life is softly exploding around us, within easy reach."

Louis Untermeyer describes his own errors in his early judgments of Moore.

> At one time I wrote that her poetry was so exact that it was a kind of witty geometry. At another time I said that her fastidiousness was almost a fault and that her very microscopic scrutiny was a limitation. . . . I now . . . think of her poems as the ultimate in improvisation, poems which have been waiting to be said in an idiom which is a curious combination of the impromptu and the precise . . . no contemporary author is more original. Her poems are not . . . craftily joined; they are *one thing*, spontaneously conceived and executed.[51]

In her essay "A Matter of Diction," May Swenson pursues Moore's own dictum that one must produce perfect verse, arguing that "it is a matter of diction, of diction that is virile because it is galvanized against inertia."[52] Swenson argues that "we women poets are often urged to be grateful for the grand and indelible example of [Moore's] work and her life." But she is not special merely because she is a woman, because of some "different Hormonal Muse." She is "inimitable because she devises her own contexts, makes her own rules, and at the point least expected, disconcertingly reverses them."[53]

Stanley Kunitz called Moore our "moral eye, saved from platitude by accuracy, honesty, by coolness, and by joy." He remembered that Moore often quoted Confucius, and he offered the Master's words in tribute to her.

> Confucius was once asked what he would do first if it were left
> for him to administer a country. "It would certainly be to correct
> language," he replied. His listeners were surprised. "Surely,"
> they said, "this has nothing to do with the matter. Why should
> language be corrected?" The master's answer was: "If language is
> not correct, then what is said is not what is meant; if what is
> said is not meant, then what ought to be done remains undone; if
> this remains undone, morals and arts will deteriorate; if morals
> and arts deteriorate, justice will go astray; if justice goes astray,
> the people will stand about in helpless confusion. Hence there
> must be no arbitrariness in what is said. This matters above
> everything." *Marianne Moore matters.*[54]

Contemporary poets also turn to Moore today because she matters. Amy Clampitt reminds us that Moore "never borrowed a stanza pattern, even from herself, but invented a new one for each occasion."[55] As Moore herself described it: "Words cluster like chromosomes, determining the procedure. I may influence an arrangement or thin it, then try to have successive stanzas identical with the first. Spontaneous initial originality—say, impetus—seems difficult to reproduce consciously later. As Stravinsky said about pitch, 'If I transpose it for some reason, I am in danger of losing the freshness of first contact and will have difficulty in recapturing its attractiveness.'"[56]

That kind of rigorous originality—one which creates a new poetic form for each new poem—is at first hard to fathom. It is easy to be impressed by a surface study of the forms; thus her formal techniques have attracted many imitators. Unfortunately only a few imitate well, usually picking up the externals of Moore's formal devices like syllabic count, subtle rhyme schemes, enjambment between lines and between stanzas, irregular capitalization, and unusual punctuation, without comprehending her sense of precision, her goal of making the form one with the meaning. They may not have assigned themselves the arduous task of precision in language, or insisted upon a kaleidoscopic view of the etymology of words and the way those words represent reality. They are unwilling to take the time to read widely and well and are unwilling to incorporate many voices from the past as well as from the present, voices that may not have the imprimatur of so-called greatness, but are valid voices nonetheless. Perhaps most of all they are unwilling to live with ambiguity, to celebrate polyphony and to understand the privilege of confronting confusion. In her essay "Humility, Concentration, and Gusto," Moore remembered Ezra Pound's remark, "The great writer is always the plodder; it's the ephemeral writer that has to get on with the job."[57]

Clampitt has recognized particularly the degree to which contemporary writers are imitating Moore's formal techniques, many of them unaware that she is the source of such original strategies. At the same time that they are absorbing formal devices, they are missing the degree to which Moore's form is totally integrated with her tone and meaning. They have, as it were, merely been imitating the imitators. As a result, their formal devices have become superficial. A return to the work of the writing master herself would uncover intricacies of technique of which the novice is usually unaware. As Clampitt puts it, "It's the unconsidered literary trickle-down that causes us to squirm." For it would appear that Marianne Moore's influence on "the poetry now being written is greater than has up to now been recognized. And if the current rash of affectations is treatable at all it can only be so through a renewed attention to its source—by paying heed, finally, not to the manner but the matter of the thing. . . . To be more imitated than read is a melancholy fate for a poet, who turns out, as one reads, to be even stronger and more surprising than one had supposed."[58]

Pursuing another theme in "Portrait of a Writing Master: Beyond the Myth of Marianne Moore," Taffy Martin takes the reader on an "archeological tour of critical attitudes towards Marianne Moore's work." She points out that originally, Moore's contemporaries admired her poetry and envied her ambition.[59] Unfortunately, over time, critics began to value Moore as what Clampitt calls more "pet than poet."[60] Her personality and mannerisms began to overshadow her work. Other critics stressed only one dimension of her work, seemingly oblivious to its larger scope. R. P. Blackmur emphasized what he saw as Moore's remoteness.[61] John Crowe Ransom found Moore's "free verse" to have "little formal clarity" and called it a "break in the poetic style book that has done service for so long."[62] Having made the early judgment that Moore was the poet of the typewriter, Hugh Kenner has had some difficulty granting her greater dignity than that of a twentieth-century amenuensis, although he ranks her with "Pound, Williams, Stevens, Hemingway, and Zukovsky into that select group of writers who rethought and altered, perhaps permanently, the novel and especially the poem."[63]

Feminist critics have made some effort to work with Moore's texts, although her chastity repels many of them.[64] One is grateful for the sane and generous critical assessments of Tess Gallagher in an essay entitled "Throwing the Scarecrows from the Garden." Among the "scarecrows" Gallagher dispels is the notion that Moore wrote "spinster" poetry, a charge implied by both Roy Harvey Pearce and Suzanne Juhasz. Gallagher writes, "Had she been inclined, she could have managed to marry. All this is beside the point. I'm interested in Moore precisely for her difference. If one has access to the ultimate in virgin thought, one ought to prize it. . . . Give me a smart woman any day, whatever her gynecological qualifications."[65] What is really important about Moore's voice was not her sexuality but her ability to speak with great precision in a woman's voice. And in *Imaginary Possessions*, Bonnie Costello has demonstrated that the "timid, frightened lady in the black hat does not exist. . . . She has been replaced by a poet whose most persuasive images are those of combat and warfare."[66] In fact, Moore's most important subjects are really inclusiveness and incongruity, while at the same time she almost paradoxically speaks for order and grace. Her most significant quality is her ability to savor wit and to find real joy in a chaotic universe. Hers was, as Gallagher points out, a relentless "team spirit," for she saw herself in the Great Chain of Being, an inheritor of Grace. In all modesty, she understood that she was a most capable writer; but that was, after all, her station in life; she was an artist-engineer. Like Anna Pavlova, who called herself "The Incomparable Ballerina Absoluta," Moore could smile and style herself the magician, the imagnifico, the wizard in words.

The last word on Marianne Moore has not been said, but fine scholars and critics like John M. Slatin, Patricia C. Willis, Bonnie Costello, and Margaret Holley are making the work more and more accessible. They are making it possible for the literary world to "get to know Marianne Moore" and to learn from the standards of poetic excellence she devised. Because she demanded perfection of language in the pursuit of the truth beyond mere words, Marianne Moore matters. Illusion is more precise than precision.

As final proof that Marianne Moore does matter, consider one of her most outstanding works—one, I would suggest, of the outstanding poems of the twentieth century. In "Approximating Paradise: 'An Octopus' and the Discovery of America," John Slatin argues that a major theme of Moore's poem is a challenge to Eliot's insistence on the primacy of the European literary tradition. Slatin feels that Moore seeks to expand the "Emersonian tradition by bringing it into its English parent-tradition; the meeting point is Paradise."[67] Moore's challenge to Eliot's view is even larger, however, for she sees a world of faith, wonder, and challenge where he had found a wasteland.

Most of Moore's major themes, forms, and interests are represented in "An Octopus," a poem published in 1924. The poem demonstrates Moore's fascination with natural science and the problems of purely scientific thought in the twentieth century, her interest in time and history, her commitment to the representation of the visual in minute detail, her fascination with "found phrases" (her objets trouvés), her sense of kaleidoscopic layers of meaning, and her notion of the necessity of self-protection. The poem also projects her own sense of herself as an American poet and, finally, celebrates her vision of herself as a believer sensitive to the knowledge of an order beyond the realm of logic; for she deals with intuition, an illusion more precise than precision.

"To write the poem of America," Emerson wrote in *The Poet*, "will require a genius with tyrannous eye," such as we have not had yet, for only such a genius knows "the value of our incomparable materials, . . . and [sees] . . . another carnival of the same gods whose picture he so much admires in Homer; . . . America is a poem in our eyes; its ample geography dazzles the imagination."[68] "An Octopus" is such a poem, for it is not about an eight-armed cephalopod mollusk but about one of America's most remarkable natural wonders, part of the unique American geography that "dazzles the imagination." It is about the place the Indians called Tacoma, "The Mountain who is God"; Americans call it Mount Rainier.

An Octopus

of ice. Deceptively reserved and flat,
it lies "in grandeur and in mass"
beneath a sea of shifting snow-dunes;
dots of cyclamen-red and maroon on its clearly defined pseudo-
        podia
made of glass that will bend—a much needed invention—
comprising twenty-eight ice-fields from fifty to five hundred feet
        thick,

of unimagined delicacy.
"Picking periwinkles from the cracks"
or killing prey with the concentric crushing rigor of the python,
it hovers forward "spider fashion
on its arms" misleadingly like lace;
its "ghostly pallor changing
to the green metallic tinge of an anemone-starred pool."
The fir-trees, in "the magnitude of their root systems,"
rise aloof from these maneuvers "creepy to behold,"
austere specimens of our American royal families,
"each like the shadow of the one beside it.
The rock seems frail compared with their dark energy of life,"
its vermilion and onyx and manganese-blue interior

                                                           expensiveness

left at the mercy of the weather;
"stained transversely by iron where the water drips down,"
recognized by its plants and its animals.
Completing a circle,
you have been deceived into thinking that you have progressed,
under the polite needles of the larches
"hung to filter, not to intercept the sunlight"—
met by tightly wattled spruce-twigs
"conformed to an edge like clipped cypress
as if no branch could penetrate the cold beyond its company";
and dumps of gold and silver ore enclosing The Goat's Mirror—
that lady-fingerlike depression in the shape of the left human

                                                           foot,

which prejudices you in favor of itself
before you have had time to see the others;
its indigo, pea-green, blue-green, and turquoise,
from a hundred to two hundred feet deep,
"merging in irregular patches in the middle lake
where, like gusts of a storm
obliterating the shadows of the fir-trees, the wind makes lanes of

                                                            ripples."

What spot could have merits of equal importance
for bears, elk, deer, wolves, goats, and ducks?
Pre-empted by their ancestors,
this is the property of the exacting porcupine,
and of the rat "slipping along to its burrow in the swamp
or pausing on high ground to smell the heather";
of "thoughtful beavers

making drains which seem the work of careful men with
                                                          shovels,"
and of the bears inspecting unexpectedly
ant-hills and berry-bushes.
Composed of calcium gems and alabaster pillars,
topaz, tourmaline crystals and amethyst quartz,
their den is somewhere else, concealed in the confusion
of "blue forests thrown together with marble and jasper and agate
as if whole quarries had been dynamited."
And farther up, in stag-at-bay position
as a scintillating fragment of these terrible stalagmites,
stands the goat,
its eye fixed on the waterfall which never seems to fall—
an endless skein swayed by the wind,
immune to force of gravity in the perspective of the peaks.
A special antelope
acclimated to "grottoes from which issue penetrating draughts
which make you wonder why you came,"
it stands its ground
on cliffs the color of the clouds, of petrified white vapor—
black feet, eyes, nose, and horns, engraved on dazzling ice-
                                                          fields,
the ermine body on the crystal peak;
the sun kindling its shoulders to maximum heat like acetylene,
                                            dyeing them white—
upon this antique pedestal,
"a mountain with those graceful lines which prove it a volcano,"
its top a complete cone like Fujiyama's
till an explosion blew it off.
Distinguished by a beauty
of which "the visitor dare never fully speak at home
for fear of being stoned as an impostor,"
Big Snow Mountain is the home of a diversity of creatures:
those who "have lived in hotels
but who now live in camps—who prefer to";
the mountain guide evolving from the trapper,
"in two pairs of trousers, the outer one older,
wearing slowly away from the feet to the knees";
"the nine-striped chipmunk
running with unmammal-like agility along a log";
the water ouzel
with "its passion for rapids and high-pressured falls,"

building under the arch of some tiny Niagara;
the white-tailed ptarmigan "in winter solid white,
feeding on heather-bells and alpine buckwheat";
and the eleven eagles of the west,
"fond of the spring fragrance and the winter colors,"
used to the unegoistic action of the glaciers
and "several hours of frost every midsummer night."
"They make a nice appearance, don't they,"
happy seeing nothing?
Perched on treacherous lava and pumice—
those unadjusted chimney-pots and cleavers
which stipulate "names and addresses of persons to notify
in case of disaster"—
they hear the roar of ice and supervise the water
winding slowly through the cliffs,
the road "climbing like the thread
which forms the groove around a snail-shell,
doubling back and forth until where snow begins, it ends."
No "deliberate wide-eyed wistfulness" is here
among the boulders sunk in ripples and white water
where "when you hear the best wild music of the forest
it is sure to be a marmot,"
the victim on some slight observatory,
of "a struggle between curiosity and caution,"
inquiring what has scared it:
a stone from the moraine descending in leaps,
another marmot, or the spotted ponies with glass eyes,
brought up on frosty grass and flowers
and rapid draughts of ice-water.
Instructed none knows how, to climb the mountain,
by business men who require for recreation
three hundred and sixty-five holidays in the year,
these conspicuously spotted little horses are peculiar;
hard to discern among the birch-trees, ferns, and lily-pads,
avalanche lilies, Indian paint-brushes,
bear's ears and kittentails,
and miniature cavalcades of chlorophylless fungi
magnified in profile on the moss-beds like moonstones in the
water;

the cavalcade of calico competing
with the original American menagerie of styles

among the white flowers of the rhododendron surmounting rigid
                                                            leaves

upon which moisture works its alchemy,
transmuting verdure into onyx.

Larkspur, blue pincushions, blue pease, and lupin;
white flowers with white, and red with red;
the blue ones "growing close together
so that patches of them look like blue water in the distance":
this arrangement of colors
as in Persian designs of hard stones with enamel,
forms a pleasing equation—
a diamond outside and inside, a white dot;
on the outside, a ruby; inside, a red dot;
black spots balanced with black
in the woodlands where fires have run over the ground—
separated by aspens, cats' paws, and woolly sunflowers,
fireweed, asters, and Goliath thistles
"flowering at all altitudes as multiplicitous as barley,"
like pink sapphires in the pavement of the glistening plateau,
Inimical to "bristling, puny, swearing men
equipped with saws and axes,"
this treacherous glass mountain
admires gentians, ladyslippers, harebells, mountain dryads,
and "Calypso, the goat flower—
that greenish orchid fond of snow"—
anomalously nourished upon shelving glacial ledges
where climbers have not gone or have gone timidly,
"the one resting his nerves while the other advanced,"
on this volcano with the bluejay, her principal companion.
"Hopping stiffly on sharp feet" like miniature icehacks—
"secretive with a look of wisdom and distinction, but a villain,
fond of human society or the crumbs that go with it,"
he knows no Greek,
"that pride producing language,"
in which "rashness is rendered innocuous, and error exposed
by the collision of knowledge with knowledge."

"Like happy souls in Hell," enjoying mental difficulties, the
                                                          Greeks

amused themselves with delicate behavior
because it was "so noble and so fair";
not practised in adapting their intelligence
to eagle-traps and snow-shoes,
to alpenstocks and other toys contrived by those
"alive to the advantage of invigorating pleasures."
Bows, arrows, oars, and paddles, for which trees provide the
wood,
in new countries more eloquent than elsewhere—
augmenting the assertion that, essentially humane,
"the forest affords wood for dwellings and by its beauty
stimulates the moral vigor of its citizens."
The Greeks like smoothness, distrusting what was back
of what could not be clearly seen,
resolving with benevolent conclusiveness,
"complexities which still will be complexities
as long as the world lasts";
ascribing what we clumsily call happiness,
to "an accident or a quality,
a spiritual substance or the soul itself,
an act, a disposition, or a habit,
or a habit infused, to which the soul has been persuaded,
or something distinct from a habit, a power"—
such power as Adam had and we are still devoid of.
"Emotionally sensitive, their hearts were hard";
their wisdom was remote
from that of these odd oracles of cool official sarcasm,
upon this game preserve
where "guns, nets, seines, traps and explosives,
hired vehicles, gambling and intoxicants are prohibited;
disobedient persons being summarily removed
and not allowed to return without permission in writing."
It is self-evident
that it is frightful to have everything afraid of one;
that one must do as one is told
and eat rice, prunes, dates, raisins, hardtack, and tomatoes
if one would "conquer the main peak" of Mount Tacoma,
this fossil flower concise without a shiver,
intact when it is cut,
damned for its sacrosanct remoteness—
like Henry James "damned by the public for decorum";
not decorum, but restraint;

it is the love of doing hard things
that rebuffed and wore them out—a public out of sympathy with
neatness.
Neatness of finish! Neatness of finish!
Relentless accuracy is the nature of this octopus
with its capacity for fact.
"Creeping slowly as with meditated stealth,
its arms seeming to approach from all directions,"
it receives one under winds that "tear the snow to bits
and hurl it like a sandblast
shearing off twigs and loose bark from the trees."
Is "tree" the word for these things
"flat on the ground like vines"?
some "bent in a half circle with branches on one side
suggesting dust-brushes, not trees;
some finding strength in union, forming little stunted groves
their flattened mats of branches shrunk in trying to escape"
from the hard mountain "planed by ice and polished by the
wind"—
the white volcano with no weather side;
the lightning flashing at its base,
rain falling in the valleys, and snow falling on the peak—
the glassy octopus symmetrically pointed,
its claw cut by the avalanche
"with a sound like the crack of a rifle,
in a curtain of powdered snow launched like a waterfall."

Observations

Marianne Moore and her mother made two trips to the Northwest while her brother, Warner, a chaplain, was assigned to the *U.S.S. Mississippi*, in drydock at Bremerton, across Puget Sound from Seattle. The first family reunion in five years (Warner had gone to sea in 1917 and married in 1918), the 1922 visit was in many ways a watershed for Moore. She was in "Paradise," in the sense of both the beautiful meadow-park named "Paradise" on the Nisqually Glacier side of Mount Rainier and the paradise of a reunion with her beloved brother. In July 1923, Moore wrote to Warner that she was attempting a poem about Mount Rainier; a second trip later that summer gave Moore ample time to contemplate the magnificence of "The Mountain who is God," a connection that did not go unnoticed by the poet.

Mount Rainier stands 14,408 feet above sea level. "From the east, its top looks like a huge ice-cream cone with a scoop removed—the result of a volcanic explosion."[69] The Moores probably approached the mountain from the east, riding to Paradise Park by automobile along a beautiful and circuitous route. The meadows in "Paradise" must have been magnificent in mid-July, a panorama of color beyond anything created by even the most talented of human "artist engineers." As one approaches the timberline, one sees the majestic Nisqually Glacier pouring slowly from the very top of the mountain. The experience is overwhelming for any traveler; it must have been dazzling to one of Moore's sensitivity.

Willis has studied the development of the poem in a 133-page notebook, a stenographer's pad of "collectibles" Moore began to gather in 1923. Among the notes are many surprises, among them the fact that Moore was working on one long poem with two possible titles: "An Octopus / of ice" *or* "Marriage / I don't know what Adam & Eve think of it by this time. . . ."[70] For the next twenty-two pages, Moore drew upon her vast reading background, trying lists of images and ideas which would ultimately become two separate and entirely different poems.

Moore also included notes from a source she used quite frequently in her poems, a popular religious text dating from the seventeenth century, Richard Baxter's *Saints' Everlasting Rest*. Somewhere during the year, "Marriage" coalesced into a separate poem, which Moore sent to Monroe Wheeler for publication in *Manikin*.

When she turned to "An Octopus" as another poem, Moore also turned her attention to researching more details about Mount Rainier. It seems certain that the *Mt. Rainier National Park Guidebook* (1922) suggested her title. The guidebook's sketch of the mountain and its pattern of glaciers as seen from above looks very much like an octopus with its icy pseudopodia extending "forward spider fashion . . . misleadingly like lace." In search of her usual precision, Moore evoked a polyphony, making notes from a text by Walter Dwight Wilcox, *The Rockies of Canada* (1900), from *Rules and Regulations: Mount Rainier* (Department of the Interior, 1922), and from Clifton Johnson's *What to See in America* (1919). Moore quoted passages from these works in her poem.

She tells us in the poem that the "octopus of ice" has "twenty-eight ice-fields from fifty to five hundred feet thick / of unimagined delicacy." Willis points out that the poem, in its original text, comprises twenty-eight sentences, scarcely a coincidence with Marianne Moore.[71] One might argue that the poem is also sometimes fifty, sometimes five hundred, feet "thick" with layers of meaning and certainly created with "unimagined delicacy."

There is an overwhelmingly visual quality to the poem, a celebration of nature's magnificence. It is like a great detailed painting with every flower and every animal sketched in and filled with color. One is reminded of Moore's tribute to Robert Andrew Parker, whom she described as "one of the most accurate and at the same time most unliteral of painters." Like Moore's own work in "Novices" and "The Steeple-Jack," Parker's work managed to combine the mystical and the actual, "working both in an abstract and in a realistic way, without contradiction . . . he is a fanaticist of great precision."[72]

In "An Octopus" Moore labors with the patience of the landscape painter ("to explain grace requires a curious hand"), sketching in pine trees, in Ruskin's words, "Each like the shadow of the one beside it." Her palette is unparalleled, rocks of "vermillion and onyx and manganese-blue" and a lake called "The Goat's Mirror" of indigo, pea-green, blue-green, and turquoise." Her flowers are a "cavalcade of calico" in

> Larkspur, blue pincushions, blue pease, and lupin;
> white flowers with white, red with red;
> the blue ones "growing close together
> so that patches of them look like blue water in the distance."

The colors remind Moore, as they had in "Marriage," of a Persian miniature of designs so mathematically perfect ("a pleasing equation") that the eye revels in them. There is great pleasure to be found in nature's patterns.

And Moore's menagerie of animals also brings the mountain alive, although interestingly ptarmigans, elk, and bears stand on equal footing with those who "have lived in hotels / but who now live in camps." The mountain plays no favorites. Of particular delight is the presence of a rat "slipping along to its burrow in the swamp / or pausing on high ground to smell the heather"; a water ouzel, with "its passion for rapids and high pressured falls"; and a marmot who produces "the best wild music of the forest." One recalls from the family correspondence that the three family members always used pet-names. Moore was sometimes the Rat from *The Wind in the Willows*, Mrs. Moore was sometimes Bunny, sometimes Weasel; and Warner was usually Badger, although he might sometimes be Weasel as well. (Perhaps an editor recommended changing "badger" to

"marmot" for accuracy in the text of "An Octopus"; the line had originally read "badger.")[73] There is also a musical quality to the composition
of the poem, with the free verse text arranged in movements, each signaled by a short line completing an idea. (The music of internal and
approximate rhyme, what Eliot called her "light rhyme," is far too complex to be thoroughly discussed here. Note the "a" sounds in "flat,"
"grandeur," "mass," "glass" in the first few lines, as well as the allitera-
tion of "picking," "periwinkles," "prey," and "python," and the echoing
"s" sounds of "spider," "fashion," "arms," "misleadingly," "lace," and
"ghostly.")

Willis finds eight movements in the orchestration of the poem, pro-
gressing from the "octopus of ice" viewed from a distance, the rock
viewed next from a closer perspective, visible among the fir trees at the
timber line, followed by a catalog of animal life arranged in ascending
order by habitat, then a catalog of plant life, moving from the forest floor
to the hardiest of plants that can exist on bald rock. There are two creatures at the apex, the goat and the Calypso orchid, the "goat flower,"
attended by a bluejay who, although fond of "human society or the
crumbs that go with it," knows no Greek. Next the poem makes what at
first may seem an odd shift to the Greeks, who "like smoothness, distrusting what was back / of what could not be clearly seen." They were
"'like happy souls in Hell,' enjoying mental difficulties."

Moving from the Greeks, the poet speaks of another breed of being:
"Relentless accuracy is the nature of this octopus / with its capacity for
fact." This creature, "creeping slowly as with meditated stealth," covers
a world too spectacular to control, too jagged to make smooth. The
glacier enjoys an unusual relationship with the mountain on which it
lives. It "exhibits the suppleness of an octopus in accommodating itself
to every surface, and yet retains the glass-like hardness and evenness of
its own character."[74] A connection begins to emerge between the glacier/
octopus and the position of the artist, particularly the poet. For although
she cannot adequately represent an entire "mountain," the poet can
strive to present an impeccable witness to the world in which she has a
part and to which she has an obligation. For she has the ability to do
honor to the mountain's magnificence with her words and her ordering,
her "neatness of finish." That is the closest any human being can get to
the reality of the mountain itself. The best one can do is point out what
one can of its symmetry and attempt to comprehend its externals, be-

cause ultimate reality will always be out of one's reach, in danger of
being

> . . . cut by the avalanche
> "with a sound like the crack of a rifle,
> in a curtain of powdered snow launched like a waterfall."

"It is a privilege to see so / much confusion," Moore said in "The
Steeple-Jack." It is a privilege to be reminded that there is a reality
beyond what even the most precise and logical of human beings can ever
understand. But there is also a privilege and a magic in being the mountain's refractor, "glass that will bend—a much needed invention," that
loves "doing hard things" so that the rest of the world might glimpse the
power and majesty of the mountain itself. That love of doing hard things
was a joy Moore shared with only a few, among them, Henry James, who
like Moore herself had been "'damned by the public for decorum,' not
decorum, but restraint." Moore would later write of Henry James as "a
characteristic American,"[75] and the whole notion of the American poet
and the American idiom is also at work in the poem.

If R. W. B. Lewis can speak of "The American Adam," Moore finds in
Mount Rainier the American Eden. But Paradise after the fall is a sur-
prisingly rough-hewn place. It is visually beautiful, but this uniquely
American Eden

> receives one under winds that "tear the snow to bits
> and hurl it like a sandblast
> shearing off twigs and loose bark from the trees."

It is a "hard mountain 'planed by ice and polished by the wind.'" It has
"lightning flashing at its base, / rain falling in the valleys, and snow
falling on the peak." One who would succeed here must be "alive to the
advantage of invigorating pleasures." But in spite of its challenges, the
mountain remains beautiful; it is no wasteland. For those brave enough to
attempt the ascent, the rediscovery of Paradise is exhilarating, although
"happiness . . . such power as Adam had . . . we are still devoid of."

For most readers, an abrupt collision of ideas occurs at the point that
Moore seems to shift the theme of the poem from Mount Rainier and its
glacier, or perhaps "Paradise," in the sense of an American Eden, to a
discussion of the Greeks. Except that is precisely where Moore had been

leading the eye—and the mind—throughout the first two-thirds of the poem. At the apex of the mountain are two figures: the goat, "its eye fixed on the waterfall which never seems to fall," and "Calypso, the goat flower— / that greenish orchid fond of snow." The name Calypso suggests Homer's *Odyssey* and the nymph on the island of Ogygia who was prepared to offer Odysseus immortality in exchange for his love. Odysseus (perhaps not unlike Adam, who chose Eve and mortality) chose to return to his mortal wife, Penelope, instead of accepting Calypso's offer. The other figure (the goat) has been associated from earliest Judeo-Christian times with the idea of sin and an awareness of a heaven. But it is also the Greek figure of Pan, a figure related to carnal desire and the power of the earth. And there lies one important consideration in the poem. In the two parallel worlds there are many ambiguities and a great deal of overlapping. But there is one overpowering difference: one world accepts the existence of sin and the awareness of a power beyond all human fathoming; the other holds for an eventual anthropomorphic explanation for everything.

Moore is willing to grant great respect to the values and the accomplishments of the Greeks, placing them even in Dante's Limbo, "Like happy souls in Hell."[76] Insofar as their logical minds could take them, they experienced success and an intellectual kind of happiness. They could amuse themselves with "mental difficulties" and with "delicate behavior." But because they had no sense of their fall from grace, no awareness of themselves in the chain of creation, no modesty or humility as it were, and because they wanted none, they were willing to resolve "benevolent conclusiveness"—refusing to understand that there are things no mortal mind can ever unwind, "complexities which still will be complexities / as long as the world lasts." The Greeks, precursors in many ways of scientists, particularly positivists, told themselves that there was an explanation and a definition for everything, even human happiness. "The Greeks liked smoothness, distrusting what was back / of what could not be clearly seen." Although they were "emotionally sensitive, their hearts were hard."

In a letter dated 2 September 1924, Moore writes to Scofield Thayer, who would soon be publishing "An Octopus" in the *Dial*, that she is worried about the work's "undesirable expansiveness"; yet she also knows the nature of her own themes and realizes that her own tendency to be "impetuous and perilously summary" in "so vital a matter" will make her guilty of trying to smooth jagged issues as the Greeks had done. She is afraid of too much "neatness."[77]

"Neatness of finish! Neatness of finish!" seem to be associated in the text with Henry James and his precise but remote method, a method Moore applauded in "Henry James as a Characteristic American." But Laurence Stapleton has suggested that the lines themselves actually come from William Carlos Williams's *Kora in Hell*, section 21, 2, which Moore had reviewed for *Contact* in 1921. Williams had written: "Neatness and finish; the dust out of every corner! You swish from room to room and find all perfect. The house may now be carefully wrapped in brown paper and sent to a publisher. It is a work of art. . . . You see, when the wheel's just at the up turn it glimpses horizon, zenith, all in a burst, the pull of the earth shaken off, a scatter of fragments, significance in a burst of water striking up from the base of a fountain."[78]

At the end of "An Octopus," Moore makes the parallel realization that one cannot control everything, that there is a remarkable scatter of fragments moved by winds that "tear the snow to bits / and hurl it like a sandblast," and a "curtain of powdered snow launched like a waterfall." But that is the very wonder of this Paradise, Tacoma, the Mountain who is God. This is the power of Bergson's élan vital, continually generating new forms and filled with glimpses of power and beauty that no man or woman could ever dream of. When, in "An Octopus," the goat stands on the highest precipice of the mountain, "a scintillating fragment of these terrible stalagmites," it watches a waterfall beyond time in the human sense, one which "never seems to fall— / an endless skein swayed by the wind"; for a moment it glimpses time eternal.

The poem reminds us that there are two ways of knowing: one, which reaches its perfection in precision, in science, is analytic, spatializing, and conceptualizing. The other is an intuition that is universal, immediate, reaching by sympathy from the heart. As Bergson had suggested, the first is useful for getting ordinary things done, but it fails to reach perfection because it leaves out duration, *durée*, and its perpetual flux, which is inexpressible by scientific fact and can be reached only by intuition. Nonetheless, the two aspects of knowing exist in a complementary relationship; in "An Octopus" Moore puts them side by side: the concrete, expressed by precise and beautiful detail; and the abstract, attainable only in fragmentary glimpses, at the highest level of human understanding—*intuition*, the "rock crystal thing to see." If one raises up one's eyes and dares to look, one will find the road to Paradise, but the trip to the summit is never easy. One may need "eagle-traps and snowshoes" and "alpenstocks" to get there. And one may have to eat "prunes, dates, raisins, hardtack, and tomatoes" if one would "conquer the main peak."

Although meticulous in its magic, "An Octopus" is not a tidy poem. It may aspire to "neatness of finish," but it must finally admit that all humans are forced into a more humble perspective before the grandeur of Tacoma, the Mountain that is God. In one way, the problem of describing this natural paradise becomes a metaphor for Western culture and its attempts to explain a world whose natural order is actually far beyond human comprehension. The epistemology of the West has been "scientific"—one might even say, male—in its desire for definition, order, and abstraction, and in its tendency to exclude the intuition, "ecstasy," inclusiveness, and enigmas of what has been thought of as Eastern thinking. Yet the latter qualities mark dimensions of women's ways of knowing that can ultimately only enrich the human experience. In many ways "An Octopus" opens up more issues than it solves, but that is typical of Moore's capacious and optimistic female mind, one that is prepared to explore, to circumnavigate her world, and to describe the myriad experiences she observes. In "Subject, Predicate, Object," Moore wrote, "It is for himself that the writer writes, charmed or exasperated to participate; eluded, arrested, enticed by felicities. . . . One may hang back or launch away. 'With sails flapping one gets nowhere. With everything sheeted down, one can go around the world.'"[79] Marianne Moore sails in pursuit of illusion, knowing full well that the only way to get even close to the kinds of piercing glances into the hearts of things she is seeking is to execute technical precision. She is a rigorous conjurer, an imagnifico, a wizard in words. Her "felicities" are conjuries that endure in a world that seeks to understand the bond between the minds of human beings and their magnificent origins.

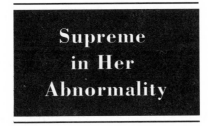

Supreme in Her Abnormality

Andrew Kappel has pointed out that during the decades of the 1960s and 1970s, the vast bulk of scholarly and critical literature on modern poetry ran to the open, the secular, and the dark; we seemed to prefer artistic visions that emphasized "total bleakness," as Wallace Stevens called it, of the chaotic particulars of reality and the consequently desperate condition of the hopelessly beleaguered self. Marianne Moore's poetry "has little in common with the poetry of the confessionals' psychic distress, with programmatic secularism, or with the banality of the Beats. Eliot and Pound were presented as more congenial figures than the fastidious Miss Moore." Unfortunately our "fascination with the romance of failure has caused us to overlook Moore's poetry of triumph."[1]

It is time for another look at the poetry of Marianne Moore because it is a new discourse, a woman's voice, and one that offers a poetry of triumph, not of despair. It is also important to reexamine Moore's discourse for all of the good reasons T. S. Eliot offered in his introduction in 1935. She is a genuine poet who has "saturated her mind with the perfections of prose." She is an original in every sense of the word. She has a particular gift for detailed observation, for finding the exact words for the experience of the eye. She is an intellectual who achieves an intense, if restrained, emotional value. She is an elegant versifier, whose forms are anything but free. But perhaps most of all, she is a fantasist of great precision; the minute details of her work are never an end in themselves but always have a service to perform in the transmission of her complex but confident and uplifting themes.

In a conversation during the latter part of his life (sometime in the 1950s), Eliot remarked to a friend that he admired Marianne Moore. "She has invented a new idiom, hitherto unused," he observed. In his view she was "quite outstanding and way above most of the men of her generation,"[2] a view that serves to reinforce my thesis. Moore's discourse seemed to Eliot to be superior because it was different, original—the invention of a poet who created a new way of looking at the world. That difference was partly due to Moore's operating within a woman's epistemology, a woman's way of knowing; she also invented the means to work out her vision with original forms. That worldview included refraction, inclusiveness, intuition, and ambiguity, while at the same time it demanded rigorous formal precision in both language and technique. As a conclusion to this book, I focus here on Moore as the creator of a new idiom, a true American original.

In assessing Moore's place among the other modernists, one must begin by acknowledging Moore's originality. Certainly the first place to look is at her formal devices, particularly her syllabic versification. The early modernists had issued the dictum "make it new," and Marianne Moore accepted the challenge, breaking words apart, rhyming in other than final syllables, exploring new possibilities of internal rhyme, and counting rhythms by syllables, all forms created by her sense of the construction of Hebrew poetry. What Pound had done with the Provençal and with the Chinese, Moore had done with Hebrew forms. But she is unique in her verbal experiments. The more one explores the intricacies of Moore's constructions, the more impressive their precision and effectiveness become. As Margaret Holley has argued in "The Model Stanza: The Organic Origin of Moore's Syllabic Prose," Moore's poems developed in the Coleridgean sense of organic form. As Moore herself puts it, once she had worked out a stanza pattern to meet her theme, "the words clustered like chromosomes." Her syllabic line scheme for any one poem "develops itself from within." Moore's experiments with syllabic measure "demythologize the traditional notion of poetry . . . to show that the metrical rhythms we have customarily assumed to be a necessary, definitive essence of poetry are, in fact, a contingent, conventional attribute of it."[3] As Moore had argued in "The Past Is the Present," it is time that the great poetic models of the past intertwine with a present that is different from them. Moore's poetic forms may appear to be shaped like traditional verses, but they certainly do not sound like them. And they force the reader to read, as Padraic Colum perceived, with new sensitivity and new alertness. What is left for us, he says, is "description by re-creation."[4]

Moore was always interested in common speech—the naturalness of prose, as she liked to think of it. And she was a fanatic about using the exact word, not the nearly exact or the decorative. In "Bowls" Moore wrote, "I shall purchase an etymological dictionary of modern English / that I may understand what is written." For although much of our language may have evolved when our ancestors "hacked things out with hairy paws," it is still our language, our words, our living history, the expression of our world. It is a thing to be treasured, polished, and renewed. When William Carlos Williams wrote that "Miss Moore gets great pleasure from wiping soiled words or cutting them clean out, removing the aureoles that have been pasted about them or taking them bodily from greasy contexts," he was being less metaphorical than accurate. That was precisely what Moore enjoyed, finding wonderful words in want only of resurrection and a little cleaning up. She found "wentletrap" and "pangolin," "testudo" and "melanchthon," "plumet basilisk, "camellia sabina," and even "Tippoo's tiger." And she made ordinary words and phrases come alive all over again. They were her "flies in amber," her found objects, jewels to be polished and set in her intricate mosaics of words. She certainly explored new rhythms and worked for the true musical phrase, never merely the "sequence of the metronome." And Moore also insisted upon absolute freedom of subject matter. As Randall Jarrell argued in "The Humble Animal," she wove her magic from homely materials.

> She not only can, but must, make poetry out of everything and anything; she is like Midas, or like Mozart choosing unpromising themes for the fun of it, or like one of those princesses whom wizards force to manufacture sheets out of nettles. And yet there is one thing Miss Moore has a distaste for making poetry of: the Poetic. She has made a principle out of refusing to believe that there is any such thing as the antipoetic; her poems restore to poetry the "business documents and school books" that Tolstoy took away.[5]

One certainly must admit that Moore was fascinated by the precise presentation of all kinds of images, the ordinary and the unusual, believing that poetry should render particulars, not deal in vague generalities, however magnificent and sonorous. One is reminded of the swan with "gondoliering legs" in "No Swan So Fine"; or of "Peter," the wonderful cat with "prune-shaped head / and alligator-eyes"; or of "the blades of the oars / moving together like the feet of water-spiders" as seen looking up from under the sea in "A Grave"; or of the "Jerboa" who "makes fern-seed / foot-prints with kangaroo speed."

As is suggested above, another area of uniqueness for Moore was her visual perceptivity, what Eliot had called "some experience of the eye." As William Pratt argues in *The Imagist Poem*, to some degree Moore is associated with the Imagist movement,[6] in spite of her own inclination to disassociate herself from the term.[7] However, Moore does seem to depart from the Imagist belief that poetry must be hard and clear, never blurred or indefinite. She enjoyed ambivalence and ambiguity. The turning and fine-tuning of her kaleidoscopic vision of truth was seldom simple and almost never perfectly clear. In "Charity Overcoming Envy" she expressed her credo well, "The Gordian knot need not be cut"; all problems do not require solutions. In "An Octopus" she wrote of "complexities which still will be complexities / as long as the world lasts," and in "Novices" she saw statements "split like a glass against a wall," a "precipitate of dazzling impressions." And yet Moore was a fanatic about detail. She demonstrates a constant commitment to the visual, in the particular, in concrete objects, both natural and human-made. She loved sketches, paintings, clippings, sculptures, and photography and found in the visual, in images, some of her richest themes.

At other times her verses involved the use of readymades, perfect quotations from every conceivable source, from great literature to catalogs. She was deeply concerned, as Kunitz pointed out, with precision in language, getting it right, expressing an idea as well and as compactly as it can be said. As she suggests in "The Pangolin," "to explain grace requires / a curious hand," in every kaleidoscopic dimension of both the words "grace" and "curious." And also in "The Pangolin," Moore celebrates the liberating wonder of humor, suggesting that "humor saves a few steps, it saves years." For after all, "Among animals, *one* has a sense of humor." Our risibility is one of our human glories, and Moore loved to delight herself and her readers with all manner of verbal sleights of hand. She loved puns and orthographic changes; she enjoyed tracing etymologies and even variations in meanings from one language to another. Recognizing the intensity of Moore's labor is significant. Her "magic" always came after tremendous effort and concentration.

Sheridan Baker suggests that when a writer's style is really good, it will hang in the memory and continue to bring wonder to the mind. He also suggests that the really great writer loves words the way some people like precious stones.[8] There is no doubt that Moore's style hangs in the memory and that she loved words, collecting her treasures over the years in her tiny notebooks, to be taken out, examined, savored, delighted in, used, and, even smiled over as the years went by. She was in every sense a collector of every manner of "imaginary possession" of the highest caliber, whether those delights were pictures, words, or ideas.

To return to Kappel's notion of Moore's work as a poetry of triumph, one recalls that Moore always experienced an amazing stability, a "susceptibility to happiness," she called it, and that philosophical outlook may prove to be the most unusual dimension of her originality of all. Clampitt makes a compelling point about Moore's uprightness—her goodness, as it were. She suggests that in our era "we are so ambivalent about the very notion of rectitude that the word *good* tends to raise our eyebrows."[9] We are oddly uncomfortable with a discourse that celebrates life rather than complaining about it and engaging in self-pity. The choice of joy amid chaos seems strangely out of place, almost confusing. As D. H. Lawrence predicted, it is hard to hear a new voice. Moore could not, or perhaps more accurately would not, wallow in what Kappel has described as the twentieth-century's "romance of failure." She once wrote to Wallace Stevens, "I loathe Sartre, am feeling didactic, moreover, and would say with Auden, 'writers are not passive recipients of good fortune; art is a vocation for which a price must be paid.'"[10]

For Moore never saw herself as the hopelessly beleaguered and lonely being at the mercy of the chaotic particulars of reality. She knew her place in the universe, in the Great Chain of being. She held a prevailing faith, one that was undogmatic and even largely unscriptural. It is never obvious in her work because it permeates it; it was part of the fiber of her every theme. One might call it a kind of clairvoyant Christian awareness of transhuman reality dependent on grace and intuition rather than on doctrine or creed. Perhaps it might be called a Pauline conviction that "the letter killeth, but the spirit giveth life" (2 Cor. 3:6). For Moore always saw in the universe a sense of order and purpose, although she could not always comprehend that order or that purpose. As she says in "The Steeple-Jack," "it is a privilege to see so / much confusion." And in "An Octopus," she is brave enough to look back at Tacoma, the Mountain that is God, and celebrate the power of an avalanche, one of the "complexities which still will be complexities / as long as the world lasts." In "Spenser's Ireland," Moore remarks,

> Whoever again
> and again says, "I'll never give in," never sees
> that you're not free
>   until you've been made captive by
>   supreme belief.

In *Babel to Byzantium*, James Dickey well summarizes the unique quality of Moore's "supreme belief."

> Heaven is a vision, and so is earth; or at least it can be. Of one of these we know something; about the other we have to speculate. . . . What poet would we most like to have construct a Heaven for us, out of the things we already have? . . . Would we prefer to inherit the cowled, ecclesiastical, distantly murmuring twilight of Eliot? Should the angels sing in a mixture of Provençal, Greek and frontier American presided over by the perfect Confucian governor as Ezra Pound might have? Or would Paradise be the artificial one of Baudelaire, a place like nocturnal Paris: a Heaven which—the maker might argue— contains those elements of Hell without which our joy could not exist? . . . I would choose Marianne Moore. And I suspect that this is so because of her persuasiveness in getting the things of this world to live together as if they truly belonged that way.[11]

"In the beginning was the Word," wrote John the Evangelist, and Moore seems to have valued the word as her most precious possession as she sought to find magical ways of granting "piercing glances into the life of things," illusions more precise than precision. Moore is very much a part of the modernist world, but she is also very much a new voice. Harold Bloom even suggests that "if we compare her with her major poetic contemporaries—Frost, Stevens, Eliot, Pound, Williams, Aiken, Ransom, Cummings, H.D., Hart Crane—she is clearly the most original American poet of her era."[12] And as Eliot suggested, she has indeed invented a new idiom. Her work is, as he had predicted it would be, "part of the small body of durable poetry written in our time." But it is a difficult new language; it is hard to hear; and if we choose to listen to it, we are going to find ourselves having to challenge the status quo.

Moore's is a discourse of inclusiveness, contradiction, paradox, intuition, and magic. It reflects a woman's reluctance to judge, to demand single answers to life's truly complex problems. As a skilled woman writer, Doris Lessing has warned that people who are hungry for answers, not hungry for ways of looking toward problems, will be disappointed with discourse like that produced by Marianne Moore. And when Keats spoke of the possibility of "negative capability," he was intuiting a mind like that of Marianne Moore. As Joseph Campbell put it, as a woman, "she is time and space itself, and the mystery beyond her is beyond all pairs of opposites."[13] She dares to operate in the world beyond abstract precision, the world of illusion. But learning to hear the "new" voice of Marianne Moore can only help us begin to connect with an important dimension of being totally human.

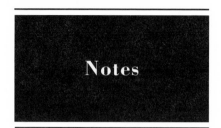

Notes

INTRODUCTION: **The Wizard in Words**

1. D. H. Lawrence, "The Spirit of Place," in *Studies in Classic American Literature* (New York: Penguin Books, 1986), p. 7.

2. Patricia C. Willis, *Marianne Moore: Vision into Verse* (Philadelphia: Rosenbach Museum & Library, 1987), p. 18.

3. John M. Slatin, *The Savage's Romance: The Poetry of Marianne Moore* (University Park: Pennsylvania State University Press, 1986), chap. 4: "The Principle of Accommodation: Moore, Eliot, and the Search for Community," pp. 120–35 passim.

4. All Moore scholars—and probably all Moore readers—would like to work from a definitive edition of Moore's poems. It would even be helpful if all of Moore's poems were still in print. Neither is, unfortunately, the case. One quickly discovers that the text of the "same" poem differs in small ways, and sometimes in great ways, from one edition to another. Occasionally a given poem appears in a new edition under an entirely new title. Unlike the case of the final and definitive editions of some poets, Moore's recently reissued *Complete Poems* does not provide a real basis for an intelligent discussion of her poetry. Certain of the works as they appeared in the first part of her career are markedly different from the later reworkings. I am not convinced that Moore ever thought of the later revisions as a means of perfecting the earlier work; they were merely reworkings done for reasons she chose not to explain. (One might make some analogies here to the various editions of Walt Whitman's *Leaves of Grass*.) Citations to Moore's poems in this book thus vary. Unless otherwise noted, however, quotations of Moore's poetry are taken from *The Complete Poems of Marianne*

Moore (New York: Macmillan/Viking Press, 1981). See Bibliography for full publication details of other volumes of poetry cited.

5. Mary Field Belenky et al., *Women's Ways of Knowing* (New York: Basic Books, 1986), pp. 6–7.

6. Ann Douglas, *The Feminization of American Culture* (New York: Doubleday, Anchor Press, 1988), p. 329.

7. Joseph Campbell, *The Power of Myth* (New York: Doubleday, 1988), p. 167.

8. Carol Gilligan, *In a Different Voice* (Cambridge: Harvard University Press, 1982), p. 17.

9. See Mikhail M. Bakhtin, "Discourse in the Novel," in *Critical Theory Since 1965*, ed. Hazard Adams and Leroy Searle (Tallahassee: Florida State University Press, 1989), pp. 666–67.

10. Belenky et al., *Women's Ways of Knowing*, p. 39.

11. Marianne Moore, "Subject, Predicate, Object," in *Tell Me, Tell Me: Granite Steel and Other Topics* (New York, Viking Press, 1966), p. 46.

12. Ibid.

13. Donald Hall, *Marianne Moore: The Cage and the Animal* (New York: Pegasus, 1970), p. 152.

14. Willis, *Marianne Moore: Vision into Verse*, p. 1.

15. Ibid.

16. T. S. Eliot, Introduction to *Selected Poems of Marianne Moore* (New York: Macmillan; London: Faber & Faber, 1935), p. xiv.

17. T. S. Eliot, "Marianne Moore (1923)," review of *Poems* and *Marriage*, *Dial* 75 (December 1923): 595.

18. William Carlos Williams, "Marianne Moore: A Novelette and Other Prose, 1921–1931," in *Selected Essays* (New York: Random House, 1954), p. 128.

19. T. S. Eliot to Marianne Moore, 20 June 1934, Rosenbach Museum & Library, V:17:25, Philadelphia (hereinafter designated Rosenbach).

20. Donald Hall, "Interview with Donald Hall," in *A Marianne Moore Reader* (New York: Viking Press, 1961), p. 266 (hereinafter designated *MMR*). All references to Donald Hall's interview with Moore hereinafter designated Hall Interview.

21. Andrew Kappel, "Introduction: The Achievement of Marianne Moore," *Twentieth Century Literature* 30 (Summer/Fall 1984): xviii.

22. Williams, *Selected Essays*, p. 292.

23. Hall, *Marianne Moore: The Cage and the Animal*, p. 179.

24. Bonnie Costello, *Marianne Moore: Imaginary Possessions* (Cambridge: Harvard University Press, 1981), p. 19.

25. Randall Jarrell, "The Humble Animal," in *Poetry and the Age* (New York: Knopf, 1953), pp. 180–81.

26. Marianne Moore, "Henry James as a Characteristic American," in *The Complete Prose of Marianne Moore*, ed. Patricia C. Willis (New York: Viking-Penguin Books, 1987), p. 317 (hereinafter designated *Complete Prose*).

27. Marianne Moore, "Conjuries That Endure," in *Predilections* (New York: Viking Press, 1955), p. 34.

28. Marianne Moore, "Anna Pavlova," in *Predilections*, p. 157. This essay appeared originally in *Dance Index* 3 (March 1944): 47–52.

29. Moore, "Subject, Predicate, Object," p. 46.

30. Marianne Moore, "A Burning Desire to Be Explicit," in *Tell Me, Tell Me* (New York: Viking Press, 1967), p. 6.

31. Willis, *Marianne Moore: Vision into Verse*, p. 100.

32. Hall Interview, *MMR*, p. 257.

33. William Carlos Williams, *The Autobiography of William Carlos Williams* (New York: Random House, 1951), p. 146.

34. Williams, *Selected Essays*, p. 292.

35. Marius de Zayas, "Femme!" *291* 9 (November 1915), as quoted in Henry M. Sayre, *The Visual Text of William Carlos Williams*, (Urbana: University of Illinois Press, 1983), p. 63.

36. Gilligan, *In a Different Voice*, p. 6.

CHAPTER 1: **What Are Years?**

1. Wyndham Lewis, *Time and Western Man*, 2d ed. (Boston: Beacon Press, 1957), p. 126.

2. William Carlos Williams, "St. Francis Einstein of the Daffodils," *Contact* 4 (1921): 2.

3. Thomas Jewell Craven, "Art and Relativity," *Dial* 70 (May 1921): 535–36.

4. Belenky et al., *Women's Ways of Knowing*, pp. 17–18.

5. Willis, *Marianne Moore: Vision into Verse*, p. 4.

6. Ibid.

7. The letter was written in 1957 and appears in Patricia Willis, ed., *Marianne Moore Newsletter* 7 (Spring and Fall 1983): 43 (hereinafter designated *MMN*).

8. Henri Bergson, *Time and Free Will: An Essay on the Immediate Data of Consciousness*, trans. F. L. Pogson (New York: Macmillan, 1959), pp. 238–39.

9. *MMN* 5 (Spring 1981): 6.

10. Bergson, *Time and Free Will*, pp. 238–39.

11. Alfred Kreymborg, *Troubadour: An Autobiography* (New York: Sagamore Press, 1957), p. 241.

12. *MMN* 6 (Spring and Fall 1982): 2.

13. Slatin, *The Savage's Romance: The Poetry of Marianne Moore*, p. 27.

14. Ezra Pound, "The Palette," in *Literary Essays*, ed. T. S. Eliot (New York: New Directions, 1968), p. 215.

15. Hugh Kenner, *The Pound Era* (Berkeley: University of California Press, 1971), pp. 192–222 passim.

16. Slatin, *Savage's Romance: The Poetry of Marianne Moore*, pp. 28–29.

17. Moore Bible Talks, Rosenbach 1252/25, VII:08:03.

18. Moore Conversation Notebook, Rosenbach 1250/23, p. 18, VII:10:06.

19. Aloysius Fitzgerald, "Hebrew Poetry," in *The Jerome Biblical Commentary*, ed. Raymond E. Brown, Joseph Fitzmyer, and Roland E. Murphy (Englewood Cliffs, N.J.: Prentice-Hall, 1968), p. 238.

20. Marianne Moore, "Humility, Concentration, and Gusto," in *Predilections*, p. 13.

21. Ibid.

22. Amy Clampitt to author, 14 March 1988.

23. Hall Interview, *MMR*, p. 260.

24. Eliot, Introduction to *Selected Poems*, p. xiii.

25. Michael H. Levenson, *A Genealogy of Modernism: A Study of English Literary Doctrine, 1908–1922* (Cambridge: Cambridge University Press, 1984), pp. 111–12.

26. Willis, *Marianne Moore: Vision into Verse*, p. 12.

27. "A Letter to Ezra Pound," from Marianne Moore, in *Marianne Moore: A Collection of Critical Essays*, ed. Charles Tomlinson (Englewood Cliffs, N.J.: Prentice-Hall, 1969), p. 17.

28. Hugh Kenner, *A Homemade World: The American Modernist Writers* (New York: Alfred A. Knopf, 1975), p. 98.

29. Hugh Kenner, "Meditation and Enactment," in *Marianne Moore: A Collection of Critical Essays*, ed. Tomlinson, p. 159.

30. Ibid., pp. 159–60.

31. Slatin, *The Savage's Romance: The Poetry of Marianne Moore*, p. 231.

32. Willis, *Marianne Moore: Vision into Verse*, pp. 40–42.

33. Personal Notebook, Rosenbach 1250/6, VII:02:02.

34. Hall, *Marianne Moore: The Cage and the Animal*, p. 84.

35. *Oxford English Dictionary*; see also "The Reign of Chintz," *House and Garden*, July 1988, p. 72.

36. Marianne Moore, "Feeling and Precision," in *Predilections*, p. 7.

37. Poetry, Rosenbach I:03:40.

38. Moore, "Feeling and Precision," p. 8.

39. Bergson, *Time and Free Will*, pp. 14–15.

40. Amy Clampitt to author, 14 March 1988.

41. Poetry, Rosenbach I:02:03.

42. Gary Lane, *A Concordance to the Poems of Marianne Moore* (New York: Haskell House Publishers, 1972), preface, n.p.

43. Willis, *Marianne Moore: Vision into Verse*, p. 54.

44. See n. 7 above.

45. Laurence Stapleton, *Marianne Moore: The Poet's Advance* (Princeton: Princeton University Press, 1978), p. 112.

46. Hall, *Marianne Moore: The Cage and the Animal*, p. 97.

47. Moore, "A Burning Desire to Be Explicit," p. 6.

48. Hall, *Marianne Moore: The Cage and the Animal*, p. 100.

49. Margaret Holley, *The Poetry of Marianne Moore: A Study in Voice and Value* (New York: Cambridge University Press, 1987), p. 10.

50. Reading Notebook, Rosenbach 1250/4, VII:01:04.

51. Tess Gallagher, "Throwing the Scarecrows from the Garden," *Parnassus, Poetry in Review* 12, no. 2, and 13, no. 1 (1985): 45.

52. Holley, *The Poetry of Marianne Moore*, pp. 111–14.

53. Hall, *Marianne Moore: The Cage and the Animal*, p. 96.

CHAPTER 2: **When I Buy Pictures**

1. Costello, *Marianne Moore: Imaginary Possessions*, p. 146.

2. Kenner, "Meditation and Enactment," p. 160.

3. Hall Interview, *MMR*, p. 253.

4. *MMN* 6 (Spring and Fall 1982): 17.

5. Marianne Moore to Warner Moore, 30 July 1911, *MMN* 6 (Spring and Fall 1982): 23.

6. Willis, *Marianne Moore: Vision into Verse*, p. 7.

7. Marianne Moore, "Education of a Poet," *Writer's Digest* 43 (October 1963): 35, 72.

8. Costello, *Marianne Moore: Imaginary Possessions*, p. 187.

9. Sayre, *The Visual Text of William Carlos Williams*, p. 4.

10. Hall, *Marianne Moore: The Cage and the Animal*, pp. 23–24.

11. William Carlos Williams to Marianne Moore, 23 December 1919, and Moore's undated response to Williams, Rosenbach V:77:25.

12. Hall Interview, *MMR*, p. 255.

13. Rosenbach V:25:02.

14. Kreymborg, *Troubadour: An Autobiography*, p. 243.

15. Williams, *Autobiography*, pp. 171–72.

16. Barbara Haskell, *Charles Demuth* (New York: Harry N. Abrams, 1987), p. 37.

17. Marianne Moore to T. S. Eliot, 10 December 1923, Rosenbach V:17:24.

18. Dickran Tashjian, *Skyscraper Primitives: Dada and the American Avant-Garde, 1910–1925.* (Middletown, Conn.: Wesleyan University Press, 1975), p. 91.

19. Reading Notebook, Rosenbach 1250/3.

20. Marianne Moore to H.D., 26 July 1921, Rosenbach V:23:32.

21. Hall, *Marianne Moore: The Cage and the Animal*, p. 100.

22. Harold Bloom, ed., Introduction to *Marianne Moore: Modern Critical Views* (New York: Chelsea House Publishers, 1987), pp. 1, 3.

23. Costello, *Marianne Moore: Imaginary Possessions*, p. 205.

24. Haskell, *Charles Demuth*, p. 135.

25. T. S. Eliot, *Selected Prose of T. S. Eliot*, ed. Frank Kermode (New York: Harcourt Brace Jovanovich/Farrar, Straus & Giroux, 1975), p. 38.

26. Slatin, *The Savage's Romance: The Poetry of Marianne Moore*, p. 139.

27. Ibid., p. 141.

28. Calvin Tomkins, *The Bride and the Bachelors: Five Masters of the Avant Garde* (New York: Viking Press, 1968), p. 15.

29. Sayre, *The Visual Text of William Carlos Williams*, p. 79.

30. Willis, *Marianne Moore: Vision into Verse*, p. 21.

31. Marianne Moore, probably to William Rose Benét, 24 February 1916, Rosenbach I:02:39.

32. Marianne Moore on E. McKnight Kauffer, Conversation Notebook, Rosenbach 1250/25, VII:11:01.

33. Willis, *Marianne Moore: Vision into Verse*, p. 21.

34. Marianne Moore, "Robert Andrew Parker," *MMR*, pp. 205–6.

35. Kappel, "Introduction: The Achievement of Marianne Moore," p. xviii.

36. T. S. Eliot to Marianne Moore, 20 June 1934, Rosenbach V:17:25.

37. Moore, *Complete Prose*, pp. 203–4.

38. Slatin, *The Savage's Romance: The Poetry of Marianne Moore*, pp. 180–81.

39. Reading Notebook, Rosenbach 1250/5, VII:02:01.

40. Grace Schulman, *Marianne Moore: The Poetry of Engagement* (Champaign: University of Illinois Press, 1986), p. 60.

41. Slatin, *The Savage's Romance: The Poetry of Marianne Moore*, p. 187.

42. *MMN* 1 (Fall 1977): 7.

43. Slatin, *The Savage's Romance: The Poetry of Marianne Moore*, pp. 196–97.

44. Reading Notebook, Rosenbach 1250/5, VII:02:01.

CHAPTER 3: **Objets Trouvés and Readymades**

1. Williams, *Selected Essays*, pp. 121–22.

2. Holley, *The Poetry of Marianne Moore*, p. 14.

3. Slatin, *The Savage's Romance: The Poetry of Marianne Moore*, p. 154.

4. Belenky et al., *Women's Ways of Knowing*, chap. 2, pp. 44–45.

5. Hall Interview, *MMR*, p. 260.

6. Moore, Foreword, *MMR*, p. xv.

7. Reading Notebook, Rosenbach 1250/4, VII:01:04.

8. Randall Jarrell, "Her Shield," in *Poetry and the Age* (New York: Knopf, 1953), p. 191.

9. William Carlos Williams to Marianne Moore, 7 November 1944, Rosenbach V:77:26.

10. Jarrell, "Her Shield," p. 191.

11. Holley, *The Poetry of Marianne Moore*, p. 39.

12. Helen Vendler, "Marianne Moore," in *Marianne Moore: Modern Critical Views*, ed. Bloom, p. 81.

13. Hall Interview, *MMR*, p. 256.

14. Kreymborg, *Troubadour: An Autobiography*, pp. 243, 244–45.

15. *MMN* 5 (Spring 1981): 15–17.

16. *MMN* 4 (Spring 1980): 14–15.

17. "Some of the Authors Speaking for Themselves," *New York Herald Tribune Book Review*, 7 October 1951, pp. 14, 16.

18. Reply to the *American Scholar*, 15 March 1965.

19. Hall Interview, *MMR*, p. 256.

20. Ibid., p. 273.

21. Holley, *The Poetry of Marianne Moore*, p. 38, citing Claude Levi-Strauss, *The Savage Mind* (London: Weidenfeld & Nicholson, 1962), pp. 16 and 35.

22. Moore, "Humility, Concentration, and Gusto," p. 12.

23. Jarrell, "Her Shield," p. 201.

24. Moore, *Complete Poems*, p. 262.

25. *MMN* 1 (Fall 1977): 17.

26. Gallagher, "Throwing the Scarecrows from the Garden," p. 56.

27. *MMN* 2 (Fall 1978): 14.

28. Jarrell, "Her Shield," p. 201; Gallagher, "Throwing the Scarecrows from the Garden," p. 50.

29. Geoffrey Hartman, record jacket from *Marianne Moore Reads from Her Works, Yale Series of Recorded Poets*, produced by Yale University Department of English, Carillon Records YP 312, 1961.

30. *MMN* 3 (Spring 1979): 11.

31. Moore, Foreword, *MMR*, p. xv.

32. Reading Notebook, Rosenbach 1250/4, VII:01:04.

33. Ibid.

34. Bloom, Introduction to *Marianne Moore: Modern Critical Views*, p. 4.

35. Moore, "Humility, Concentration, and Gusto," p. 15.

36. Williams, *Selected Essays*, p. 122.

37. Ibid., p. 293.

38. Ibid., p. 123.

39. Quoted in Gallagher, "Throwing the Scarecrows from the Garden," p. 52.

40. Moore, "Feeling and Precision," p. 3.

41. Taffy Martin, *Marianne Moore: Subversive Modernist* (Austin: University of Texas Press, 1986), p. 132.

42. Slatin, *The Savage's Romance: The Poetry of Marianne Moore*, pp. 121–55 passim.

43. Marianne Moore, "The Cantos," review of a draft of *XXX Cantos*, by Ezra Pound (Hours Press), in *Collected Prose*, p. 272.

CHAPTER 4: Kaleidoscope

1. William Carlos Williams to Marianne Moore, 24 May 1936, Rosenbach V:77:26.

2. Marianne Moore, "Idiosyncrasy and Technique," in *MMR*, p. 172.

3. Moore, "A Burning Desire to Be Explicit," p. 5.

4. *MMN* 5 (Spring 1981): 3.

5. Moore, "A Burning Desire to Be Explicit," p. 5.

6. Marianne Moore to Mrs. Moore, 19 February 1907, *MMN* 5 (Spring 1981): 5.

7. Marianne Moore, "Impact, Morals and Technical; Independence versus Exhibitionism; and Concerning Contagion," in *The Harvard Summer School Conferences on the Defense of Poetry* (Cambridge: Harvard University Press, 1951), p. 71, as it appears in *Complete Prose*, p. 435.

8. Marianne Moore, "Reticent Candor," from a series of comments on selected contemporary poets, Bryn Mawr, 1952; also in *Predilections*, p. 60.

9. Ezra Pound, *Selected Poems of Ezra Pound* (New York: New Directions, 1957), p. 32.

10. Willis, *Marianne Moore: Vision into Verse*, p. 13.

11. Eliot, *Selected Prose*, p. 62.

12. Williams, "Marianne Moore: A Novelette and Other Prose, 1921–1931," in *Selected Essays*, p. 12.

13. Hall Interview, *MMR*, p. 262.

14. Harold Monro, "The Imagists Discussed," *Egoist* 2 (May 1915): 77–80. See also Harriet Monroe, "A Symposium on Marianne Moore," *Poetry* 19 (January 1922): 208–16, and Louis Untermeyer, *American Poetry since 1900* (New York: Henry Holt, 1923), pp. 362–68.

15. Reading Notebook, Rosenbach 1250:12/17.

16. Willis, *Marianne Moore: Vision into Verse*, p. 16.

17. Hall, *Marianne Moore: The Cage and the Animal*, p. 50.

18. *London Times Literary Supplement*, 21 July 1921, p. 471.

19. Slatin, *The Savage's Romance: The Poetry of Marianne Moore*, p. 65.

20. Robert Herrick, "To the Virgins, to Make Much of Time," in *Norton Anthology of English Literature*, 4th ed., ed. M. H. Abrams (New York: W. W. Norton, 1979), 1:1320.

21. Andrew Marvell, "To His Coy Mistress," in *Norton Anthology of English Literature* 1:1361.

22. Hall Interview, *MMR*, p. 262.

23. Moore, "Idiosyncrasy and Technique," p. 171.

24. Moore, "Subject, Predicate, Object," p. 48.

25. Wallace Stevens, "A Poet That Matters," *Life and Letters Today* 13 (December 1935), reprinted in *Opus Posthumous* (New York: Alfred A. Knopf, 1957), pp. 247–48.

26. Sue Renick, "Moore's 'The Fish,'" *The Explicator* 21 (September 1962): n.p.

27. Hall, *Marianne Moore: The Cage and the Animal*, p. 47.

28. Kenner, *A Homemade World*, pp. 99–102. See also Kenner, *The Pound Era*, pp. 87–89.

29. Bernard Engel, *Marianne Moore* (New Haven, Conn.: College and University Press, Twayne Series, 1964), p. 57.

30. Costello, *Marianne Moore: Imaginary Possessions*, p. 70.

31. Kenner, *A Homemade World*, pp. 99–100.

32. Stapleton, *Marianne Moore: The Poet's Advance*, p. 17.

33. Schulman, *Marianne Moore: The Poetry of Engagement*, p. 85.

34. Slatin, *The Savage's Romance: The Poetry of Marianne Moore*, p. 74.

35. Holley, *The Poetry of Marianne Moore*, p. 62.

36. Elizabeth Bradburn, "The Machinery of Grace," unpublished honors paper, Amherst College, Amherst, Mass., 1987.

37. *MMN* 4 (Fall 1980): 21.

38. Elizabeth Bishop to Marianne Moore, 19 January 1957, Rosenbach V:05:05.

39. Eliot, Introduction to *Selected Poems*, p. xiii.

40. Moore, "Impact, Morals and Technical," *Complete Prose*, p. 435.

CHAPTER 5: **Armor's Undermining Modesty**

1. Monroe, "A Symposium on Marianne Moore," pp. 213–16.

2. Slatin, *The Savage's Romance: The Poetry of Marianne Moore*, p. 17.

3. Williams, *Autobiography*, "The Waste Land," p. 146.

4. Alyse Gregory to Hildegarde Watson, 6 June 1964, transcript in the Watson Collection, Bryn Mawr College Library, as it appears in Holley, *The Poetry of Marianne Moore*, p. 157.

5. Jarrell, "Her Shield," p. 199.

6. Marianne Moore to T. S. Eliot, 18 January 1934, Rosenbach V:17:25.

7. Moore, "Humility, Concentration, and Gusto," p. 13.

8. Gallagher, "Throwing the Scarecrows from the Garden," p. 45.

9. Ibid., p. 49.

10. Moore, "Anna Pavlova," pp. 150–51.

11. Ibid., p. 151.

12. Moore, *Complete Prose*, appendix, p. 659.

13. Moore, "Anna Pavlova," pp. 148–50.

14. Elizabeth Bishop to Marianne Moore, 5 December 1936, Rosenbach V:04:30.

15. Moore, "Ezra Pound," in *Predilections*, pp. 74–75.

16. Pound, *Selected Poems*, p. 32.

17. Moore, "A Felicitous Response," *Christian Science Monitor*, 7 February 1952, p. 7, remarks before the National Book Committee on the acceptance of the National Book Award; also in *Collected Prose*, p. 649.

18. Slatin, *The Savage's Romance: The Poetry of Marianne Moore*, p. 81.

19. Henry James, *Portrait of a Lady* (Boston: Houghton Mifflin, 1963), 1:287–88.

20. Ibid. 2:57.

21. Slatin, *The Savage's Romance: The Poetry of Marianne Moore*, p. 81.

22. Ibid., p. 78.

23. A.L.S. [American Library Society?], 4 March 1927, *MMN* 4 (Spring 1980): 2.

24. Hall, *Marianne Moore: The Cage and the Animal*, p. 96.

25. Moore to Eliot, 2 July 1934, Rosenbach V:17:25.

26. Holley, *The Poetry of Marianne Moore*, p. 79.

27. Bergson, *Time and Free Will*, pp. 14–15.

28. Moore, "Feeling and Precision," pp. 7–8.

29. Moore, "Humility, Concentration, and Gusto," p. 13.

30. Bradburn, "The Machinery of Grace," p. 13.

31. Ibid., p. 14.

32. Ibid., p. 16.

33. Ibid., p. 30.

34. A. Kingsley Weatherhead, *The Edge of the Image: Marianne Moore, William Carlos Williams, and Some Other Poets* (Seattle: University of Washington Press, 1967), p. 58, in chap. 3: "Marianne Moore."

35. Kenner, *A Homemade World*, "Disliking It," p. 92.

36. Weatherhead, *The Edge of the Image*, pp. 18–19.

37. Bradburn, "The Machinery of Grace," p. 34.

38. Martin, *Marianne Moore: Subversive Modernist*, pp. 17–18.

39. Moore, "Feeling and Precision," p. 8.

40. Bradburn, "The Machinery of Grace," p. 35.

41. Kenner, *A Homemade World*, p. 92.

42. *New York Times*, 19 February 1919.

43. Willis, *Marianne Moore: Vision into Verse*, p. 62.

44. Princess Asfa Yilma, *Haile Selassie: Emperor of Ethiopia* (New York: Appleton-Century, 1936), p. 77.

45. Willis, *Marianne Moore: Vision into Verse*, p. 62.

46. T. S. Eliot to Marianne Moore, 20 September 1935, Rosenbach V:17:26.

47. Marianne Moore to Ezra Pound, 31 July 1946, Rosenbach V:50:08.

48. William Wasserstrom, "Irregular Symmetry: Marianne Moore's *Dial*," in *Festschrift for Marianne Moore's Seventy-Seventh Birthday*, ed. M. J. Tambimuttu (New York: Tambimuttu & Mass, 1964), p. 34.

49. Kenner, personal conversation, May 1988.

50. Moore, "Humility, Concentration, and Gusto," in *MMR*, p. 130.

51. Marianne Moore on the inspiration for poetry from a WEVD broadcast, "The World of Books," corrected transcript, 13 July 1951, as it appeared in *MMN* 3 (Fall 1979): 2.

52. Marianne Moore to her brother Warner, 5 July 1911, *MMN* 6 (Spring and Fall 1982): 10–11.

53. Hall, *Marianne Moore: The Cage and the Animal*, p. 133.

54. Ibid., p. 131.

55. "Poetry," in *Selected Poems*, p. 36.

56. Jack Martels, *The Beer Can Collector's Bible* (New York: Ballantine Books, 1976), p. 105.

CHAPTER 6: **Conjuries That Endure**

1. Marianne Moore to T. S. Eliot, 23 October 1934, Rosenbach V:17:25.

2. T. S. Eliot to Marianne Moore, 4 April 1921, Rosenbach V:17:24.

3. Eliot, Introduction to *Selected Poems*, p. xiv.

4. See John Tytell, *Ezra Pound: The Solitary Volcano* (New York: Doubleday, 1987).

5. Willis, *Marianne Moore: Vision into Verse*, p. 16.

6. Marianne Moore to Ezra Pound, 10 May 1921, Rosenbach V:50:06.

7. Willis, *Marianne Moore: Vision into Verse*, p. 17.

8. Ibid., p. 19.

9. Kappel, "Introduction: The Achievement of Marianne Moore," p. v.

10. *Festschrift*, p. 71.

11. William Carlos Williams to Marianne Moore, 7 December 1936, *MMN* 7 (Spring and Fall 1983): 33.

12. William Carlos Williams to Marianne Moore, 21 January 1917, and Moore to Williams, 23 February 1917, Rosenbach V:77:25.

13. *Festschrift*, p. 61.

14. Willis, *Marianne Moore: Vision into Verse*, p. 1.

15. Marianne Moore, *"The Dial*: A Retrospect," in *Complete Prose*, p. 356; appeared first in *Life and Letters To-Day* 27 (December 1940): 175–83.

16. Hall Interview, *MMR*, p. 267.

17. Willis, *Marianne Moore: Vision into Verse*, p. 19.

18. William Carlos Williams to Marianne Moore, 23 March 1921, Rosenbach V:77:25.

19. Marianne Moore to William Carlos Williams, 22 June 1951, Rosenbach V:77:26; see also Celeste Goodrich, "Private Exchanges and Public Reviews: Marianne Moore's Criticism of William Carlos Williams," *Twentieth Century Literature* 30 (Spring/Fall 1984): 160.

20. Willis, *Marianne Moore: Vision into Verse*, p. 21.

21. Eliot, Introduction to *Selected Poems*, p. ix.

22. Hall, *Marianne Moore: The Cage and the Animal*, p. 30.

23. Hall Interview, *MMR*, p. 260.

24. Moore, "Humility, Concentration, and Gusto," p. 13.

25. Willis, *Marianne Moore: Vision into Verse*, p. 1.

26. W. H. Auden to Marianne Moore, 14 November 1939, Rosenbach V:02:47.

27. *Festschrift*, p. 130.

28. Marianne Moore to Wallace Stevens, 1935 (no day or month found), Rosenbach V:63:22.

29. Wallace Stevens to Marianne Moore, 3 February 1937 and 24 February 1945, Rosenbach V:63:22.

30. Kappel, "Introduction: The Achievement of Marianne Moore," p. xvii.

31. Ibid., p. xviii.

32. Marianne Moore to Ezra Pound, 9 January 1919, Rosenbach V:50:06.

33. Willis, *Marianne Moore: Vision into Verse*, p. 17.

34. Ezra Pound to Marianne Moore, 26 May 1948, Rosenbach V:50:08.

35. Hall, *Marianne Moore: The Cage and the Animal*, p. 117.

36. James Laughlin, *Pound as Wuz* (St. Paul: Graywolf Press, 1987), p. 30.

37. Willis, *Marianne Moore: Vision into Verse*, p. 22.

38. Bonnie Costello, "Marianne Moore and Elizabeth Bishop: Friendship and Influence," *Twentieth Century Literature* 30 (Summer/Fall 1984): 130.

39. Marianne Moore to Elizabeth Bishop, 21 June 1959, in ibid., p. 148.

40. Costello, "Marianne Moore and Elizabeth Bishop," p. 142.

41. Moore to Bishop, 7 March 1935, in ibid., p. 139.

42. Bishop to Moore, [1940?], in ibid., pp. 137–38.

43. Randall Jarrell, "The Poet and His Public," *Partisan Review* 13 (1946): 488.

44. Robert Lowell, "Thomas, Bishop, and Williams," 55 *Sewanee Review* (Summer 1947): 497.

45. Elizabeth Bishop to Marianne Moore, 8 August 1969 and 15 October 1970, Rosenbach V:05:06.

46. Costello, "Marianne Moore and Elizabeth Bishop," p. 148.

47. *Festschrift*, pp. 15, 119.

48. Ibid., p. 117.

49. Ibid., p. 113.

50. John Ashbery to Marianne Moore, 20 November 1960, Rosenbach V:02:39.

51. *Festschrift*, p. 114.

52. Moore, "Feeling and Precision," p. 4.

53. *Festschrift*, p. 48.

54. Ibid., p. 63.

55. Amy Clampitt, "The Matter and the Manner: Another Look at the Poetry of Marianne Moore," adapted from a paper originally given on 20 May 1987 at the Chicago Public Library Cultural Center, n.p.

56. Hall Interview, *MMR*, p. 263.

57. Moore, "Humility, Concentration, and Gusto," p. 20.

58. Clampitt, "The Matter and the Manner," n.p.

59. Taffy Martin, "Portrait of a Writing Master: Beyond the Myth of Marianne Moore," *Twentieth Century Literature* 30 (Summer/Fall 1984): 194.

60. Clampitt, "The Matter and the Manner," n.p.

61. R. P. Blackmur, "The Method of Marianne Moore," in *Marianne Moore: A Collection of Critical Essays*, ed. Tomlinson, p. 77.

62. John Crowe Ransom, "On Being Modern with Distinction," *Quarterly Review of Literature* 4 (1948): 136.

63. Kenner, *A Homemade World*, p. xviii.

64. Suzanne Juhasz, *Naked and Fiery Forms: Modern American Poetry by Women: A New Tradition* (New York: Harper, 1976).

65. Gallagher, "Throwing the Scarecrows from the Garden," p. 57.

66. Costello, *Marianne Moore: Imaginary Possessions*, p. 196.

67. Slatin, *The Savage's Romance: The Poetry of Marianne Moore*, pp. 156–57.

68. Ralph Waldo Emerson, "The Poet," in *Selections from Ralph Waldo Emerson*, ed. Stephen E. Whicher (Boston: Houghton Mifflin, 1960), p. 238.

69. Patricia C. Willis, "The Road to Paradise: First Notes on Marianne Moore's 'The Octopus,'" *Twentieth Century Literature* 30 (Summer/Fall 1984): 245.

70. Ibid., p. 247.

71. Ibid., p. 249.

72. Marianne Moore, "Robert Andrew Parker," in *Collected Prose*, pp. 500–501.

73. Willis, "The Road to Paradise," p. 245.

74. Ibid., p. 263.

75. Marianne Moore, "Henry James as a Characteristic American," in *Predilections*, pp. 130–38; also in *Collected Prose*, pp. 316–22, and in *Homage to Henry James*, by Moore and Edmund Wilson (Mamaroneck, N.Y.: Paul P. Appel, 1971), pp. 7–16.

76. Willis, "The Road to Paradise," p. 245.

77. Quoted in Stapleton, *Marianne Moore: The Poet's Advance*, p. 36.

78. Stapleton, *MMN* 1 (Fall 1977): 16.

79. Moore, "Subject, Predicate, Object," p. 47.

CONCLUSION: **Supreme in Her Abnormality**

1. Kappel, "Introduction: The Achievement of Marianne Moore," p. xxii.

2. Lyndall Gordon, *Eliot's New Life* (New York: Farrar, Straus & Giroux, 1988), p. 217.

3. Margaret Holley, "The Model Stanza: The Organic Origin of Moore's Syllabic Verse," *Twentieth Century Literature* 30 (Spring/Fall 1984): 190.

4. *Festschrift*, p. 117.

5. Jarrell, "The Humble Animal," pp. 179–80.

6. William Pratt, *The Imagist Poem* (New York: E. P. Dutton, 1963). Pratt includes Moore's work among the Imagist poets. I am also using the "principles of imagism" on pp. 18–22.

7. Hall Interview, *MMR*, p. 260.

8. Sheridan Baker, *The Practical Stylist* (New York: Thomas Y. Crowell, 1969), p. 1.

9. Clampitt, "Getting to Know Marianne Moore," n.p.

10. Marianne Moore to Wallace Stevens, 2 March 1953, Rosenbach V:63:22.

11. James Dickey, *Babel to Byzantium: Poets and Poetry Now* (New York: Farrar, Straus & Giroux, 1968), pp. 160–61.

12. Bloom, Introduction to *Marianne Moore: Modern Critical Views*, p. 1.

13. Campbell, *The Power of Myth*, p. 167.

Bibliography

Works by Marianne Moore (arranged chronologically)

Poems. London: Egoist Press, 1921.

Marriage. Appeared in *Manikin*, no. 3. New York: Monroe Wheeler, 1923. 200 copies.

Observations. New York: Dial Press, 1924.

Selected Poems. Introduction by T. S. Eliot. New York: Macmillan; London: Faber & Faber, 1935.

The Pangolin and Other Verse. London: Brendin Publishing, 1936.

What Are Years. New York: Macmillan, 1941.

Nevertheless. New York: Macmillan, 1944.

Marianne Moore Reading Her Own Poems. Harvard Vocarium Records P-1064, 1944.

Rock Crystal: A Christmas Tale, by Adalbert Stifter. Translated by Elizabeth Mayer and Marianne Moore. New York: Pantheon Books, 1945.

"Selections from a Poet's Reading Diary and Sketchbooks." *Tiger's Eye* 1 (October 1947): 20–35. Reprint. New York: Kraus Reprint Editions, 1967.

Face. Cummington, Mass.: Cummington Press, for *The New Colophon*, 1949.

Collected Poems. London: Faber & Faber; New York: Macmillan, 1951.

The Fables of La Fontaine. Translated by Marianne Moore. New York: Viking Press, 1954.

Marianne Moore Reading Her Poems and Fables from La Fontaine. Caedmon TC 1025, 1955.

Selected Fables. Translated by Marianne Moore. London: Faber & Faber, 1955.

Predilections. New York: Viking Press, 1955.

A Talisman. Cambridge, Mass.: Adams House & Lowell House Press, 1955.

Like a Bulwark. New York: Viking Press, 1956.

Idiosyncrasy & Technique. Inaugurating the Ewing Lectures at the University of California, Los Angeles, 3 and 5 October 1956. Berkeley and Los Angeles: University of California Press, 1958.

Letters from and to the Ford Motor Company. New York: Pierpont Morgan Library, 1958.

O to Be a Dragon. New York: Viking Press, 1959.

A Marianne Moore Reader. New York: Viking Press, 1961.

The Absentee: A Comedy in Four Acts. Based on Maria Edgeworth's novel of the same name. New York: House of Books, 1962.

Eight Poems by Marianne Moore, with Drawings by Robert Andrew Parker, Hand-Colored by the Artist. New York: Museum of Modern Art, 1962. 195 copies.

Puss in Boots, Cinderella, Sleeping Beauty, by Charles Perrault. Retold by Marianne Moore from the French. New York: Macmillan, 1963.

The Arctic Ox. London: Faber & Faber, 1964.

Poetry and Criticism, by Marianne Moore and Howard Nemerov. Cambridge, Mass.: Adams House & Lowell House Press, 1965.

Dress and Kindred Subjects. New York: Ibex Press, 1965.

Tell Me, Tell Me: Granite Steel and Other Topics. New York: Viking Press, 1966.

The Complete Poems of Marianne Moore. New York: Macmillan, 1967.

Selected Poems. London: Faber & Faber, 1969.

The Accented Syllable. New York: Albondocani Press, 1969.

Prevalent at One Time. Philadelphia: Cypher Press, 1970. Occasioned by Miss Moore's eighty-third birthday.

Homage to Henry James, by Marianne Moore and Edmund Wilson. New York: Appel, 1971.

Unfinished Poems by Marianne Moore. Philadelphia: Philip H. & A. S. W. Rosenbach Foundation, 1972.

The Complete Poems of Marianne Moore. New York: Macmillan/Viking Press, 1981.

The Complete Prose of Marianne Moore. Edited and with an introduction by Patricia C. Willis. New York: Viking-Penguin Books, 1987.

Secondary Sources

Abbott, Craig S. *Marianne Moore: A Descriptive Bibliography.* Pittsburgh: University of Pittsburgh Press, 1977.

Angoff, Charles. "The Little Magazine." *American Mercury* 63 (1946): 370–74.

Auden, W. H. *The Dyer's Hand and Other Essays.* New York: Vintage Press, 1968.

Bar-Yaacov, Lois. "Marianne Moore: An In-Patriot." *Hebrew Studies in Literature* 3 (1975): 165–95.

———. "Moore's 'The Mind Is an Enchanting Thing.'" *Explicator* 43 (Spring 1985): 36–37.

Belenky, Mary Field, et al. *Women's Ways of Knowing.* New York: Basic Books, 1986.

Bergson, Henri. *Time and Free Will: An Essay on the Immediate Data of Consciousness.* Translated by F. L. Pogson. New York: Macmillan, 1959.

Bishop, Elizabeth. "As We Like It." *Quarterly Review of Literature* 4 (Spring 1948): 129–35.

———. "Efforts of Affection: A Memoir of Marianne Moore." In *The Collected Prose,* p. 155. New York: Farrar, Straus & Giroux, 1984.

Blackmur, R. P. "The Method of Marianne Moore." In *Marianne Moore: A Collection of Critical Essays,* ed. Charles Tomlinson. Englewood Cliffs, N.J.: Prentice-Hall, 1969.

Bloom, Harold, ed. *Marianne Moore: Modern Critical Views.* New York: Chelsea House Publishers, 1987.

Bogan, Louise. *Achievement in American Poetry, 1900–1950.* Chicago: Henry Regnery, 1951.

Borroff, Marie. *Language and the Poet: Verbal Artistry in Frost, Stevens, and Moore.* Chicago: University of Chicago Press, 1979.

Bradburn, Elizabeth. "The Machinery of Grace." Unpublished honors paper. Amherst College, Amherst, Mass., 1987.

Brownjohn, A. "With Sincerity and with Gusto." *Times Literary Supplement,* 28 May 1982, p. 577.

Brumbaugh, Thomas B. "In Pursuit of Miss Moore." *Mississippi Quarterly* 15 (Spring 1962): 74–80.

Burke, Kenneth. "Likings of an Observationist." In *Marianne Moore: A Collection of Critical Essays,* ed. Charles Tomlinson. Englewood Cliffs, N.J.: Prentice-Hall, 1969.

———. "Motives and Motifs in the Poetry of Marianne Moore." In *A Grammar of Motives.* Englewood Cliffs, N.J.: Prentice-Hall, 1945.

Campbell, Joseph. *The Power of Myth.* New York: Doubleday, 1988.

Carrington, Ruth Gibson. *What Are Years? The Late Poems of Marianne Moore.* Ann Arbor, Mich.: Dissertation Abstracts, 1985.

Cecilia, Sister Mary. "The Poetry of Marianne Moore." *Thought* 38 (1963): 354–74.

Clampitt, Amy. "Getting to Know Marianne Moore." Unpublished paper. 1987.

———. "The Matter and the Manner: Another Look at the Poetry of Marianne Moore." Adapted from an unpublished paper given 29 May 1987 at the Chicago Public Library Cultural Center.

Cole, Thomas. "The Revised Poems of Marianne Moore." *Imagi* 6 (1952): 11–12.

Coleridge, Samuel Taylor. *Biographia Literaria.* Edited by James Engell and W. Jackson Bate. Princeton: Princeton University Press, 1983.

Costello, Bonnie. "The Feminine Language of Marianne Moore." In *Women and Language in Literature and Society*, ed. Sally McConnell-Ginet et al. New York: Praeger, 1980.

———. *Marianne Moore: Imaginary Possessions.* Cambridge: Harvard University Press, 1981.

———. "Marianne Moore and Elizabeth Bishop: Friendship and Influence." *Twentieth Century Literature* 30 (Summer/Fall 1984): 130–49.

Cowley, Malcolm. *Exile's Return.* New York: Viking Press, 1951.

Dickey, James. *Babel to Byzantium: Poets and Poetry Now.* New York: Farrar, Straus & Giroux, 1968.

Donoghue, Denis. *Connoisseurs of Chaos: Ideas of Order in Modern American Poetry.* New York: Columbia University Press, 1984.

———. "The Proper Plentitude of Fact." In *The Ordinary Universe.* London: Faber & Faber, 1968.

Douglas, Ann. *The Feminization of American Culture.* New York: Doubleday, Anchor Press, 1988.

Durso, J. "Marianne Moore, Baseball Fan." *Saturday Review* 52 (12 July 1969): 51–52.

Edsal, Constance H. "Values and the Poems of Marianne Moore." *English Journal* 57 (April 1969): 516–18.

Eliot, T. S. Introduction to *Selected Poems* by Marianne Moore. New York: Macmillan; London: Faber & Faber, 1935.

———. "Marianne Moore." In *Marianne Moore: A Collection of Critical Essays*, ed. Charles Tomlinson. Englewood Cliffs, N.J.: Prentice-Hall, 1969. Essay originally published in 1923.

———. "Observations." *Egoist*, May 1918, pp. 59–70.

———. *Selected Prose of T. S. Eliot.* Edited by Frank Kermode. New York: Harcourt Brace Jovanovich/Farrar, Straus & Giroux, 1975.

Engel, Bernard F. *Marianne Moore.* New Haven, Conn.: College and University Press, Twayne Series, 1964.

———. "Moore's 'A Face.'" *Explicator* 34 (1975), item 29.

Festschrift for Marianne Moore's Seventy-Seventh Birthday—by Various Hands. Edited by M. J. Tambimuttu. New York: Tambimuttu & Mass, 1964.

Fraiser, Julius Thomas. *The Voices of Time.* New York: George Braziller, 1969.

Friedman, Alan J., and Carol C. Donley. *Einstein as Myth and Muse.* Cambridge: Cambridge University Press, 1954.

Gallagher, Tess. "Throwing the Scarecrows from the Garden." *Parnassus, Poetry in Review* 12, no. 2, and 13, no. 1 (1985): 45–60.

Garrigue, Jean. *Marianne Moore*. Minneapolis: University of Minnesota Pamphlets, 1963.

Gilligan, Carol. *In a Different Voice*. Cambridge: Harvard University Press, 1982.

Glatstein, Jacob. "The Poetry of Marianne Moore." *Prairie Schooner* 47 (1973): 133–41.

Goodrich, Celeste. "Private Exchanges and Public Reviews: Marianne Moore's Criticisms of William Carlos Williams." *Twentieth Century Literature* 30 (Spring/Fall 1984): 160–74.

Gregor, Arthur. "Omissions Are Not Accidents: Reminiscences." *Twentieth Century Literature* 30 (Summer/Fall 1984): 150–59.

Gregory, Horace, and Marya A. Zaturenska. "Marianne Moore: The Genius of the Dial." In *A History of American Poetry, 1900–1940*, pp. 317–25. New York: Harcourt Brace, 1946.

Hadas, Pamela White. *Marianne Moore: The Poetry of Affection*. Syracuse, N.Y.: Syracuse University Press, 1977.

Hall, Donald. "Interview with Donald Hall." In *A Marianne Moore Reader*, pp. 253–73. New York: Viking Press, 1961. Originally published in *Paris Review*, Winter 1961.

———. "An Interview with Marianne Moore." *McCall's* 93 (December 1965).

———. *Marianne Moore: The Cage and the Animal*. New York: Pegasus, 1970.

Hartt, Frederick. *Art: A History of Painting, Sculpture, Architecture*. Vol. 2. Englewood Cliffs, N.J.: Prentice-Hall, 1985.

Haskell, Barbara. *Charles Demuth*. New York: Harry N. Abrams, 1987.

Hoffman, Frederick J. *The Little Magazine: A History and Bibliography*. Princeton: Princeton University Press, 1947.

———. *The 20s: American Writing in the Postwar Decade*. New York: Free Press, 1962.

Holley, Margaret. "The Model Stanza: The Organic Origin of Moore's Syllabic Verse." *Twentieth Century Literature* 30 (Spring/Fall 1984): 181–90.

———. *The Poetry of Marianne Moore: A Study in Voice and Value*. New York: Cambridge University Press, 1987.

James, Henry. *The Portrait of a Lady*. Boston: Houghton Mifflin, 1963.

Jarrell, Randall. "Her Shield." In *Poetry and the Age*, pp. 185–207. New York: Knopf, 1953. Reprinted in *Marianne Moore: A Collection of Critical Essays*, ed. Charles Tomlinson. Englewood Cliffs, N.J.: Prentice-Hall, 1969.

———. "The Humble Animal." In *Poetry and the Age*, pp. 179–84.

———. "Thoughts about Marianne Moore." *Partisan Review* 19 (November–December 1952): 687–700.

Jenkins, D. "Marianne Moore: A Presbyterian Poet?" *Theology Today* 41 (April 1984): 34–41.

Joost, Nicholas. *Scofield Thayer and the Dial*. Carbondale: Southern Illinois University Press, 1964.

Joost, Nicholas, and A. Risdon. "Sketches and Preludes: T. S. Eliot's London Letters in the Dial." *Pennsylvania Language and Literature* 12 (Fall 1976): 366–83.

Joost, Nicholas, and Alvin Sullivan. *D. H. Lawrence and the Dial*. Carbondale: Southern Illinois University Press, 1970.

Juhasz, Suzanne. *Naked and Fiery Forms: Modern American Poetry by Women: A New Tradition*. New York: Harper, 1976.

Kappel, Andrew J. "Introduction: The Achievement of Marianne Moore." *Twentieth Century Literature* 30 (Summer/Fall 1984): v–xxx.

Keller, Lynn. "Words with a Thousand Postcards: The Bishop/Moore Correspondence." *American Literature* 55 (October 1983): 405–29.

Kenner, Hugh. "The Experience of the Eye: Marianne Moore's Tradition." In *Modern American Poetry: Essays in Criticism*, ed. Jerome Mazzaro, pp. 204–21. New York: David McKay, 1970.

———. *A Homemade World: The American Modernist Writers*. New York: Alfred A. Knopf, 1975.

———. "Meditation and Enchantment." In *Marianne Moore: A Collection of Critical Essays*, ed. Charles Tomlinson. Englewood Cliffs, N.J.: Prentice-Hall, 1969. Originally published in *Poetry* 102 (May 1963): 109–15.

———. *The Pound Era*. Berkeley: University of California Press, 1971.

———. "Supreme in Her Abnormality." In *Marianne Moore: A Collection of Critical Essays*, ed. Charles Tomlinson. Englewood Cliffs, N.J.: Prentice-Hall, 1969.

Kreymborg, Alfred. *Troubadour: An Autobiography*. New York: Sagamore Press, 1957.

Lane, Gary. *A Concordance to the Poems of Marianne Moore*. New York: Haskell House Publishers, 1972.

Lawrence, D. H. *Studies in Classic American Literature*. New York: Penguin Books, 1986.

Leavis, F. R. "Marianne Moore," *Scrutiny* 4 (1935): 87–90.

Levenson, Michael H. *A Genealogy of Modernism: A Study of English Literary Doctrine, 1908–1922*. Cambridge: Cambridge University Press, 1984.

Lewis, Wyndham. *Time and Western Man*. Boston: Beacon Press, 1927. 2d ed., 1957.

Lourdeaux, Stanley. "Marianne Moore and a Psychoanalytic Paradigm for the Dissociated Image." *Twentieth Century Literature* 30 (Summer/Fall 1984): 366–71.

———. "Toads in Gardens for Marianne Moore and William Carlos Williams." *Modern Philology* 88 (November 1982): 166–67.

Martin, Taffy. *Marianne Moore: Subversive Modernist*. Austin: University of Texas Press, 1986.

―――. "Portrait of a Writing Master: Beyond the Myth of Marianne Moore." *Twentieth Century Literature* 30 (Summer/Fall 1984): 192–209.

Monroe, Harriet. "Symposium on Marianne Moore." *Poetry* 19 (January 1922): 208–16.

Moore, Richard. "William Carlos Williams and the Modernist Attack on Logical Syntax." *English Literary History* 53 (Winter 1986): 895–916.

Newlin, M. "Unhelpful Hymen! Marianne Moore and Hilda Doolittle." *Essays in Criticism* 27 (January 1977): 216–30.

Nitchie, George. *Marianne Moore: An Introduction to the Poetry*. New York: Columbia University Press, 1969.

Norman, Charles. *Ezra Pound*. New York: Macmillan, 1960.

Okeke-Ezijba, E. "Moore's 'To a Snail' and Gunn's 'Considering the Snail.'" *Explicator* 42 (Winter 1984): 17–18.

Ostriker, A. "What Do Women Poets Want? H.D. and Marianne Moore as Poetic Ancestresses." *Contemporary Literature* 27 (Winter 1986): 475–92.

Pearce, Roy Harvey. "Marianne Moore." In *Marianne Moore: A Collection of Critical Essays*, ed. Charles Tomlinson. Englewood Cliffs, N.J.: Prentice-Hall, 1969.

"People." *Time*, 14 February 1969.

Perkins, David. *A History of Modern Poetry: From the 1890's to the High Modernist Mode*. Cambridge: Harvard University Press, Belknap Press, 1987.

―――. *A History of Modern Poetry: Modernism and After*. Cambridge: Harvard University Press, Belknap Press, 1987.

Perloff, Marjorie. *The Poetics of Indeterminacy: Rimbaud to Cage*. Princeton: Princeton University Press, 1981.

Phillips, Elizabeth. *Marianne Moore*. New York: Frederick Ungar Publishing, 1982.

Plimpton, George. "The World Series with Marianne Moore." *Harper's Magazine* 233 (October 1964): 627–33.

Pound, Ezra. *Letters, 1907–1941*. Edited by D. D. Paige. New York: Harcourt Brace & World, 1950.

―――. *Literary Essays*. Edited by T. S. Eliot. New York: New Directions, 1968.

―――. "Marianne Moore and Mina Loy." In *Marianne Moore: A Collection of Critical Essays*, ed. Charles Tomlinson. Englewood Cliffs, N.J.: Prentice-Hall, 1969. Essay originally published in *Little Review* 10 (March 1918): 57–58.

Pratt, William C., ed. *The Imagist Poem*. New York: E. P. Dutton, 1963.

Ransom, John Crowe. "On Being Modern with Distinction." In *Marianne Moore: A Collection of Critical Essays*, ed. Charles Tomlinson. Englewood Cliffs, N.J.: Prentice-Hall, 1969.

Rees, Ralph. "The Imagery of Marianne Moore." Ph.D. diss., Pennsylvania State University, 1956. The first full-length study of Moore's poetry.

———. "The Reality of Imagination in the Poetry of Marianne Moore." *Twentieth Century Literature* 30 (Summer/Fall 1984): 231–41.

Rosenthal, Erwin. *The Changing Concept of Reality in Art*. New York: George Wittenborn, 1962.

Rosenthal, M. L. *The Modern Poets: A Critical Introduction*. New York: Oxford, 1965.

Ross, Bruce. "Fables of the Golden Age: The Poetry of Marianne Moore." *Twentieth Century Literature* 30 (Summer/Fall 1984): 327–50.

Rothenburg, Jerome, ed. *The Revolution of the Word*. New York: Seabury Press, 1974.

Sayre, Henry M. *The Visual Text of William Carlos Williams*. Urbana: University of Illinois Press, 1983.

Schulman, Grace. "Conversation with Marianne Moore." *Quarterly Review of Literature* 16 (1969): 154–71.

———. *Marianne Moore: The Poetry of Engagement*. Champaign: University of Illinois Press, 1986.

———. "Marianne Moore and E. McKnight Kauffer: Two Characteristic Americans." *Twentieth Century Literature* 30 (Summer/Fall 1984): 175–80.

Sheehy, Eugene, and Kenneth Lohf. *The Achievement of Marianne Moore*. Folcroft, Pa.: Folcroft Library Editions, 1958.

Slatin, John M. "Advancing Backward in a Circle: Marianne Moore as Natural Historian." *Twentieth Century Literature* 30 (Summer/Fall 1984): 273–326.

———. "American Beauty, William Carlos Williams, and Marianne Moore." *Library Chronicle of the University of Texas* 29 (1984): 49–73.

———. *The Savage's Romance: The Poetry of Marianne Moore*. University Park: Pennsylvania State University Press, 1986.

Sprout, Rosalie. "After the Fables: The Translator as Poet." *Twentieth Century Literature* 30 (Summer/Fall 1984): 351–65.

Stapleton, Laurence. *Marianne Moore: The Poet's Advance*. Princeton: Princeton University Press, 1978.

Stearns, Catherine M. *Poetic Decorum and the Problem of Form: Louise Bogan, Marianne Moore, and Elizabeth Bishop*. Ann Arbor, Mich.: Dissertation Abstracts, 1985.

Steinman, Lisa M. *Made in America: Science, Technology, and American Modernist Poets*. New Haven: Yale University Press, 1987.

———. "Modern America, Modernism, and Marianne Moore." *Twentieth Century Literature* 30 (Summer/Fall 1984): 210–30.

Stevens, Wallace. "About One of Marianne Moore's Poems." In *The Necessary Angel*, p. 95. New York: Random House, 1951.

———. "A Poet That Matters." *Life and Letters Today* 13 (December 1935). Reprinted in *Opus Posthumous*, pp. 247–54. New York: Alfred Knopf, 1957.

Tashjian, Dickran. *Skyscraper Primitives: Dada and the American Avant-Garde, 1910–1925*. Middletown, Conn.: Wesleyan University Press, 1975.

Taupin, René. *The Influence of French Symbolism on Modern American Poetry*. Translated by William C. Pratt and Anne Rich Pratt. New York: AMS Press, 1985.

Therese, Sister. *Marianne Moore: A Critical Essay*. Grand Rapids: Eerdmans, 1969.

Tomkins, Calvin. *The Bride and the Bachelors: Five Masters of the Avant Garde*. New York: Viking Press, 1968.

Tomlinson, Charles. "Abundance, Not Too Much: The Poetry of Marianne Moore." *Sewanee Review* 65 (Autumn 1957): 677–87.

———, ed. *Marianne Moore: A Collection of Critical Essays*. Englewood Cliffs, N.J.: Prentice-Hall, 1969. See especially "A Letter to Ezra Pound."

Vendler, Helen. *Part of Nature, Part of Us: Modern American Poets*. Cambridge: Harvard University Press, 1980.

Wasserstrom, William. *The Time of the Dial*. Syracuse: Syracuse University Press, 1963.

———, ed. *A Dial Miscellany*. Syracuse: Syracuse University Press, 1963.

Weatherhead, A. Kingsley. *The Edge of the Image: Marianne Moore, William Carlos Williams, and Some Other Poets*. Seattle: University of Washington Press, 1967.

Whittemore, Reed. *Little Magazines*. Minneapolis: University of Minnesota Press, 1963.

Williams, William Carlos. *The Autobiography of William Carlos Williams*. New York: Random House, 1951.

———. "Marianne Moore." In *Marianne Moore: A Collection of Critical Essays*, ed. Charles Tomlinson. Englewood Cliffs, N.J.: Prentice-Hall, 1969. Essay originally published in 1925.

———. *Selected Essays of William Carlos Williams*. New York: Random House, 1954. See especially pp. 35, 256.

Willis, Patricia C. *Marianne Moore: Vision into Verse*. Philadelphia: Rosenbach Museum & Library, 1987.

———. "The Road to Paradise: First Notes on Marianne Moore's 'An Octopus.'" *Twentieth Century Literature* 30 (Summer/Fall): 242–66.

———, ed. *The Complete Prose of Marianne Moore*. New York: Penguin, 1987.

———. *Marianne Moore Newsletter*. Spring 1977–Fall 1981. Philadelphia: Philip H. & A. S. W. Rosenbach Foundation.

Winters, Yvor. "Holiday and Day of Wrath." *Poetry* 26 (April 1925): 39–44.

———. *In Defense of Reason*. Denver: University of Denver Press, 1947.

Zabel, Morton Dauwen. "A Literalist of the Imagination." *Poetry* 47 (March 1936): 326–36. Reprinted in *Literary Opinion in America*, pp. 385–92. New York: Harper & Row, 1951.

Zingman, Barbara. *The Dial: An Author Index*. Troy, N.Y.: Whitson Publishing, 1975.

Zukofsky, Louis. "Sincerity and Objectification." *Poetry* 37 (February 1931): 277.

Index

About the Author

Darlene Williams Erickson is Assistant Professor of English at Ohio Dominican College. She holds a doctorate in twentieth-century American literature from Miami University. Her scholarly writing includes papers on Toni Morrison, Amy Clampitt, and Marianne Moore. She is currently at work on a book-length study of Anne Sexton.